Gestural Listening In and Beyond the Classroom

Gestural Listening in and Beyond the Classroom

Laura Feibush

Utah State University Press
Logan

Published by Utah State University Press
An imprint of University Press of Colorado
1580 North Logan Street, Suite 660
PMB 39883
Denver, Colorado 80203-1942

 The University Press of Colorado is a proud member of Association of University Presses.

The University Press of Colorado is a cooperative publishing enterprise supported, in part, by Adams State University, Colorado School of Mines, Colorado State University, Fort Lewis College, Metropolitan State University of Denver, University of Alaska Fairbanks, University of Colorado, University of Denver, University of Northern Colorado, University of Wyoming, Utah State University, and Western Colorado University.

ISBN: 978-1-64642-816-8 (hardcover)
ISBN: 978-1-64642-817-5 (paperback)
ISBN: 978-1-64642-818-2 (ebook)
https://doi.org/10.7330/9781646428182

Library of Congress Cataloging-in-Publication Data

Names: Feibush, Laura author
Title: Gestural listening in and beyond the classroom / Laura Feibush.
Description: Logan : Utah State University Press, [2026] | Includes bibliographical references and index.
Identifiers: LCCN 2025054764 (print) | LCCN 2025054765 (ebook) | ISBN 9781646428168 hardcover | ISBN 9781646428175 paperback | ISBN 9781646428182 ebook
Subjects: LCSH: English language—Rhetoric—Study and teaching (Higher) | Listening—Study and teaching (Higher) | Gesture—Psychological aspects—Study and teaching (Higher) | Nonverbal communication in education—Study and teaching (Higher)
Classification: LCC PE1404 .F375 2026 (print) | LCC PE1404 (ebook)
LC record available at https://lccn.loc.gov/2025054764
LC ebook record available at https://lccn.loc.gov/2025054765

Contents

Gestural Listening In and Beyond the Classroom

Introduction

Invocation: Toward Listening as a Rhetorical Force

It's October 2020, just after the vice-presidential debate between Senator Kamala Harris and then–Vice President Michael Pence. Stills and GIFs of Harris's facial expressions while listening to Pence go viral online, commented upon by both sides of the political spectrum. Widely memed photos of her facial expressions during the debate are captioned by viewers who react to her measured yet stern attitude. Some register her comportment as "strength," while some find it "condescending" (Astor; Eustachewich).

There's something going on with Harris's debate listening and with viewers' responses to it. Her listening is not "just" listening—it exceeds reception, expanding into a multifaceted expressive resource in which viewers recognize meaningful communication. Moments when she is not just speaking, but listening and reacting, emerge as important ways Harris contributes to the conversation, moments that carry indelible communicative weight and nuance. Further, public responses to Harris's moment-to-moment debate reactions recognize multiple levels of meaning within her gestural behaviors. In *The New York Times*, for instance, Maggie Astor describes some of her behaviors as "laughs, head shakes and 'are you kidding me' expressions." Viewers recognize

https://doi.org/10.7330/9781645428182.c000

that Harris needs to perform attentive listening during the debate but that her listening also needs to retain a quality of skepticism, of resistance—"are you kidding me?" Her reactions need to be legible in the context of the debate as respectful toward her opponent while also reflecting the mood of many spectators at the time, tiring of the inflammatory distraction tactics characteristic of the first Trump administration. To this end, Harris must enact politeness on one level, even as she gesturally registers and conveys frustration, disbelief, and skepticism on another, as she is repeatedly interrupted and confronted with incorrect or misleading statements.

But Harris's listening behaviors do more than simply veil outrage with politeness. Viewers find still more shades of meaning in her expressions, layers of significance that are connected to her identity as a Black woman. Quoted by Astor in *The New York Times*, Nadia E. Brown notes: "Her facial expressions and the eye rolls and neck movements were quintessential Black woman—she was signaling, 'Don't start.'" Viewers like Brown articulate the elements of lived experience that shape Harris's body language, a verbal and gestural way of being that American audiences are unaccustomed to seeing on a national debate stage. On that stage, Harris speaks in a situation where Black women have never appeared. That makes it a place where she has a complex and unenviable task: winning over voters while navigating the minefield of stereotypes that harangue Black people and women when speaking in public. She must avoid appearing to be "too much" of anything: too angry or aggressive to be palatable to a wide range of voters; too shrill and querulous to be taken seriously as a female politician; or, on the other hand, too accommodating or gentle to be an effective leader. Even as she works to sidestep stereotypes of Black folks and women, however, Harris draws upon the communicative techniques of women, Black people, and other marginalized groups who have historically found ways to convey meaning outside the typically recognized discursive bounds.

The year 2024 saw Harris on a national debate stage again, this time as a presidential candidate opposite Donald Trump. Facing off with a more unpredictable opponent, Harris's listening behaviors have at once a sharper edge and a wider range, from "raising her eyebrows and shaking her head to letting out the occasional chuckle, resting her hand on her chin and even just blinking" (Keith and Treisman). Indeed, while 2020 saw a more constrained debate with Pence, the Harris of 2024 is not afraid to laugh. Her laughter, along with her lightly smiling expressions of incredulity, works to register an ongoing doubtfulness about what's being said, a nonverbal means of calling out her opponent. The Associated Press writes: "At various points she looked amused or befuddled by whatever Trump was saying, as if wordlessly saying he was lying . . . Other times she laughed." When comparing Harris's 2024 debate performance to her turn against Pence four years earlier, perhaps what stands out most is not how her style has evolved but rather how consistently expressive her listening is compared to her opponents in either year. In 2024, Trump maintains a limited gestural vocabulary, keeping "a serious expression on his face, while sometimes smiling with pursed lips or shaking his head" (Mason). He refrains from gestural engagement with Harris, with the Associated Press noting: "He rarely looked at Harris while she spoke, instead pointing his face forward toward the cameras or ABC News moderators" (*For Harris and Trump*). By contrast, one reporter writes: "The vice president maintained an expressive face throughout the evening, raising her eyebrows, laughing, and looking on as if in disbelief as Trump spoke" (Mason). Another notes that "Harris in particular leaned into the nonverbal communication" (*For Harris and Trump*). Strikingly, this article goes on to frames her nonverbal behaviors as a means to communicate continuously, suggesting that through her gestural comportment, she is " 'speaking' to the audience even while Trump ostensibly had the floor."

In short, Harris's listening behaviors are remarkably communicative. What's more, Harris's embodied listening behaviors reveal dimensions of power and identity that warrant further investigation.

In the following five chapters, I will illustrate and analyze how listening behaviors communicate. Situations like the Harris debates highlight how rich and nuanced listening communication can be, especially when people question and complicate some of the ideas that often prevail about listening in our wider culture: that it is primarily passive and receptive, for instance, and that it should generally take a backseat to the more productive and readily visible skills of speaking and writing. Listening, when understood as possessing its own repertoire of dually impressive and expressive capacities, emerges as a fascinating site of study, particularly for those engaged in sensitive communicative work such as teaching and counseling. A central thesis of this book is that listening *moves*, listening *brings about*, listening *causes*, listening *pressures*, listening *catalyzes*. In particular, the moving, conductive, forceful aspect of listening that I focus on here is its embodied manifestation—what I call "gestural listening." I define gestural listening as the expressive, embodied ways in which people manifest the otherwise silent, interior act of listening. Harris, as previously described, enacts gestural listening through her expressions, posture, and even her choice about where to direct her gaze. In doing this work, I examine how people listen by watching the listener instead of the speaker, the audience instead of the stage. I attend to, among other things, hands and faces, nods and other forms of nonverbal backchanneling, where people sit, when they interrupt, and when they engage in impactful quietness.

It would be easy to assume that what I mean by gestural listening here comprises only quiet, nonverbal gestures: intermittent nods or sighs, the play of eye contact, and so on. But in fact, it is sometimes in speaking or, at times, through vocalizations like "hmm . . ." or "right!" that listeners demonstrate their listening. In many situations, it is those types of vocalizations that shape the discursive space and give it a palpable character: a vocally responsive listener might make a speaker feel attended to, signaling a caring engagement. At other times, it is nonverbal elements of gestural listening that influence the communicative situation: sustained eye contact, nods, or even the purposeful stillness of putting aside other endeavors in order for the listener to show that listening is their top priority in that moment. Often, listeners draw both from gestural and vocal repertoires as part of their listening behavior. So what I mean by gestural listening is more than "just" gesture, or rather, it expands ready notions of the gestural to include a flow between modes: gestural listening can, at times, encompass both audible vocalization and quiet, embodied responses. That multimodal flow, further, suggests that what is meant by gestural listening is actually a third thing—something not "just" receptive or silent and not purely expressive, either. Rather, it is a kind of "influential reception," a purposeful collecting, a gathering that draws forth and arranges the language that it gathers.

Throughout this book, I analyze situations through the lens of gestural listening and teach readers to do so as well. Developing the ability to do this gives rise to two valuable outcomes: (1) we become aware of the many, various differences in how people enact attentiveness across aspects of identity like race and gender, and (2) we gain the use of gestural listening as a powerful rhetorical tool—one that warrants a more fully developed vocabulary.

In the aftermath of the 2020 and 2024 debates, memes and GIFs provided ways to capture and circulate gestural listening behavior, isolating pieces of Harris's communicative repertoire that struck viewers as important, humorous, or profound. In doing so, they provide a fuller vocabulary to describe listening phenomena and their effects on communicative situations. The need for a richer, shared vocabulary for listening behavior can be seen even in writers' syntax as they invoke listening's power to move. For example, after a violent accident in Carson McCullers's *The Heart Is a Lonely Hunter*, the protagonist, Mick, searches for her younger brother. Bubber has disappeared, causing panic among the family. At long last, Mick finds Bubber hiding in a tree. She implores him to come down, using every persuasive technique in her youthful reper-toire, and at a certain moment, she pauses. Here, McCullers writes: "It was like she could hear Bubber listening" (169). As she is unable to see him fully, a dual listening takes place: Mick listens for evidence of movement, in hopes of discerning the quality of her brother's attention, his receptivity to her verbal persuasion; at the same time, Bubber himself listens powerfully to what Mick is saying, as if listening in hope of something that would absolve him, or at least allow him to come down and move forward. Upon realizing that Bubber seems to be listening to her, seems to be open to what she has to say, Mick goes on to speak again, this time eventually convincing her brother to come down from the tree and return home with her.

I mention this moment from McCullers's novel for two reasons. First, it gives us an example of a situation in which listening behaviors actually *cause things* to happen. That is, they act as a palpable force in this communicative—and rhetorical—situation. I also note this sentence because of how McCullers stretches for a way to convey the impact of listening in this moment of height-ened tension. At first glance, being able to "hear listening" doesn't seem to make sense. Isn't listening generally a quiet thing, unable to be heard at all? Isn't listening something that must be registered after the fact, once the lis-tener becomes a speaker and says something that retroactively proves their lis-tening attention? Or perhaps listening can be seen, rather than heard, but only in the expressive face of a particularly responsive person. McCullers's choice of wording—"she could hear Bubber listening"—demonstrates the slipperi-ness of listening, its dual inward and expressive qualities, and the difficulty of conveying its complex presence in communicative situations. In finding ways to better identify and describe listening behaviors, which I endeavor to do throughout this book, we enrich our understanding of rhetorical situation.

This book argues, in short, that listening is a rhetorical force. By "rhetorical force," I mean that listening behaviors can influence communicative situations in profound ways that can be fruitfully understood through rhetorical frame-works, much like speaking, reading, and writing can. On the debate stage, Har-ris's skeptical listening spoke for her even before she began to speak, and, at times, when she was verbally silent, her particular listening behaviors sent clear messages of resistance to her opponent while also resonating with the mood of sympathetic audience members. Her listening was as intentional and pur-poseful as her speech, and it impacted the communicative situation: in other words, her listening acted as a rhetorical force. Further, I contend that listening behaviors form a crucial component to establishing a full picture of any given rhetorical situation. Without noting Mick's strained attention toward Bubber's own listening in the tree, readers would not have a full picture of that urgent rhetorical situation. Likewise, ignoring Harris's precise, expressive gestural listening erases a crucial dimension of meaning from an analysis of the debate.

Accounting for listening as a rhetorical force has the power to reveal communicative dynamics that many readers will recognize but that may not have been fully articulated in scholarship before now. Spoken and written language has always been the main location for the study of rhetoric, while listening's quiet, nonverbal qualities have made it a difficult site for rhetorical inquiry until recently. Dubbed "the other side of language" by philosopher Gemma Fiumara, the vagaries of listening have gone largely unstudied in rhetorical history, which I trace throughout this book and which takes a decisive turn with Krista Ratcliffe's 2005 *Rhetorical Listening: Identification, Gender, Whiteness*.

Waking Up to Gestural Listening

My journey to this project began when I found myself deep in conversation with my classmates. As an undergraduate writing tutor at a women's college, I worked with classmates on many aspects of their writing: drafting, organization, and argumentation but also understanding challenging texts and interpreting assignment directions. In my capacity as a writing tutor, I often found myself in dialogue with classmates where neither of us had definitive answers. Indeed, in undergraduate peer tutoring, tutors are usually not subject-matter experts. More often, peer tutors are simply students a bit more experienced at navigating the writing process, or perceptive writers with an awareness of writing pedagogy they have gained through training. Nevertheless, in writing consultations, as tutor and tutee, we often felt equally invested in finding some way to move forward—and we did. By the end of our consultations, students had generated new ideas, located relevant textual evidence, revised thesis statements, and reorganized paragraphs. So what did I really offer to my classmates in the Writing Center? I offered my intentional listening. I noticed that by my offering a sustained, encouraging listening presence, the student who sought the consultation ended up articulating things they otherwise wouldn't have: asking questions they hadn't asked in class, hazarding the beginnings of new arguments, and identifying what they didn't yet understand. We enacted classic Writing Center pedagogies, like sitting side-by-side rather than face-to-face and making sure the student held the pen or piloted the laptop—small choreographies of writing tutoring that physically reinforced the peer relationship and the student's ownership over their own writing. These are Writing Centers' "sacred cows," though now rightly critiqued and complicated by a growing awareness of how they are culturally shaped. But for me, at the time, they framed the listening space of writing tutorials like a tableau. Effective tutoring is more than just showing up and listening expectantly, to be sure. But, as a young peer tutor, I found listening emerged as the most crucial constitutive element of the consultation: it occasioned, encouraged, and ultimately brought about learning.

My failures, too, brought me to this project. One semester, I was partnered as a writing tutor for the term with a young Latina woman entering her first year of college. First-year students taking part in this program were often first-generation college students and/or came from backgrounds historically underrepresented in the academy. Elena struggled to address course writing assignments, the instructions for which, in retrospect, often operated on assumptions about prior knowledge and what is meant by terms like "write an essay in which . . . ," "reflect," "synthesize," or "analyze." In our sessions, we often looked at her rough drafts together, and I found myself telling her that she likely needed to significantly change what she had already written, sometimes rewriting entirely—a lot of work, and discouraging for a student to hear. I noticed that in the midst of these conversations, as I was explaining issues in her paper, sometimes Elena's eyes would well up with tears. The tears never fell, and she was able to continue with our conversations. For my own self, I felt embarrassed and unsure of how to proceed but decided it was best to ignore the emotional display and forge ahead with the tutoring sessions. In doing so, I enforced damaging beliefs: I reified a power structure that positioned me as an in-control expert and her as a newbie whose unseemly emotions would not be acknowledged in academic writing and research. With discouragement written on her face, my classmate's gestural listening communicated volumes but I did not recognize them. I only moved forward based on her calm, business-as-usual verbal responses, ignoring the embodied listening behaviors that more strongly shaped our communicative situation.

When I began to teach first-year composition courses as a graduate student, I brought what I had learned about listening in peer tutoring. The success of my classes depended, as do many discussion-based courses, on my students' willingness to speak up about what they understood and about what they did not yet understand. So, I worked on my rapport with students, trying to create the right kind of environment. I noticed that creating an encouraging, participatory atmosphere could be linked to a specific quality in my listening. If I allowed students to see me listening to them, they often became more willing to engage in class discussion. In the classroom, I found myself in postures of listening, with my head bent forward, eyes gazing into a middle distance. I followed up by checking that I understood what the student had expressed before moving forward. My own more intentional performance of listening was, in the beginning, mainly just a way to facilitate richer and easier class discussions.

What I am writing about here may also remind readers of the term "active listening." Many people, like me, have encountered this term in conjunction with school or work, likely pertaining to how to be a better listener or, at least, a more productive one. "Active listening" skills usually include techniques like strategic note-taking, asking follow-up questions, and maintaining eye contact (Rogers and Farson). Active listening skills can be extremely helpful in retaining information and avoiding conflict. I want to challenge, however, the assumption that "good" listening is only the kind of listening that the classroom or the conference room deems productive or helpful. Instead, I consider a broad range of listening behaviors without immediate judgment or assuming that I can determine what constitutes "good" listening. Rather, I investigate listening however it appears and consider the many ways it acts upon discursive situations, suspending, for a moment, assumptions about what constitutes "good" and "bad" listening, as well as the usefulness of that categorization. So, while active listening may be a useful touchpoint for entering the discussion about listening as a rhetorical force, what I mean by the rhetorical power of listening is not limited to active listening strategies.

In addition to noticing my own listening behaviors in my classroom, I looked for listening in my students. Becoming aware of their listening behaviors catalyzed an important realization for me in my first semester of teaching. In particular, my experiences with one student—I will call him David—illuminated an urgency behind this project that I had not originally seen. David stood out in a class of first- and second-year students for his stillness. Initially, I interpreted his still, quiet behavior as a stony silence, one that might indicate he did not like the class or think it worth his while. Other times, I interpreted his behavior as a lack of engagement. While I could see David—the only Black, male student in the class—speaking with his classmates in small-group work, he rarely spoke up in class-wide discussions.

My impression was overturned a few weeks later, however, in a one-on-one conversation with David during my office hours. There, David offered observations and asked questions in a way that reflected a deep, lively engagement with our main course text.

He had, in fact, been listening.

That conversation was a turning point, one that brought me to question myself and my perceptions. As an instructor, I had not known how to identify or interpret David's listening behaviors. Further, I wasn't aware of the way my own expectations of listening behaviors had been culturally shaped. Due to that lack of awareness, instead of defaulting to a stance of compassion, of giving David the benefit of the doubt, I reverted to a stance of defensiveness, suspicion, and dismissal. My profound misperception of this student made me realize that the listening performances of historically underrepresented students might look different from the performances of listening usually recognized and rewarded in classroom spaces.

My experiences with David were an overdue wakeup call. With those interactions on my mind, I wondered how instructors tell the difference between quiet actions in the classroom: on the one hand, when students are daydreaming or feigning attention with their minds elsewhere and, on the other hand, when they are thinking, processing, dwelling in the pause of cogitation. When are they listening? How do we know what listening looks like, especially if it looks different across a range of students? How can instructors recognize and think critically about listening performances in the classroom?

Rethinking Capture and Code in the Study of Gesture

Initially, my impulse in answering these questions was to create a catalogue of listening gestures, in hopes of arriving at a kind of "key" for listening, where *this* gesture means *that*. But gesture resists easy codification: never free of meaning, at the same time, gestures attach less readily to particular semantic meanings than words do. So while it is possible to become more sensitized to the role of gesture in day-to-day life, no such definitive gestural "key" exists.

That is not for lack of trying, though, throughout the tradition of gesture studies. As far back as John Bulwer's *Chirologia* and *Chironomia*, published in 1644, which strove to catalogue the hand gestures underscoring certain rhetorical appeals in public speaking, those studying gesture have gone to great lengths to create codices of movement (see figure 0.1). More recently, twentieth-century gesture scholars have used many modes of capture in their attempts to code gesture. In particular, members of the "Chicago School" of gesture take pride in exacting transcriptions of gesture onto the page. For example, in *Hearing Gesture*, Susan Goldin-Meadow exemplifies this attitude when she writes: "Overall, the key to any study of gesture is its coding system—isolating gesture from the stream of motor behavior, describing its form, and assigning it meaning (and, of course, going through the steps to ensure that meaning codes are reliable and valid)" (11). In the early days of this inquiry, I too began assembling a catalogue of listening gestures that I hoped would comprise a sort of "gestural vocabulary" with which to look for listening. A few of them are as follows:

1. Catches: "catching" or "receiving" a message of some kind; for example, nodding.
2. Looping: catching and "elaborating," or indicating reception with a response of some kind; for example, a nod with a smile.
3. Reflecting: mirroring the expression of the speaker.
4. Holding: when a listener holds, or sustains, a gesture to indicate the sustained quality of their attention; for example, a teacher asks a question gesturing with one hand, and then keeps the hand up for a moment while students consider.
5. Taking-the-floor: audible signals of a person trying to "take the floor" during conversation; for example, an audible intake of breath overlapping with the previous speaker's words.

The desire to isolate and transcribe gesture, to capture and code it, points to a major pattern in thinking about gesture and language over time. Both the Chicago School and ancient rhetoricians share a tendency to center spoken words as the primary material of meaning and communication. In exploring silence as a form of political agency in his 2003 article "Silence: A Politics," Kennan Ferguson encapsulates this focus in noting how communication is often "presumed to reside within, or be constituted by, language; words might be demarcated by the lacuna between them, but the words remain the elementary objects of analysis" (115). Linguistics, largely ascribing to this orientation, takes the word as its basic unit of analysis. In turn, gesture studies that derive from the field of linguistics often position gesture as a kinesthetic "parallel" to the word. The Chicago School's methods of transcription and coding spring from its academic roots in linguistics. While this has been a useful analytical lens, its findings in the linguistics world are limited to what words tell, while the other communicative modalities that words operate in tandem with receive short shrift. Similarly, when we take a gesture as a kind of "kinesthetic word," we tend to ignore the other embodied context within which those gestures take place. This orientation separates specific gestures from their broader, embodied contexts. Predictably, relatively few writers examine the stillness enacted in *between* movements or dwell on the idea of stillness *as* movement, as a particular

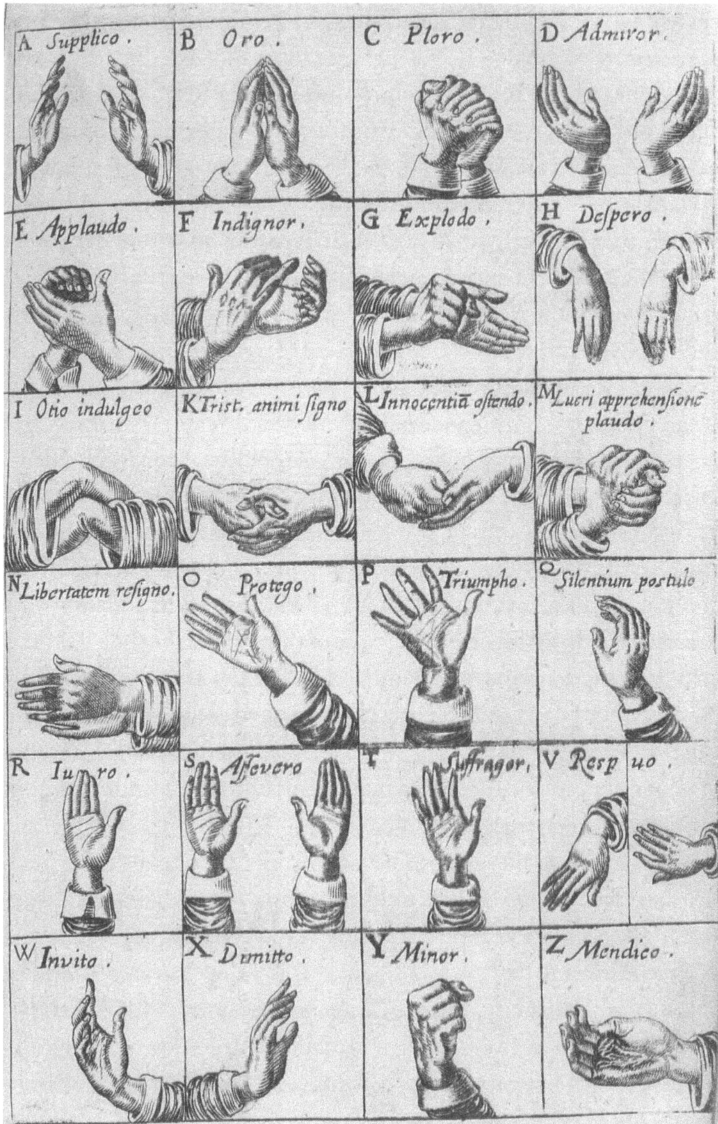

FIGURE 0.1. Illustration from John Bulwer's 1644 Chirologia, detailing types of hand gestures that may be made during speeches by orators.

kinesthetic choice that a person makes. By ignoring these elements, we render invisible certain embodied meaning-making and ways of being.

It is important to note here that only certain categories of gesture are understood by gesture theorists to "contain" or convey semantic meaning;

such gestures are called "emblematic," as defined by eminent gesture theorist Adam Kendon (*Gesture*). Emblematic gestures are those that can directly "stand in" for a word or phrase, like the thumb-to-pointer-finger "OK" hand gesture. Although this is only one category of gesture, equating gesture to language nevertheless lends itself to the sense that, methodologically, gestures might be isolated and transcribed with something like the semantic precision of words. The desire to identify a similarly small unit of analysis can be seen to drive gestural inquiry. But that effort to encode, Aristotelian in its drive to subdivide and name, often falls short of the richness of people's movements in day-to-day situations. Although GIFs and stills of Vice President Harris go some way toward capturing gestural moments, for instance, it is only by looking at a fuller picture that we can grasp the significance of her individual gestural "units." That fuller picture includes knowledge of expectations for political debate behavior, awareness of how categories of identity shape individuals' public appearances (like Harris's femininity, and Indian and Black heritage), and a sense of how a television broadcast circumscribes movement and how those broadcasts circulate further online in digital formats like GIFs and stills, as well as a memory for the highly polarized national feeling at the time of the debate. Further, gestural "units" are challenging to demarcate, embedded as they are into a person's habitus. Where do they begin and end, exactly? In short, coding gesture in the style of linguistics—or in similar conversation analysis methods characteristic of sociology—does not provide me with a flexible enough framework to unfold the richness of gestural listening dynamics.

The limitations in our ability to codify and reliably "decode" gesture push some gesture-based inquiries—including this book—in a different direction, one that highlights the complex interplay between language, gesture, and culture. Providing a different approach in this vein, Gunther Kress, in *Multimodality: A Social Semiotic Approach to Contemporary Communication* (2009), views speech and gesture as two different modal resources for communication, each with their own limitations and affordances. His theory of multimodality sees language as one semiotic resource among many, rather than as a full, "complete" mode of communication unto itself. In any given situation, communicators usually draw on multiple available semiotic resources, shifting between and among them based on the values and conventions of a given community, what it is they need to express, and which mode seems most apt to fulfill that communicative need. Kress calls this combination of communicative modes a "modal ensemble." While it's true that twentieth- and twenty-first-century gesture theorists also see communication as inherently multimodal, by incorporating dimensions of speech and gesture, Kress's notion of modal ensembles differs from other gesture theorists insofar as it does not *prioritize* or *centralize* speech as the main site of concern, as most gesture theorists do. Kress understands communication more broadly: even seeming "lacks" of communication are in themselves communicative. I find Kress's approach useful because it possesses the flexibility and richness to sustain inquiry into complex, real-world communicative situations, often encompassing a range of communicative resources.

Inspired in part by Kress's modally fluid and capacious approach, I understand gestural listening as a modal ensemble—a communicative and rhetorical force that flows between and encompasses, at different times embodied gestures like nods or hand movements, words and other vocal expressions, moments of silence and stillness. I also take into consideration larger physical configurations like where people sit and stand within rooms or other built environments like hallways and sidewalks. Methodologically, the idea of gestural listening as a modal ensemble moves its study away from *transcription* and toward *description*. It asks us to look at whole scenes of embodied interaction, to examine the social and cultural forces that come to bear on how different people listen, and how gestural listening is perceived by others. We need to consider the gestural listening we encounter in classrooms and elsewhere on a case-by-case basis and in relation to larger categories of identity, such as race, gender, and authority. In order to do that, I supplement Kress's framework of modal ensembles by drawing upon the resources of ethnography and auto-ethnography. Throughout this book, I describe moments of gestural listening I have observed in my own classrooms and those of others to illustrate and analyze what their dynamics can teach us about our lives as listeners and the listened-to. In answer to Stacey Waite's assertion in *Teaching Queer* that "there is no bodiless pedagogy, no disembodied scholarship to represent disembodied students and teaching," I incorporate moments of autobiography, too, to more fully acknowledge the way I have been shaped as a listener and as an observer of listening (23). My hope is for this book and its findings to be used, implemented in a range of pedagogical settings—to that end, at the end of each chapter, I offer pedagogical materials that can be used by readers in different ways to explore or enact aspects of listening that have emerged in my research. for instance: questions for self-reflection, survey questions with which to better understand students' gestural listening, suggestions for syllabus policies, guiding questions for research on listening, and two classroom activities.

Contextualizing Gestural Listening in Rhetoric and Writing Studies

In the chapters to come, I dive deep into moments in rhetorical history that highlight the role of embodied listenership. Here, I present some very brief context on contemporary rhetoric and writing studies.

Listening has enjoyed a burst of attention in recent years, creating a new terrain of scholarship in which I situate my own. Lately, listening has been studied from the perspective of archival rediscovery, as Jonathan Stone does in his analysis of the Lomax recordings, as well as listening's pedagogical possibilities (Ahern and Mehlenbacher; Ceraso; Comstock and Hocks; Detweiler). Scholars in English and cultural studies like Brenda Jo Brueggemann, Shannon Walters, and Jennifer Lynn Stoever have analyzed listening with regard to dimensions of ability and race, as well as from historical and philosophical angles, as do Alain Corbin, Emily Thompson, Jonathan Sterne, and Daniel Gross. Others, like Michael Bull and Brandon LaBelle, have focused on sound in relation to media and environment. My work has been made possible by the ways these scholars conceptualize sound as a rich site of critical inquiry.

Perhaps most notably, listening has been framed as a feminist rhetorical practice by Cheryl Glenn (*Unspoken*) and Krista Ratcliffe (*Rhetorical Listening*). While reading my work, those familiar with recent literature in English studies may think primarily of our field's most widely read champion of listening in rhetoric—Krista Ratcliffe—and her formulation of "rhetorical listening." Indeed, in many ways, my book exists because hers paved the way for listening to be part of what people think about when they analyze a rhetorical situation. *Rhetorical Listening: Identification, Gender, Whiteness* offers one of the first direct theorizations of listening at the intersection of rhetoric and the teaching of writing. Ratcliffe's assertion there that listening can be a generative "trope for interpretive invention" is a powerful one and highlights listening's place as part of discursive processes in reading and speaking (17). Ratcliffe's work also leverages listening's considerable power toward urging individuals to become better aware of their power and privilege, acknowledge their positionality, and assume a stance of accountability. Understanding listening as having specific, usable affordances—the idea that listening can be an interactional tool—is one way in which I follow in Ratcliffe's footsteps.

I especially appreciate Ratcliffe's theorization of rhetorical listening for the specificity and definition that it brings to the idea of listening. In our moment, to "really listen" often acts as a kind of "cue" for profundity or connection. Due to these vague cultural codings, however, writers frequently stop short of examining what listening really is, how to do it, or what it brings about. For instance, a recent *Canadian Geographic* article on bioacoustics quips: "Earth is talking. Are we listening?" (Mitchell) while myriad public apologies in the iPhone-Notes-App style or its successor, the gridded Instagram apology, follow patterns of "I made a mistake, but now I'm listening" (Diop). Listening as a catch-all for paying sympathetic attention, being open to feedback, or responding to "something more" is often deployed as a flexible platitude. By contrast, Ratcliffe outlines specific roles and functions for listening, explaining that rhetorical listening consists of "(1) Promoting an understanding of self and other, (2) proceeding within an accountability logic, (3) locating identifications across commonalities and differences, [and] (4) analyzing claims as well as the cultural logics within which these claims function" (26).

Ratcliffe offers a welcome corrective to the impulse in op-eds, sermons, and public apologies to use listening as a loose, generic cue. Here, I build upon her ideas by further attending to elements of embodiment, and acknowledging elements of uncertainty about what might be going on inside a person's head when that person appears to be listening. In doing so, I also follow the leads of a number of scholars writing on listening's intersections with cultural studies, like Charles Hirschkind's analysis of listening in Islam, in which he asserts that "the rhetorical act is accomplished by the hearer and not the speaker" (35) when listening publics in Egypt hearken to the words of *khatibs*, or preachers. I respond to Jennifer Lynn Stoever, who argues that "American listening habits are shaped by our experiences as raced subjects and by dominant ideologies of 'correct,' 'proper,' and 'sensitive' listening" (277). I also constellate thinkers about sound and listening with scholars like Edward Corbett and Debra Hawhee, who argue that rhetoric's nexus extends to, and occurs through, the body ("Rhetoric"; *Bodily Arts*).

Indeed, as full of possibility as listening is, it is also rife with complexity with regard to agency and materiality. While Ratcliffe focuses on how rhetorical listening can be activated by choice by the listener, Steve Goodman frames sonic perception as a form of vulnerability when listening occurs far outside the realm of civil discourse, abused by sonic weapons: "The ear, which transforms vibration into electric impulses addressed to the brain, can be damaged, and even destroyed, when the frequency of a sound exceeds 20,000 hertz, or when its intensity exceeds 80 decibels" (10). Is this listening, or is it just hearing? When does sonic assault cause individuals to cross from mere hearing into forced listening? Goodman and others also remind us that sound functions powerfully including outside the realm of language, its rhetorical impact moving beyond the semantic content of words. Julian Henriques examines the way the sound systems used in reggae music exert "sonic dominance" and need to be understood physically as well as discursively. J. Martin Daughtry brings to our attention still more aspects of listening's slippery material nature, explaining in *Listening to War* how wartime audition in Iraq constitutes both a crucial source of information for military and civilians alike, as well as a source of trauma located deep in the body. Daughtry gives a striking example of gestural listening informed by the listener's wartime experiences when he describes a father and son hearing a cruise missile approach their Amman neighborhood in 2006, early in the Iraq War. As Ali Zayouna hears his first cruise missile, he listens and waits, unaware of when or where the missile's landing will produce an earthquake-like impact. His father, a veteran of the Iran-Iraq War, quickly realizes that while the sound is moving away from them, the missile will likely detonate nearby, causing a deafening blast: "As Ali stood, uncomprehending, still holding his glass of water, his father's reaction was as instantaneous as it was surprising: he yanked his hearing aid out of his ear" (Fragment #1). Simultaneously a strength and a vulnerability, expressive and outward even as it acts to receive and internalize, listening emerges as deeply corporeal, bearing the marks of personal memory and experience as well as the listener's habitus and culture.

Chapter Overview: Methods and Sites of Study

As I mention earlier, in the scholarly tradition of rhetoric and writing studies, listening has long been positioned as subordinate to its more overtly productive counterparts: speech and writing. This, in turn, may reflect a well-documented "hierarchy of the senses," with its roots in the Enlightenment, which ranks listening second after vision. Those studying visual rhetorics, for instance, will likely be able to draw upon the textual and intellectual resources of more continually robust discourses over time. But while listening has experienced a kind of (sonic?) boom in the couple of decades, including a proliferation of auditorily focused research and the coalescing of a multidisciplinary field known as "sound studies," in the longer scope of history, listening remains on the margins. Investigating a topic that has often been on the fringes, I have been compelled to reach beyond scholarship in rhetoric and writing studies—my disciplinary home—to find texts and theorists who center listening. In doing so, I found that except for certain audio-centric fields like music, listening has hovered on the periphery of many other fields of study, too. Faced with this situation, I have developed a tactic of what I am calling "necessary eclecticism," in which I draw upon fields of study both adjacent to my own and those more far flung in order to paint a fuller picture of gestural listening. Readers will see that each chapter is generally anchored in the works of teacher-scholars located within the broad fields of rhetoric and composition, or rhetoric and writing studies. Beyond that, however, as readers will see in the chapter outline that follows, my efforts to "flesh out" the embodiment of listening have taken me to not only to history, literature, cultural studies, and disability studies but also to religion, psychology, primary-school education and music education, gesture studies, anthropology, and even architecture. My pursuit of gestural listening has taken me as far back as foundational texts in Western culture, such as the Old and New Testaments, and as far up to the minute as the sources in chapter 4 who assess contemporary technologies like video-conferencing software (VCS) and apply critical frameworks to computer hardware and software interfaces. This approach runs the risk of coming across as a hodgepodge or a patchwork; my turns to sources in various fields may at first strike readers as tangents. I aim to make it clear why these moves are necessary, however. The "necessary eclecticism" on display here is intentional, a synthetic approach to a project that brings a quiet, historically "fringe" topic to the center.

In chapter 1, "Looking for Listening: A Rhetorical History of Gestural Listening," I outline the longer intellectual history in which I situate my project. The story of the history of rhetoric that I tell constellates texts and thinkers mainly in rhetoric but also in a range of other disciplines (with necessary eclecticism in mind), to bring together pedagogy, sound, and the body. Tracing these contours through the history of rhetoric illuminates the ways listening has been conceptualized over time that influence gestural listening behaviors, and perceptions of it, up to the present. These include the conflation of hearing with obedience, and what it means to become the right "type" of listener—ideas with origins that can be located in the Old and New Testaments, and then later in Christian and Muslim settings examined by Carol Harrison and Charles Hirschkind. I ask, in this chapter: What is "good" listening, and how did our sense of what "good" listening is develop over time? A set of rhetoricians focusing on aspects of inclusion and exclusion—including Jacquelyn Jones Royster, J. Logan Smilges, and Brenda Jo Brueggemann—show how what counts as "good" listening can play out with unexpectedly tangible consequences, especially in academic spaces. Dwelling, too, on theorists who locate rhetorical praxis in the bodies of participants, such as Edward Corbett, Cory Holding, and Deborah Hawhee in her readings of Kenneth Burke, this chapter identifies several precedents for conceptualizing listening as a rhetorical force in its own right. Carl Rogers's ideas about "active listening" form important benchmarks here, as he, along with Kenneth Burke, exemplifies the more expansive capacities associated with listening in the twentieth century—beyond the neutral or "just" receptive. Building on their understandings of listening as generative and constructive, eminent rhetoricians Krista Ratcliffe and Cheryl Glenn have ushered in silence and listening as key terms in rhetorical scholarship, illustrating in particular how silence and listening operate as feminist rhetorics. Inspired by the feminist tradition of attending to the role of personal, lived experience, throughout chapter 1, I also reflect on who I am as a listener, offering vignettes of classroom interactions that highlight my positionality as I seek to understand the intricate dynamics of gestural listening. Altogether, this chapter establishes a kind of genealogy for the idea of gestural listening as a rhetorical force, a deceptively quiet form of influence that shapes the conditions of discourse.

In chapter 2, "Listening in the Classroom: Respect, Resistance, and Self-Regulation," I synthesize findings from a study that captures gestural listening behaviors and attitudes toward listening in two classrooms, which I filmed and surveyed, then understood better through follow-up interviews with participants. Throughout, results suggest notable patterns in how students present themselves, their attention, and their gestural listening in classroom spaces, including surprising findings about what and whom students believe gestural listening is for. Informed by my findings, I argue that gestural listening behaviors move between three main functions: displays of respect and resistance, and efforts at self-regulation that enable students to become their "classroom selves." I suggest that gestural listening behaviors coalesce into a what I refer to as a "gestural idiom of the classroom," one that instructors should recognize and question. To help make this argument, I engage with a set of teacher-scholars steeped in the teaching of writing; all pay special attention to belonging and what belonging looks like in classroom spaces. Mary Reda, Stacey Waite, and S. Brooke Corfman all turn their attention to quiet students: Reda to the compromises they make to become the "right" or "preferred" kind of student; Waite to the participation strategies carved out by students who can't or won't perform that preferred, classroom "correctness"; and Corfman to the limitations of student self-disclosure. All three articulate contested aspects of classroom comportment in ways that cast light on the role of gestural listening. Toward the end of chapter 2, I turn to Tina Campt's book *Listening to Images*. In a chapter guided mainly by a classroom study, student responses, and teacher-scholars in writing studies like Reda, Waite, and Corfman, it may seem like a digression to dwell on how Campt interprets a photo series, an inquiry situated more squarely within visual culture and, specifically, image making. But Campt's understanding of the Gulu Real Art photo series, and certain physical qualities of its subjects, provides a new way of seeing students and their listening, too. To see classrooms, and the students and instructors within them, in new ways is one of the main aims of this book, so here I draw upon the powerful ways of seeing articulated by those working in visual culture and contemporary art. Campt's notions of "stasis" and "muscular stillness" thread through subsequent chapters, as well, a touchstone for understanding the strategic stillness of listeners.

Of the "preferred" gestural listening idiom of the classroom I identify in chapter 2, I ask: Who is served by it? What else might it be expanded to allow for? With those questions in mind, chapter 3, "Gestural Listening across Identity," investigates the impact of aspects of identity such as race, gender, and neurodiversity on gestural listening. Crucially, I show that listening does not always look like what we expect it to, as the realities of listening come into conflict with classroom environments and expectations shaped by the historical and cultural patterns that I outline in chapter 1. In this effort, I'm guided by the ideas of scholars like Shannon Walters and Melanie Yergeau, who work to reconfigure the perceived rhetorical agency of disabled and neuro-atypical rhetors. Especially with regard to how gender inflects performances of gestural listening, I engage with the editorial legacy of Ratcliffe and Glenn as I draw upon essays from their edited collection *Silence and Listening as Rhetorical Arts*, in particular the contributions from Lisa Suter and Nancy Myers. Both demonstrate how embodied manifestations of silence have often been leveraged by women as a purposeful, rhetorical choice. Last, I assemble a set of writers focused on intersections of race and gender, including Perry Gilmore, Vershawn Ashanti Young, and Jennifer Lin LeMesurier, to better understand how gestural listening is inflected by overlapping aspects of identity. I contend that by becoming aware of "preferred" demonstrations of gestural listening, educators can then begin to question assumptions about who is listening "well" and who is not. This questioning clears the path, I argue, for a broader range of embodied ways of being in classrooms that are recognizable as acceptable, a badly needed expansion in perspective on the part of students and instructors.

In classrooms today, students and instructors bring more than just themselves. Where they may once have brought a notebook and pencil, they now bring laptops, tablets, and cell phones. Indeed, they may even log into an online class using one of those devices, conjuring the classroom itself through a device's smooth screen. Chapter 4, "Listening with Technology," examines the roles of personal devices and digital technologies like VCS on gestural listening behaviors, especially the ways that they interact with and, at times, shape gestural listening as a rhetorical force. This chapter unfolds in two halves: First it investigates how the presence of personal mobile devices, like cell phones and laptops, fits into perceptions of classroom listening behaviors. To do this, I draw once again upon the results of the study I conducted that informs chapters 2 and 3, with the responses of students and instructors influencing my findings about how students and teachers perceive listening to be happening—or not happening, or not happening in the right way—with the presence of mobile phones and laptops in class. I begin with the way these personal mobile technologies have the effect of making people seem to be "absently present," or mentally absent even when physically present—an idea set forward and explored extensively by Sherry Turkle in *Alone Together*. Complicating and enriching Turkle's findings, I then move to examine a set of contemporary researchers, especially Takashi Nakamura, about the effects of personal mobile technology on social perceptions. Bringing these findings home to the writing classroom are a growing number of researchers in rhetoric and composition, led here by Derek Mueller and his sense of how devices like phones and laptops help students construct a "digital underlife" within the classroom.

In the second half of chapter 4, I expand my arguments about gestural listening into digital and online territories, considering how gestural listening behaviors—and what it means to show "good" listening—have been shaped in unexpected ways by video-conferencing technologies. Of course, an enormous shift to teaching and learning in online environments was dramatically catalyzed by the COVID-19 pandemic, bringing a new urgency to understand how listening plays out in online educational spaces. Drawing on the interdisciplinary field of critical interface studies, I introduce the term "interface thinking," through which I aim to show how technologies like Zoom create new options for listening behaviors—like the self-protective (or self-effacing) move of turning off one's camera—though it also circumscribes gestural listening's possibilities by limiting listeners to interface-enabled responses, such as laptop-embedded camera framing. In my approach to the idea of interface, I am in conversation with the work of scholars who map critical frameworks from art and media studies onto contemporary digital technologies, especially Johanna Drucker, Lori Emerson, and Michael L. Black. In particular, I argue that the concept of "Zoom fatigue"—used generally here to refer to fatigue associated with synchronous, online VCS—can be readily explained in terms of gestural listening as a rhetorical force. Investigating the nascent world of research on VCS, I engage with another collection of contemporary researchers in various fields about Zoom fatigue, particularly Jeremy Bailenson and Robby Nadler, who elaborate on how social and sensory interactions are inflected by virtual experiences. This chapter rounds out my inquiry into gestural listening across a variety of educational sites, arguing that the dynamics of listening remain a vital rhetorical force even—and especially—in contested, contemporary online environments.

As my references to the Harris debates suggest, the dynamics of gestural listening are not limited to classroom spaces. While I believe classrooms heighten the play of gestural listening as a rhetorical force due to their particular expectations for respect and authority, I see gestural listening as a tool for understanding many types of interactions that span far beyond educational settings. Through an array of examples in chapter 5, "Gestural Listening Currents beyond the Classroom," I aim to show what gestural listening as a theoretical lens has to offer our understanding of diverse types of gatherings. Specifically, this chapter focuses on three sites of collective listening outside the classroom and their flowing "currents" of gestural listening: protest, worship, and choral singing. While these arenas may at first seem auditorily, gesturally, and rhetorically disparate, the work of Paul Prior aids me in showing how they can in fact be interconnected or, to use his term, "laminated" as sites of intentional listening practice. I start by examining two types of public protest: college campus demonstrations and the NFL "kneeling protests" led by Colin Kaepernick. To analyze the campus protests, I bring together the ideas of journalist Laurie Penny and rhetoricians Louis Maraj and Tamika Carey; each helps make visible forms of refusal and urgency that play out via gestural listening behaviors. In a similar vein, Kevin Quashie's discussion of "quietness," especially in his analysis of the well-known photograph of Tommie Smith and John Carlos at their 1968 Olympic medal ceremony, sheds light on how the gestural—a raised fist, a stance, a facial expression—can reorient, and add dimension to, an act of collective listening. Kneeling's gestural overlap with the body language of prayer and mourning allows me to segue to another site of gathered listening: the listening of congregants in places of worship. Here, three scholars' different approaches to the built environment, especially the position of pews and pulpits, provide starting points for examining the gestural listening currents in congregational settings: gesture theorist Adam Kendon's investigation into proxemics, historian Richard Cullen Rath's study of acoustics in various houses of worship, and rhetorician Roxane Mountford's observations about gender and preaching in Protestant congregations. Finally, the deep ties between religious ritual and choral singing bring me to my last site of gestural listening—the somatic and constantly unfolding listening of choral singing. I suggest that ensemble singers develop "somatic alignment" with each other through the gestural listening that choral singing requires, especially its emphasis on breathing and affective exchange. In making this suggestion, I draw upon the ideas of conductor and music-educator James Jordan and ethnographer Deborah Kapchan, who both examine sites of ensemble singing with potent gestural manifestations of listening. In all, with this chapter, I aim to show how gestural listening operates as a rhetorical force not just in the classroom but also beyond it, and to further articulate its special rhetorical capacities.

Throughout this book, I suggest that listening is not only a silent, internal process but also something that can be visibly and outwardly expressed. And yet, I don't want to imply through my formulation of "gestural listening" that listening is, instead, something that can simply be seen and thus fully decoded, demystified. Rather, listening emerges as a phenomenon that flows modally between the auditory, the haptic, and the visual. Already, quite literally, listening is more than meets the eye. In terms of what listening can do, too—what it can achieve, bring about, catalyze, cause—I call for an expansion of the way we understand its potential. In communicative situations, listening can receive and absorb, to be sure. It can recognize, making people "feel heard," one of its most profound functions. But gestural listening can also encourage and provoke, drawing out what might otherwise go unsaid. Further still, gestural listening can work to resist, refuse, reorient; it can serve to self-regulate, or register a listener's mental presence or absence. It's in more than one way, then, that I invite readers to join me in my investigation of gestural listening with the watchword that listening, it turns out, is truly more than meets the eye.

1

Looking for Listening

A Rhetorical History of Gestural Listening

One winter day, I walk into my writing classroom and begin to get class started, settling my bag and chalking a few key terms on the board. Students have assembled, each seated within their own arrangements of laptop, notebook, jacket, coffee cup, backpack, or phone. Turning around, I see that one student, Meredith, who is usually a lively contributor, has her head down on the table in front of her, cheek pressed to the tabletop, eyes closed. Self-conscious, I think: Wow. Am I off to such a boring start today that sleeping is preferable? Then I remember: Meredith has mentioned struggling with the effects of a long-term concussion.

Headaches, vision difficulties, and trouble with concentration can characterize persistent post-concussive symptoms, any of which might explain Meredith's unusual posture. Nevertheless, her actions have an impact, even if unintended—I notice my immediate move to negative self-talk, its self-focus, self-blame. From there on some days, it can be a short jump to the frustration, discouragement—or, for me, the sense of frozenness—of feeling disrespected, ignored. Meredith illustrates to me, once again, that listening does not always look like what we expect it to and that many factors come to bear on how people enact their listening, even as those behaviors wordlessly, ongoingly communicate. She reminds me of how strong my expectations for "correct" gestural

https://doi.org/10.7330/9781646428182.c001

listening are by appearing in the classroom in a way that seems, at first, "incorrect." She highlights how the physical arrangements of bodies, furniture, and built environment in the classroom space reflect, and continually reconstitute, the classroom's dynamics of authority: one leader at the front of the room, faced by an ensemble of others seated together.

Compare this to Suellyn Duffey's experience with a student's unusual listening choreography. In "Student Silences in the Deep South," Duffey describes the following encounter in a one-on-one meeting with a student. In doing so, she shows how gestural listening is inflected not just by dynamics of authority in classroom spaces but by other categories of identity, such as race:

"Her Body Made Me Listen"
A Scene

Her body is the color of latte. Mine is white. Hers faces the desk at which we sit, and one of her arms stretches across the desktop and supports her head, adorned with intricately braided designs. She appropriates the space for herself.

She makes no eye contact with me. She makes no perceptible movement but rests, still. I do not think her asleep, as she may seem.

I sit beside her, my chair angled toward her, my body half facing her and half facing her essay on the desk between us.

I speak. She listens. (Duffey 296)

The first detail Duffey offers refers to Ashley's skin color, centering an awareness of race. The paragraph also notes Ashley's hair, further implying that Ashley's race is something to consider in conjunction with her listening behavior during this interaction. Only after these details does Duffey move on to the spatial orientation of herself and her student, and their body positions, with Ashley resting her head on her arm and Duffey ostensibly sitting upright in a chair. Notably, Duffey does not mention her own body position very specifically, only that she half-faces Ashley and half-faces the essay on the desk. Only body positions that are considered unusual for the given situation, it seems, warrant mention, and in fact it is Ashley's departure from commonly accepted and expected gestural listening norms that occasions the writing of this vignette. In noting that "she makes no eye contact with me," Duffey reminds the reader that eye contact is a common expectation for what "good" gestural listening looks like, and that in this moment Ashley rejects that expectation.

Duffey has come to see Ashley's body language through a different lens, however. "Even though Ashley gave me none of the usual signals that she was attentive," she writes, "I had learned to recognize her ways of listening—and of showing that she was listening—were different from those of students I was accustomed to" (297). Sensitive to the usual embodied patterns of classroom settings, it would have been easy for Duffey to react in a corrective way—"Sit up straight now, Ashley"—or in a way that made Ashley's listening comportment seem like a concern—"Are you okay? Are you feeling sick?" However, Duffey goes on to interpret Ashley's gestural performance this way: "Since Ashley's silence and body at rest are ways I behave in communicative situations in which I am very close to the person I'm in dialogue with—someone I love, a family member, a trusted colleague—I had to look beyond my own experience to listen to what Ashley's silence was telling me" (297). While Duffey refers to "listening" to Ashley's silence, it is really Ashley's listening that takes center stage here, which Duffey needs to become aware of as something that is already present, already happening, something that "appropriates the space." As Ashley listens gesturally "against the grain," against deeply naturalized patterns of classroom behavior, Duffey realizes she must interpret her listening behaviors using a different rubric altogether. Although it would be easy to fall back on normative expectations for what "good" listening looks like in the context of a college classroom, Duffey suspends judgment, allowing for Ashley's particular way of being.

Students and instructors often labor under profound yet unacknowledged assumptions about what "good" listening is supposed to look like in classroom environments, assumptions that Meredith and Ashley call us to reexamine. With that in mind, instructors should become aware of how those assumptions may affect their interpretations of student behavior. While the classroom heightens the dynamics of gestural listening via its structures of authority, in fact many situations in daily life come with their own norms for "correct" gestural listening. In *The Sonic Color Line: Race and the Cultural Politics of Listening*, Jennifer Lynn Stoever recounts the 2015 death of Sandra Bland after a traffic stop, showing in tragic detail how correctness in gestural listening is shaped by race and power. After Bland expresses annoyance at being pulled over by an officer, Encinia, Stoever writes:

> Encinia became angry; he called her noncompliant and commanded her to step out of her car. Bland told him she knew her rights and did not need to exit the vehicle or put her cigarette out. Encinia then told her he would "light [her] up" with his Taser, dragged her from the car, and pulled her along the ground until out of his dashboard camera's range. After tackling and handcuffing her, Encinia arrested Bland for "assaulting an officer." Three days later, Bland was found hanged in her cell. (2)

In this tragic altercation, Encinia expects Bland's listening behaviors to look like immediate obedience, a vision of nonthreatening compliance. Instead, her listening behaviors deviate from his particular vision of "good" listening. They are not legible to the white officer as "correct" listening responses in that situation. Gestural listening that deviates from certain expectations is extremely dangerous in situations where dynamics of race collide with structures of authority that demand a certain vision of embodied obedience. Stoever continues: "Even though the Texas Department of Safety director maintains that 'citizens have the right to be objectionable—they can be rude,' Encinia's actions reveal how white authority figures continue to expect black people to perform more visible, overt, and extreme forms of compliance—through speech, vocal tone, eye contact, and physical behavior—than they ask of white subjects" (2). Stoever calls attention to the double standard for gestural listening that exists between differently raced bodies. When gestural listening behaviors are not legible according to a particular rubric, the consequences can be lethal.

How did we get here? How did our notions of what "good" listening looks like take shape, powerful yet largely unacknowledged? How can we better recognize gestural listening's profound capacity to affect communicative situations? In this chapter, I investigate the way embodied listening has been conceptualized rhetorically and how notions of "good" listening have developed over time. The sources I constellate here are those that get at how listening recruits the body in various rhetorical traditions and those that set precedents for understanding listening and embodied presence as rhetorically significant. Older, historical notions of listening do not disappear to be replaced with new ones; rather, contemporary understandings of "good" listening are complex and situation-specific, thickly layered with at-times paradoxical ideologies of respect, receptivity, and obedience, as well as with orientations that are often not acknowledged as being a part of listening, like expression, judgment, and resistance. As I aim to show throughout this book, historical conceptualizations of listening come to bear on how students and instructors listen—and perceive the listening of others—even today. Further, as instanced in the tragedy of Bland, perceptions of gestural listening reach far beyond classroom settings and into public spaces, with stakes as high as we can imagine.

As I mention earlier, and which bears repeating, Stacey Waite observes in *Teaching Queer* that "there is no bodiless pedagogy" (23). Just as Waite and Duffey, in the preceding discussion, interrogate the way their own identities come to bear on their experiences as students and instructors, I recognize that my own positionality informs my investigation into gestural listening. That is, the way I see the listening of others depends on who I am, and who I am in turn informs my own listening behaviors. With that in mind, I begin sections of this chapter with autobiographical vignettes, which serve to do two things: First, they are intended to illustrate some of the ways that I have been shaped as a listener and as an observer—as a particular person who listens and looks for listening. My hope, throughout, is that readers may also begin to reflect on aspects of their own lives that shape them as listeners, and I include a set of questions at the end of the chapter intended to help readers deepen that inquiry. Second, the personal moments I have chosen to include here provide points of entry to several of the important ways that listening has been conceptualized over time. The cultural history of listening that I trace here moves through seemingly far-ranging texts and sites, but our notions about listening, especially what counts as "good" listening, ultimately show up in our everyday experiences; I acknowledge listening's day-to-day impact by including some of mine.

"Good" Listening and Obedience

I'm in Hebrew school on Sunday morning with a dozen other eleven-year-olds. Our teacher, always fighting for our attention, is admonishing us about how it used to be: children were expected to sit completely still and silent in class. There's a complete understanding—by her and us—that those were "the olden days," in a religious community that must have been ideologically distant from the synagogue in our own New Jersey suburb.

"So, for the rest of class," she says, "let's play a game. Let's see who can sit still and be the quietest."

It's easy for me. I zip myself into a state of quiet attention—relieved even, to have reason to be still, to not have to raise my hand or interact too much with my classmates, most of whom I don't know well, because they don't go to my public middle school during the week. Everyone else forgets about the game. At the end of class, when no one is paying attention, our teacher congratulates me for winning.

In my Sunday school class that day, I am explicitly rewarded for my still, quiet gestural listening—I "win." Many school-age students have benefited from my same propensity toward quietness, the ability to sit still. We are often referred to as "good kids." The game, of course, functions in part as our teacher's plea to her rambunctious class to shout out less, to reduce distracting whispers to classmates, to sit still—to be, in short, "better behaved" in the context of the classroom environment. That day, my ability to produce an embodied "goodness," or "correctness," makes me a model citizen of the classroom. I reproduce its preferences, my listening falling easily into a show of obedience. Being a model citizen of a particular locale, however, often comes with a cost.

It may seem that being still and quiet is a kind of not-doing, an absence of movement or sound. But at the same time, there's an activeness to it. While it's not too hard for me to pull off this performance, I am, in fact, *trying to win*. In her 1996 article "When the First Voice You Hear Is Not Your Own," Jacqueline Jones Royster offers particularly sharp descriptions of what "correct" gestural listening looks like in professional academic settings. In doing so, she highlights how listening that conveys correctness, obedience, and acceptance often requires a kind of effortful inner suppression. She writes:

> I have been compelled on too many occasions to count to sit as a well-mannered Other, silently, in a state of tolerance that requires me to be as expressionless as I can manage, while colleagues who occupy a place of entitlement different from my own talk about the history and achievements of people from my ethnic group, or even about their perceptions of our struggles. I have been compelled to listen as they have comfortably claimed the authority to engage in the construction of knowledge and meaning about me and mine, without paying even a passing nod to the fact that sometimes a substantive version of that knowledge might already exist. (30)

Here, Royster illustrates the type of gestural listening that is often required as a form of "citizenship" in professional scholarly environments. She refers to the gestural performance that is required of her, "to be as expressionless as possible," a phrase that accentuates the stoicism, the limited emotional and expressive range that is de rigueur among academic audiences. This she does in order to appear as a "well-mannered Other," something she is "compelled" to do even as it helps to mask presumptuous speakers who wrongly claim authority. For Royster, maintaining a studied, expressionless stillness even in the face of insult is part of what grants a membership card to the arena of academic knowledge-making. The phrase "well-mannered" reveals her sense of being an outsider: after all, coming across as well mannered is an imperative when visiting the homes of others, or when in shared spaces; it is not necessary in one's own home. In the phrase "as expressionless as I can manage," she further emphasizes the effort—the effort of remaining still—involved in maintaining what would be considered appropriate gestural listening for that particular context. While listening is often thought of as speaking's passive, receptive counterpart, we get the sense here that it actually demands its own form of work and self-regulation, especially in settings where correct gestural listening must be maintained even when listening to something that may be deeply objectionable.

Royster writes of a concerted effort to gesturally listen in a way that is highly legible, a form of gestural listening that grants her access and membership to an exclusive discourse community. What it means to be legible as a listener, in this case, means adopting obedient norms of "expressionless" audiencing. In fact, the trope of listening-as-obedience is one of the most enduring ways in which listening has been shaped culturally. We can locate it as far back as in the Old Testament, for instance, especially in moments that emphasize the relationship between the Old Testament God and the Israelites. There, while Moses alone speaks with God "mouth to mouth," or "face to face," the patterns of interaction between God and the Israelites in the Old Testament set up the expectation that for regular people, God is often heard but not seen. The Israelites must come to trust a voice that is separate from any normal physical form. Largely, the Israelites hear the word of God through Moses. At Mount Horeb, for example, Moses says: "The Lord spoke with you face to face at the mountain, out of the fire. (At that time I was standing between the Lord and you to declare to you the words of the Lord; for you were afraid of the fire and did not go up the mountain)" (*The HarperCollins Study Bible* [used throughout for scriptural citations] Deut. 5:4–5). Moses acts as a kind of go-between, standing between the Lord and the rest of the Israelites and listening on their behalf, precisely because the "words of the Lord" must be received "out of the fire," which the others were "afraid of" and would not approach. Indeed, this moment exemplifies how in the Old Testament, God is often heard in conjunction with a frightening or jarring visual accompaniment, like fire. The unusual sensory paradigm through which the Israelites hear from God results in a sense of God's majesty, power, and otherworldliness.

It also makes direct, face-to-face listening challenging. According to the Old Testament, coming into too-direct sensory contact with God can, in fact, be deadly. Great pains are taken to make sure the Israelites, especially those with priestly duties, do not come too close to the presence of God without extensive preparations. Again at Mount Horeb, Moses asks the convened Israelites: "Who is there of all flesh that has heard the voice of the living God speaking out of fire, as we have, and remained alive?" (Deut. 5:26). Already, biblical listening takes on certain contours: the voice of God is disembodied, or embodied in an unusual, non-humanlike form. It must often be transmitted through a go-between. In the biblical context, hearing God is often dangerous and must be treated with the utmost caution, even as the Israelites yearn for ongoing reassurance, struggling to bolster their faith. The Israelites often do not hear God directly. As a result, they must show their listening after the fact: through obedience.

Obedience is layered with the language of listening in the Old Testament in various ways. Freed from 400 years of Egyptian bondage, the Israelites from late Exodus onward face the issue of how to live as a newly coalesced state—how to order their new society and whose leadership to follow. They ask, implicitly: Who is it that we can hear, and who is it that we should obey? In Deuteronomy, the Israelites further ask Moses, for instance, to "go near, you yourself, and hear all that the Lord our God tells you, and we will listen and do it" (Deut. 5:27). Agreeing to treat Moses as a divine go-between, they also establish a pattern of synonymy between listening and heeding, hearing and obeying with the phrase "We will listen and do it." Here, it is as though listening and doing are essentially the same—that "good" listening results in specific behaviors enacted thereafter. The "Shema," which is one of the central prayers in modern Judaism and which also stems from Deuteronomic scripture, highlights the overlap between listening and doing, usually translated as follows: "Hear, Israel, the Lord is our God, the Lord is One." Notably, the word for listening has previously been translated as "obey," and in some contexts the terms are essentially synonymous. In Old Testament traditions, the imperative to obey is blended into the very language of listening, as though they are one and the same.

Several problems arise from the Old Testament's conception of listening as obedience. First, listening can have many functions, going far beyond simple obedience. For Royster, gestural listening is not just about accepting what she hears; rather, it is also a performance that contributes to her at-times troubled sense of "citizenship" in her professional environment. As we will see going forward, listening can take on varied valences of expression and can serve a range of communal and interpersonal functions. Nevertheless, in many spaces that are shaped by hierarchical power dynamics, the imperative for obedient gestural listening persists, although it is thickened with other ideas about listening.

A second problem is that obedience does not look the same for all types of listeners in all instances. For some, it may not look like tolerant, accepting, or meek behavior, as mine did in my Sunday school seat. Further, some listeners may not be able to convey a sense of listening-obedience in a way that is legible to the presiding authorities. In "Bad Listeners," for instance, J. Logan Smilges writes: "As a neurodivergent person, I have sensory limits that are different than those of my nondisabled peers." They continue to point out how obedient listening is not always accessible: "Sometimes Bad Listeners won't listen because it's not the right time or not the right place ... But there are also times and places that nondisabled people assume are meant for listening, that seem to invite listening to happen. In these times and places, we imagine listening occurring spontaneously, suddenly, naturally." As we have already seen, however, listening, and especially the embodied enactment of gestural listening, is often far from natural and far from effortless. Or, it feels "natural" for some to listen "appropriately" at those times, while it feels unnatural for others—like Royster, they may feel "compelled."

As an example of an environment that may seem to "invite listening to happen," Smilges continues:

> Seminars come to mind. My class is scheduled to meet from 3 PM to 6 PM in the room next to the elevator. Someone speaks, and someone responds. Someone else speaks. They are looking at me, the instructor ... It's been a bad day, and I'm not *feeling up to any of it*. I'm tired; my head hurts; my body hurts ... I want to cancel class and send everyone home, but here everyone is: looking at me, listening to me, as if I were listening to them. I feel bad that I'm not listening. I'd feel worse if I did listen. I make a judgement call: we'll continue with class, but I won't be responding to questions. *Write them down, and I'll respond via email tomorrow. Talk amongst one another.* I turn on my phone's voice recorder. I'll listen better later.

Smilges may appear as though they are listening—students are "listening to me, as if I were listening to them"—but Smilges actually recognizes a moment when their "correct" gestural listening performance as a classroom instructor is about to break down—they are not "up to any of it," but "here everyone is: looking at me," expecting behavior that aligns with expectations for an instructor in the classroom. So Smilges moves to turn on a voice recorder, in order to be able to "listen better later." In fact, turning on the phone's voice recorder constitutes a different kind of gestural listening, a move that changes the materiality and temporality of listening and implies that Smilges will listen to take in the information and respond to the students' discussion later. That is, listening is still happening. However, switching on the voice recorder releases Smilges from the immediate necessity for the embodiment of "correct" gestural listening in the moment.

In turning on their phone's voice recorder in order to "listen later," Smilges extends and re-sequences the act of listening to encompass "crip time": "Operating on crip time, our listening will likewise need to be broken into new rhythms and patterns, as well as perhaps new modes and modalities, that reflect each participant's needs in the moment," Smilges writes. While Smilges refers to this as being a "bad listener," it is only "bad listening" according to a narrow rubric of listening-as-obedience, or listening-as-correctness. In calling themselves a "bad listener" in this instance, Smilges points once again to the strong expectations for gestural listening that exist in specific contexts—and, crucially, how obedient gestural listening ultimately ends up becoming entwined with normative gestural listening. Gestural listening refers to obviously gestural expressions like nodding, verbal backchanneling, and posture, but by my definition it encompasses any form of expressive, materially embodied listening. With this in mind, switching on the voice recorder constitutes gestural listening, too. It is simply a nonnormative, even "disobedient" form of gestural listening.

Another perspective on the strength of our expectations for normative gestural listening is introduced by Brenda Jo Brueggemann, who writes about her experiences both as a student and as a teacher who is severely hard of hearing. Brueggemann makes observations about what it means for her as a hard-of-hearing woman to "appear" correctly, especially when it comes to listening. In *Lend Me Your Ear: Rhetorical Constructions of Deafness*, she writes: "I tend to control conversations . . . It is safer this way: if I don't shut up, if I keep talking, then voila, I don't have to listen" (93). Here, Brueggeman positions listening as a form of vulnerability, one that often exposes her disability and makes her subject to a set of associations and reactions that people often have toward deaf and/or hard-of-hearing individuals. "And if I don't have to listen," she continues, "I don't have to struggle, don't have to ask for repeats, don't have to assume any of the various appearances that I and other deaf/hard-of-hearing people often appear as—stupid, aloof, disapproving, suspicious" (93). Brueggemann confronts and negotiates daily the expectations that exist for what listening should look like, how it should gesturally manifest. But in fact, those expectations depend on sensory abilities within the range of normal. "If I keep talking," Brueggemann asserts finally, "I pass" (93). With the idea of "passing," she may put readers in mind of the citizenship that I mention with regard to myself and Royster earlier: the belonging, and the set of rights and privileges granted to those who can produce the correct forms of comportment in any given situation. What we think listening looks like takes on serious consequences for those negotiating disability.

Brueggemann is conscious about the "look" of her listening both as a student and as a teacher. About teaching, she writes: "I avoid, at all costs, leading large group discussions in which students might speak from the back of the room"

(99). Instead, she writes, "I put them in small groups for discussion and then I walk around, lean over their shoulders, sit down with a small group for a short time" (99). In this way, Brueggemann not only readjusts classroom practices for the kind of hearing she can and can't do; she also gesturally listens in a different way, walking around, leaning over students' shoulders, and sitting down with individual groups. "Then," she continues, "I bring one group to the front of the class to help me lead the whole class through discussion, branching from what they were talking about in their smaller groups. In this way, the students take charge of receiving the questions and become interpreters for me and each other" (99). Brueggemann finds a way to have her students actually *do* most of the listening, and in doing so, they also coordinate or facilitate the class discussion. What emerges here is a model of listening in which a group of students serves as a kind of aural conduit for their instructor, becoming, as she writes, "interpreters." Another image for this situation is to see the discussion-leading group as an adaptor, with one end connected to Brueggemann and the other end bearing multiple ports that can connect to their roomful of classmates.

Listening conceptualized as obedience gives rise to the sense that "correct" gestural listening in any given context is listening that aligns with normativity—neurotypicality and having the "right kind" of body. An illustrative case in point are individuals with autism spectrum disorder (ASD). For people with autism, the usual ways of establishing connections with other people via nonverbal signals can cause distraction and even discomfort. People with autism are often uncomfortable with eye contact, for example. In an article for the Indiana University's Indiana Resource Center for Autism, Kozella Stewart asks if eye contact should be insisted upon by parents and especially teachers working with autistic children. Educators, after all, are often taught to gather and recapture students' attention when starting instruction and when attention seems to have diffused. "To accomplish this task," Stewart writes, "teachers often first attempt to get attention by cuing 'Look at me'":

> They also often assume that they have individuals' attention when they "get eye contact" and that those who do not conform cannot be paying attention. Thus, when individuals who have autism seem to avoid looking into the eyes of teachers and others with whom they interact, the strategy that comes most naturally and is often pursued quite intently is the verbal cue "Look at me." If an individual who has an autism spectrum disorder fails to respond within what is viewed as a reasonable length of time, the cue may be repeated more forcefully. If the person still fails to look as directed, misinterpretations of why the person isn't "complying" may fuel futile power struggles that only

> frustrate everyone concerned and further thwart the abilities of individuals with autism to respond. (Stewart)

Insisting on gestural manifestations of listening that are the "normal" or expected ones, then, can backfire completely for students with autism. Eye contact often serves as a gestural assurance that attention is being paid and that listening is occurring. The implications of Rozella's observations, though, is that listening doesn't always look like what we expect listening to look like in neurodiverse individuals. Furthermore, insisting on any gestural performance of listening may actually be a disservice to some students. Stewart goes on to note that some students with autism struggle to simultaneously process information coming in through different sensory channels. This struggle leads to situations where a student may appear to be looking out the window all during class but can then demonstrate, upon being asked, exact knowledge of what's been said.

The variety of embodied forms listening can take may seem to bring about a death knell to an inquiry into gestural listening. If listening can look so diverse depending on the individuals in question, why look for listening at all? But investigating how listening manifests for neurodiverse individuals changes the angle on that inquiry in a useful way. It reminds people, teachers in particular, that we have, already, certain expectations for what paying attention looks like and even for what respect and resistance look like in classroom settings. Those preconceptions can affect our perceptions of students as people, as well as our perceptions of their abilities and potentials. Nothing crystallizes expected norms for listening behaviors more than their subversion by those negotiating atypical forms of cognitive perception.

Thus far, we have a sense of several important concepts in this rhetorical history of embodied listening. First, listening has long been conceptualized as obedience, or acquiescence. Second, we see that in many communicative situations, gestural listening comes under pressure to be legible according to certain rubrics. What reads as "recognizable" gestural listening, furthermore, tends to be listening behaviors that reflect norms for categories of identity like race, gender, and ability, among others. Last, we get the sense that listening, especially gestural listening, carries rhetorical power—the ability to influence and exert pressure, even to persuade. Whether correct or incorrect, obedient or defiant, listening moves beyond the body to have a palpable impact on discursive situations.

Becoming the "Right" Listener

The choir has rehearsed all term, and now we file onto flood-lit risers in a darkened auditorium, filled with an expectant audience of parents and classmates. Taking our places, we feel the formality of our uniforms: floor-length, black dresses alternating with crisp tuxedoes. The conductor lifts his hands—it's time to sing. After a short opening phrase, a soprano rises up to a high solo note, exposed, and the rest of the choir is supposed to enter again then, like a supporting wave—but no, we miss our entrance somehow, and a ripple of uncertainty runs through the group. For split-second direction, everyone looks to the conductor, who collects our attention with a buoyant, gathering gesture and cues the entrance again. Watching even more closely now, the choir catches the new cue with a palpable focus, leaning forward. Will the soloist sustain her high note long enough for us to play off our mistake? Will we reach the next cadence together? We follow the conductor's movement closely as he, too, listens for the way forward.

Singing in choir, I learned a type of listening that is multidimensional. Choral listening extends from individual singers to the conductor, as they watch each other carefully to give and catch cues for breaths, entrances, movements, and cutoffs. But choral listening also encompasses a web that connects each singer to all the others, as they listen "out" to each other, listening "around" themselves, in order to enter and cut off together, for instance, or to make the vocal micro-adjustments that help achieve a smooth blend of voices. The old poster on the choir room wall instructs: "Listen louder than you sing." Choral listening takes shape as obedient and disciplined—as singers uniformly "take orders" from the conductor—but also participatory and constantly unfolding in the moment, flowing in many directions, sustained continually alongside the act of singing.

While choir is a kind of special case, one that heightens gestural listening dynamics, it nevertheless helps illustrate an important idea that runs through cultural constructions of listening: that being a "good" listener in any given situation is not necessarily something that comes naturally but rather something that a person needs to *become*. It is something taught and learned, something culturally shaped according to the nuances of any given situation. Further, if listening is something that needs to be learned, it follows that there exist types of "preferred" listening in different environments that need to be learned or cultivated in order to be successful in those settings. In Sunday school, I "won" the game by demonstrating the "preferred listening" for that context.

One might think that preferred listening is always obedient, quiet, acquiescent listening, but in reality the picture is more complex. For instance, preferred listening, or "good listening," in choir is obedient, following the conductor's cues closely. Simultaneously, however, choral listening requires active participation, listening "out" toward the other choir members into order to blend, breathe, and respond together as a cohesive whole, as we did in the case of the mistake my choir made in performance. So preferred listening in that setting actually layers obedience and acquiescence onto participatory, interactive listening networked in several directions between the self and many other nodes.

Similarly, while I have written that "preferred" classroom listening is obedient, quiet, and acquiescent, in fact that is an oversimplification of what classroom spaces tend to demand of students. In classroom environments, what emerges as "preferred listening" is a nuanced gestural listening profile incorporating several, often-competing values and expectations. Ultimately, preferred gestural listening in the classroom aligns students with success in academic settings, yet often it is only at the foreclosure of other available ways of being. Meredith and Ashley, for instance, risk having their gestural listening behaviors punitively misunderstood. In Sunday school, I gained my teacher's gratitude by being quiet and manageable, but due to the self-containment that required I likely did not connect with my classmates as fully as I could have.

Returning again to biblical sources, the New Testament provides a site for locating textual patterns that conflate hearing and obedience but that further establish the need to *make oneself* into the right kind of listener. In the Gospels of Matthew, Mark, and Luke, for instance, Jesus famously urges those he preaches to with the formula "listen, those with ears to hear." This formulation is repeated, in particular, before or after Jesus relays a cryptic parable. The exhortation to "listen, those with ears to hear" reinforces the relationship between listening, understanding, and subsequent actions of obedience: Jesus, in the Gospel of Matthew, declares: "Everyone then who hears these words of mine and acts on them will be like a wise man who built his house on rock . . . And everyone who hears these words of mine and does not act on them will be like a foolish man who built his house on sand" (Matt. 7:24–27). In the Gospels, if a person listens, and listens rightly, they will then act in ways consistent with Jesus's reinterpretation of Mosaic law. Again, hearing and obeying are conceptualized as being of a piece.

The New Testament further implies, however, that it may not be enough to "just listen," to "come as you are," so to speak. The question remains of how to listen so that one can "build a house on rock." Those who would hear divine truths, and the deeper meanings of the parables, must listen in the right way, even making themselves into the right kind of listener—a listener of faith, primed to receive the word of Jesus correctly. When questioned by the disciples about his choice to use parables in his preaching, Jesus invokes scripture stemming from Isaiah: "The reason I speak to them in parables is that 'seeing they do not perceive, and hearing they do not listen, nor do they understand'" (Matt. 13:13–14). The text in Isaiah referred to here is, as biblical scholars know, not itself readily decipherable; it refers, though, to those who listen without understanding, again implying that people must cultivate not just any listening within themselves but the *right* listening. While this intertextual reference does little to bring clarity to the type of listening Jesus might see as right, directly after this moment in Matthew he offers another parable, the Parable of the Sower. This parable is about seeds sown on different types of soil—those cast hopelessly on the dry, bare path, those sown in rocky soil, those sown in soil choked by thorns, and, finally, "what was sown on good soil": "this is the one who hears the word and understands it, who indeed bears fruit and yields, in one case a hundred-fold, in another sixty, and in another thirty" (Matt. 13:18–23). Here, the parable seems to imply that listening creates the conditions for right understanding, even if a given teaching is not immediately clear. In Luke, Jesus further warns to "pay attention to *how* you listen; for to those who have, more will be given; and from those who do not have, even what they seem to have will be taken away" (Luke 8:18; emphasis mine). Not all listening is created equal, it seems.

While the embodied idiom of what Jesus refers to as good listening is not visible in the words of the New Testament, the takeaway remains that to be like "good soil," and to be the type to whom "more will be given," one must listen correctly. A person must endeavor to become the right kind of listener, another idea about listening that persists over time.

So what might it look like to become the right kind of listener? Sources in rhetorical history that highlight how "right listening" might look are hard to come by. However, those that do exist point to a particular balance between demonstrations of normative obedience and participatory engagement. In *The Art of Listening in the Early Church*, Carol Harrison excavates a vision of preferred listening habits for early Christian listeners. According to Harrison, right listening for early Christians has to do with the stamp of faith on the heart, listening through a speaker's phrasings—eloquent or not—to extract truth. In her reading of Plutarch's *The Art of Listening to Lectures* (*De recta ratione audiendi*), a pagan text that also influenced early Christian rhetorical practice, Harrison highlights Plutarch's description of the gestural, participatory listening that should accompany right audition. Reading Plutarch, Harrison writes:

> Just as bodily gesture and facial expressions were regarded as an intrinsic part of the way in which a speaker communicated their message, so Plutarch urges that the hearer should also ensure that they encourage the speaker by making their friendly disposition evident to them in, for example, "a gentleness of glance, a serenity of countenance, and a disposition kindly and free from annoyance." (129)

Harrison interprets this moment from Plutarch to mean that "right listening or right reception, is thus the beginning of right speaking or right delivery" (131). This is a departure from the biblical listening I outline earlier, and an orientation that invests the gestural responses of audience members with remarkable importance. Listeners, here, have the ability to influence the speaker, creating conditions for "right speaking or right delivery." To help contextualize this development in listening sensibilities, Harrison writes that due to norms in their juried legal system, theater, and other sites of civic life, early Christian audiences were "used to being treated not so much as an audience as a conversation partner; someone who could influence the speaker by their expressions, gestures, applause, laughter, and groans, or, indeed, their silence" (144). Listeners' behaviors affect what is being spoken, but certain affects are preferred, recommended, or expected of "encouraging" listeners. Here, a new vision of embodied listening takes shape, involving a particular mix of reception and participation.

Similarly seeking the roots of listening behaviors in religious practice, Charles Hirschkind traces the contemporary phenomenon of listening to recorded sermons in Egypt all the way back to Muslim liturgical traditions. In those traditions, he identifies a particular rhetorical paradigm with consequences for what "right listening" looks like. According to Hirschkind, the most important rhetorical act in Muslim liturgical traditions rests within the listener, rather than in the preacher (*khatib*). On "sam,'" or correct hearing, Hirschkind writes, "what the divine message requires within this tradition is not so much a rhetor as a listener, one who can correctly hear what is already stated in its most perfect, inimitable, and untranslatable form" (35). By contrast to rhetorical traditions that emphasize the artfulness of the speaker, and the speaker's ability to craft persuasive language on a given topic, Hirschkind argues that Islamic traditions place the responsibility within the listener to receive properly the already-perfect word of God.

At first, this may remind readers of the listening paradigm I have identified here as characteristic of the New Testament and the necessity of Jesus's followers to develop "ears to hear." The type of faithful listening that Hirschkind identifies, however—listening that correctly responds to the already-perfect words of the Qur'an—recruits not just the ears but a range of sensorimotor responses. Hirschkind finds that correct gestural listening in this tradition can be seen and felt in the "listener's lips as they subtly trace the salutation to the Prophet following the *khatib*'s mention of his name, in the barely audible phrases of supplication uttered when a certain dire event of the eschaton has been described . . . or in adjustments of posture" (124). While the New Testament does not vividly describe the actions of listeners, Hirschkind and Harrison locate embodied listening practices that are crucial to reception in Islamic and early Christian traditions.

What emerges is the sense that "preferred listening," which is socially shaped, combines obedience with interactivity in ways that are situation specific. Gestural listening becomes a form of reception that is, itself, expressive. So listening, here, is far from speaking's passive counterpart—rather, it is a thickly layered site of receptivity that simultaneously reaches outward to express, able to influence discursive situations.

Generative Listening

While in college, I teach practice lessons to a group of adults learning English as a foreign language as I work toward an ESL teaching certificate. Afterward, our teaching is evaluated by the teacher-trainer, who helps us hone techniques like prompting students with yes-or-no questions that test their comprehension. Laughing, he says, "Laura, I would love to play poker with you. You have a terrible poker face. You're giving them the answers with your expressions." By my first job out of grad school, teaching writing at a small liberal arts college in central Pennsylvania, I've become a cliché of the overactive listener. When a reticent student speaks in class, I'm nodding and vocalizing before they've even finished a sentence, using all my expressive resources to encourage and affirm their contribution as it's happening. *Keep going,* I'm saying, without words. *I'm with you. Yes.*

Becoming a teacher is a process that reshapes my listening behaviors, exaggerating some aspects while minimizing others. In the ESL classroom, I may have "given away the answers" with my face because active, expressive gestural listening is often coded as feminine in the United States, deriving from the expectations American women face to perform care and likeability. In that moment, I enacted habitual gestural listening performances coded as female. Alternatively, I may have given "hints" with my face because I was ill at ease with the dynamic in that classroom, uncomfortably aware of being the representative authority on spoken English while the students, all of them considerably older than I was, struggled to express themselves in basic English phrases. Perhaps, without really realizing it, I tried to level the playing field. Here, gestural listening reflects elements of gender, age, and authority, even as I leverage it to quietly disrupt those dynamics.

By my first postgraduate job, my gestural listening is highly visible and directly responsive to what's being said. I often feel that its primary function is simply to be ongoingly encouraging, something especially crucial in classes that rely on discussion. It is a tool that I deploy still more when students seem unsure of themselves, especially with first-years or with students new to a discipline. Sometimes, through my gestural listening, I can draw students out, receiving in a way that encourages, that creates conditions for them to express ideas, especially ideas that may be tentative, partially formed, but for those very reasons important moments in the learning process.

What I want to point out here is that in these instances, my gestural listening is generative, even as it works to continuously—including when I am not actually speaking—to cultivate a particular rapport with the students. Tracing another thread through rhetoric scholarship that focuses on the influence of embodied listening, I locate precedents for conceptualizing gestural listening as generative, continuous, and instantiated by gathered, embodied presence. Further, listening begins to serve an expanded range of functions that gain definition in twentieth-century thought. Those functions retain elements of obedience and respect, as well as imperatives for becoming the "preferred" type of listener inflected by situation and identity, even as they build upon those constructions of listening.

Historically, rhetoricians often considered gesture to be secondary to the "main" material of classical rhetoric: speech. More recent scholarship in rhetoric and gesture, however, suggests a different relationship between gesture, language, and thought. Cory Holding's "Rhetoric of the Open Fist" rereads John Bulwer's treatises on rhetorical gesture, *Chironomia* and *Chirologia*, in a way that challenges existing narratives of gesture as merely ornamental or coercive, ideas associated historically with Quintilian, and from Bulwer's London contemporaries. Holding argues instead that gesture during speech should be understood as something quite different—as a form of invention located within the body. By suggesting that "reasoned engagement is also entirely bodily," her work draws upon insights from twentieth-century gesture studies, exemplified by the researchers David McNeill, Susan Goldin-Meadow, and Adam Kendon. These researchers find that gestures are not just illustrative in a mime-like way for a hearer's benefit; rather, they fuel and contribute to the unfolding of thought and language for the speaker, as well. As McNeill puts it: "Gestures . . . are themselves thinking in one of its many forms—not only expressions of thought, but thought, i.e., cognitive being, itself" (99). That is, embodied gestures bring about thought, catalyzing and shaping it, rather than simply being an after-the-fact decoration to speech.

If gestures constitute an important part of invention and, even more fundamentally, of cognition, as Holding and the gesture theorists argue, the gestures of listening warrant our attention as richly informative, especially as they arise in groups. Edward Corbett answers that call in "Rhetoric of the Open Hand and Rhetoric of the Closed Fist," in which he further carves out context for an embodied, responsive rhetoric of assembled listeners. What Corbett calls "muscular rhetoric," or "body rhetoric," refers to a range nonverbal forms of persuasion characterized by "massed physical presence," often accompanied by other nonverbal forms of expression like flags, pins, armbands, or "bizarre costumes" (291). Rhetoric of the closed fist, as Corbett defines it, tends to be nonverbal, coercive rather than traditionally persuasive, and is often practiced by those without ready access to other types of participation in the public sphere. While protestors often protest to gain a voice in reforming or creating policy, the end goal of Corbett's "body rhetoric" is not necessarily speech. Rather, it signifies, in and of itself, a form of generative presence that exerts pressure. By focusing on how rhetors use nondiscursive means—means beyond verbal expression—to influence communicative situations, Corbett presages the work of feminist scholars in the later twentieth-century who reread silence and listening as feminist rhetorical tactics.

Debra Hawhee's investigations of rhetoric, both ancient and modern, also focus on assembled bodies as sites of rhetorical generativity. In her reading of Kenneth Burke's early-career musical criticism, Hawhee investigates Burke's preoccupation with the rhetorical role of bodies, especially those "audiencing" at musical and dance performances. Hawhee argues that Burke's "inquiry into music's effects on bodies takes him to the edges of language, particularly language as rhythm, wherein rhythm becomes not merely an aesthetic feature but an enlivening force—sheer energy—with a unique capacity to mingle with and transform bodily energies and rhythms already churning, humming, and moving" (*Moving Bodies*, 28). In focusing on the bodies of audience members, Burke, illuminated through Hawhee, is careful not to neutralize or homogenize those bodies, as though they are passive, simplistically receptive, or obedient. Rather, they are already "churning," producing "bodily energies" with which the music interacts. In short, the people of the audience are listening, and what listening means, here, is listening with the whole body, a nonneutral act already "humming," already taking place. Duffey has the same realization about Ashley's listening, as described earlier, enabling her to avoid chastising Ashley, asking her if she's unwell, or otherwise responding in a way that misunderstands the student's self-presentation. Duffey assumes, as Burke does, that Ashley already arrives on the scene with an inner life that churns, hums, and moves.

By favorably "identifying" with an audience, in Burke's own terms, a rhetor creates conditions for persuasive success in part by inclining the audience to listen. Identification allows for audience members to "activate receptivity"—that is, to begin to use listening's affordances both to express and receive. If audience members find themselves nodding, leaning forward, or resting their gaze on the speaker, those elements of receptive body language may serve to further open them to what they hear. Upon seeing those nods or indications of interest and openness, the speaker may in turn be emboldened, and the cycle of identification perpetuates. With this in mind, Burke's conceptualizing of identification powerfully homes in on the dynamics of mutual listening, and ways in which listening acts as a force on communicative situations. When I nod to my students in the preceding vignette, I use that gestural mode to intentionally open myself to their contributions. Gestural listening changes me, even as it creates an atmosphere of mutual exchange in the classroom.

Already, through Burke, twentieth-century thought affords an expansion of what listening is and does—no longer is it simply an enactment of obedience and respect, or even a learned, preferred performance. Instead, listening emerges as a capacity that can be offered to others, with functions including the therapeutic and the pedagogical. Contributing to that expansion, just a few years after *A Rhetoric of Motives* was published, the psychologist Carl Rogers began to articulate his ideas on "person-centered" therapeutic practices. Notably, Rogers identifies new functions for listening, beyond obedience or performative respect. In the therapeutic context, Rogers writes:

> Being empathic involves a choice on the part of the therapist as to what she will pay attention to, namely the inner world of the client as that individual perceives it. Thus it does change the interpersonal politics of the relationship.

> It in no way, however, exercises control over the client. On the contrary it
> assists the client in gaining a clearer understanding of, and hence a greater
> control over, her own world and her own behavior. (11)

Here, the listening of the therapist to the client has a remarkable influence on
the client. The nature of that influence is more reminiscent of Burke's identification than of earlier models of listening I have traced in this chapter, which
emphasize obedience and respect. Rather than trying to bring about any particular outcome, Rogers's understanding of listening is meant to create a climate
in which the client grows and changes in constructive ways.

Implications of Rogerian listening for educational situations are rich. Listening plays an important role in creating the "facilitative conditions" that
Rogers lays out as essential parameters for successful person-centered work
in educational settings, commonly called "student-centered" teaching. Among
them is the condition that "*a facilitative learning climate is provided*" (7; emphasis
in original). Rogers continues: "In meetings of the class or of the school as a
whole, an atmosphere of realness, of caring, and of understanding listening is
evident. This climate may spring initially from the person who is the perceived
leader. As the learning process continues, it is more and more often provided
by the learners for one another" (73). Rogers figures "understanding listening" as something a "perceived leader" can instantiate simply by enacting it.
He further indicates that, ideally, this behavior "catches," inviting others to
enact it for each other as well. Of a graduate course that started off resistant
to his approach but nevertheless ended productively, Rogers writes: "It was
learning and therapy; and by therapy I do not mean illness, but what might be
characterized by a healthy change in the person, an increase in his flexibility,
his openness, his willingness to listen" (86).

Taken together, Burke and Rogers represent a trend in twentieth-century
thinking that emphasizes the idea of listening as a capacity that can be offered
to others, activated within others by a skillful rhetor, and even one that may
benefit both listener and listened-to as they fluidly exchange roles. Rogers
and Farson write: "Not the least important result of listening is the change
that takes place within the listener himself. Besides providing more information than any other activity, listening builds deep, positive relationships and
tends to alter constructively the attitudes of the listener." Both listener and
listened-to are participating, and both can be changed—for the better, Rogers
believes—by purposeful listening. In short, this period brings about a new set
of functions for the role of listening in rhetoric. While its historical valences

remain, the twentieth century emphasizes strong movements away from ear-lier formulations of listening, toward distinctly different possibilities.

Listening Bodies

In fifth grade, we do a craft for Father's Day where we create a "hug" by trac-ing our hands on construction paper, cutting them out, and attaching them to either end of a piece of string the length of our arm spans. We're measured at the blackboard to determine the length of our strings. My arm span, coordinat-ing with my height, is the widest in my class by a longshot.

Throughout my childhood and adolescence, most people's first reactions to me had to do with my prodigious height. By age eleven, I was five-foot-five, reaching five-nine by fourteen. There are certain narratives that follow tall kids: becoming an exceptional athlete, for instance, can act as an explanation for "excessive" height. Another narrative is the tall kid who slouches, whose standout height makes them shy. Easily winded and not especially shy, my experiences fall into another category: I was often treated as though I were older than I really was. I wonder, my own personal chicken and egg, whether I tended to act in a more mature way—think "mom friend" and "pleasure to have in class"—because I was treated with the expectation that I was, or if I truly was advanced, meriting that treatment regardless of my size. Similarly, I'm not sure if my still, contained body language, even as a kid, came naturally from my energy level and personality or if it came from a sense that I needed to match others' perceptions of myself. As a big kid, if I acted too young and childish, I felt I would look more foolish than my more average-sized classmates doing the same things. Either way, throughout childhood and early adulthood, my size influenced the way I comported myself and how I showed my listening. The development of my gestural listening "way of being" was shaped by my specific, embodied lived experience. This aspect of gestural listening brings it squarely into the orbit of feminist rhetorical approaches, many of which explic-itly acknowledge such situated approaches to rhetorical praxis.

In the last few decades of rhetorical history, listening has been richly con-ceptualized as a feminist rhetorical practice. Krista Ratcliffe, in particular, theorizes listening as an intentional, effortful choice with rhetorical possibili-ties and consequences. Her work brings about valuable insights such as the assertion in *Rhetorical Listening: Identification, Gender, Whiteness* that listening can be a generative "trope for interpretive invention" (17). Here, Ratcliffe makes the important argument, connected to the legacy of Burke and Rogers, that listening as a feminist rhetorical practice can be generative and constructive, moving beyond displays of obedience or normativity and building on the idea of listening as a capacity that affects both listener and listened-to In a similar vein, Cheryl Glenn focuses on the rhetorical power of silence—one way in which listening can manifest—in *Unspoken*, insisting upon an understanding of rhetoric that is not "constituted solely of purposeful language use"; it also encompasses the "purposeful uses and deliveries of silence" (155). Paying special attention to who has had access to rhetorical agency in centuries past, Ratcliffe and Glenn emphasize that silence and listening are often tools used to exert rhetorical pressure when other means are not available. That is, they become especially important forms of rhetorical agency in rhetors for whom more overt or verbally explicit defiance could be dangerous, as was the case for Sandra Bland, for instance. As I intend to show further in the next chapter, gestural listening is most definitely a quiet way of demonstrating resistance and refusal, a tool leveraged in particular by students, who navigate displays of respect and resistance through discursive and nondiscursive means.

Even as they are mobilized by those without full recourse to the arts more traditionally under the purview of rhetorical study, speaking and writing, silence and listening as conceptualized by Ratcliffe and contemporaries have certain limitations. For instance, Glenn quotes Gary Planck's research on Dineh students (referred to in Planck's text as Navajo). He writes, of a program bringing Dineh students to Dartmouth University: "Navajos are taught from the youngest age never to draw attention to ourselves. So Navajo children do not raise their hands in class. At a school like Dartmouth, the lack of participation was seen as a sign not of humility but lack of interest and a disengaged attitude" (Plank 30, quoted in Glenn 141). In this situation, the Dineh students make concerted choices to present themselves as respectful students. They enact a powerful silence and may be adopting rhetorical listening stances, but their embodied idiom is at odds with the expectations of a Dartmouth classroom. Rather than ceasing to signify altogether, their listening registers, but in a negative way, as "disengaged." Simply noting the presence of student silence and listening, in this case, is not enough to bring about understanding.

This is where the need emerges for a rhetorical framework of listening that extricates listening from its frequent delivery in silence with greater precision and that further attends to dimensions of embodied experience. Glenn opens the door to embodied experience when she writes: "We live inside the act of discourse, to be sure, but we cannot assume that a *verbal* matrix is the only one in which the articulations and conduct of the mind take place—regardless of the measure of inward or outward persuasion" (153). But while possibilities for nonverbal suasion are hinted at, or implied, in Ratcliffe and Glenn's work, the bodies doing the listening are not yet foregrounded. In a recent volume of *Peitho*, for instance, Michael J. Faris points out a gap in prior discussions of rhetorical listening when he notes that "the body barely surfaces." As I came to learn through experience in my own tall body, however, listening behaviors are based in the lived experiences of specific bodies. Like other embodied qualities, gestural listening signifies constantly, whether we like it or not, operating upon communicative situations immediately and continuously. A fully "fleshed-out" theory of gestural listening requires careful attention to these nuances, enabling those analyses of the full communicative picture in any given rhetorical situation that encompass multiple dimensions of identity.

In the anecdotes from my own life that I have included here, for instance, my height is not the only operative factor. My age and gender, too, come into play, like when a student tells me one day, at the end of class: "I like your dress." It's a comment off-handedly delivered by a young woman in my class, on her way out. She is always impeccably dressed in stylish and coordinating outfits, even if casual, and artfully made up with softly drawn brows and winged eyeliner. It's my first semester of teaching as a graduate student; I am twenty-three years old and figuring out "work clothes" on a budget. When my student tells me she likes my dress, I just respond with a quick "thank you!" But on the inside, I feel the particular glow of a compliment from another young woman.

In this interaction with my student, I have been bestowed a particular seal of approval. The student's comment has the informality of an offhand exchange between girls and women, the type of remark that builds a casual yet positive rapport. It also indicates, in an instant, that my presence is readily legible as female, so much so that the student can give me a quick compliment on my outfit as one gal to another, as though we are on the bus or at the coffeeshop. This aspect of my identity is so recognizable that for a moment, it overcomes the typical classroom rule of not commenting on each other's appearances. What counts for me, in the eyes of others, as "good" gestural listening may be circumscribed in a limiting way by my being a young woman—I need to appear responsive, likeable, caring. At the same time, I benefit in other ways from being squarely legible as a woman.

Gestural listening manifests in bodies that are constantly in a state of change, however. When I went through the teacher-training program as part of my graduate degree, several of my classmates mentioned their struggles with being mistaken for younger than they are. Women, in particular, spoke of feeling like they need to "dress up" more on days they went into campus to teach. There was the sense that their attire needed to help signal their age and thus their authority, at times when their bodies or faces alone might not. I did not relate. For all its attendant awkwardness throughout my early years, my height seemed to protect me from that issue, offsetting my young age. I never had to worry that students wouldn't know I was the teacher; kids have regularly "thought I was the teacher" since I was around fourteen. Indeed, existing as a young person with an unusually tall body constantly put me in touch with other people's general sense of surprise at my physical self, with the ways in which I was outside the norm.

And yet these dynamics continue to change as I move through different identity categories, gaining professional advancement and simply getting older. Recently, at a faculty meeting, I announced an event I was organizing, as did two other new hires, around my age in their early thirties. Behind me, a longtimer in the department said to a colleague next to him in a carrying whisper: "Why do some of these professors look like they're about nineteen years old?" Ironically, I've now "aged out" of looking older than I am. That is, for a professor, at the time of this writing, I now "look young," even though throughout all my formative years, I appeared older than I was.

And I know that this, too, shall pass. How I present physically has been changing throughout my life and will continue to. My gestural listening, and the way it comes across to others, will change along with me. More recent scholarship focusing on silence and listening as rhetorical arts works to further emphasize the feminist valuing of the lived, embodied, specific, and explicitly situated experience, central to the way I formulate gestural listening as a rhetorical force.

Gestural Listening as a Rhetorical Paradigm

One of listening's special affordances is its ability to shape the conditions for further engagement, to allow new ideas and sentiments to be spoken in arenas from which they have previously been dismissed. In this sense, I propose that listening is not simply one rhetorical move to be deployed strategically among others but rather a more fundamental condition, containing and shaping—far from neutrally—whatever discourse takes place within it. Constant complex, and flowing with characteristic slipperiness between the verbal and nonverbal, gestural listening moves toward a new paradigm for rhetoric that emphasizes the listener as much as the speaker, the nondiscursive as well as the discursive, and the inclusive rather than the agonistic. In this sense, it shares the aim of invitational rhetoric, formulated by Sonja Foss and Susan Griffin in 1995, of shifting the end goal of rhetorical encounter from persuasion to understanding and mutuality, even as it provides a more observable lexicon for those aims.

Arriving at the end of this chapter, I hope to have conveyed the sense that gestural listening springs from a deep lineage of ideas in the history of rhetoric and that gestural listening performances carry layers of often contradictory ideologies with them into the present. Going forward, I focus further on gestural listening's implications for classroom presence and practice. Throughout the cultural history of listening that I have traced here, we have seen notions of obedience and acquiescence, normativity and becoming, generativity and capacity, participation and responsiveness, cultural specificity, and lived embodied experience, among others, layer together into the way listening gesturally manifests. In the contemporary classroom, I argue that competing presentations of respect, resistance, and self-regulation are the most important elements of gestural listening that students must navigate. Further, these complex displays of respect and resistance are inflected in important ways by the same types of identity categories I have highlighted in my own experience throughout this chapter.

Questions for Discussion, Free-Writing, or Reflection

The following questions are designed for readers, especially teachers, to reflect on their perceptions of what makes for "good" listening, both in themselves and in others. These questions are particularly useful in the context of a teacher-training or professional development workshop for instructors, mentors, coaches, or counselors of many kinds.

1. What types of listening do we ask of students in our classrooms?
2. What does listening "look like" for you? That is, how do you listen gesturally?
3. Do you listen differently in different spaces or contexts?
4. When might we assume that listening looks like obedience?
5. When might our students' listening look like something else?
6. What ideologies or experiences have shaped us as listeners? That is, how have we each *become* listeners? In other words, what experiences have you had that taught you how to listen?

7. What models for listening do you have in your life (people, such as a parent, or environments like church or school, etc.)?

8. What might some of your preferred listening behaviors be?

9. When do you expect listening behaviors to be expressive? What types of expressiveness are preferred, and which are not?

10. How have aspects of your identity shaped you as a listener?

11. How are listening behaviors inflected by group dynamics?

2

Listening in the Classroom

Respect, Resistance, and Self-Regulation

One day in class, we are studying topic sentences. My students have drafted a paragraph in a free-write, and I have just prompted them to reread their topic sentences with an eye toward revision. I ask: "How might you need to change your topic sentence to fit the paragraph that you actually ended up writing?" I give them five minutes to revise. Glaring critically at his laptop screen with a hand to his chin, Frankie lets out an exasperated sigh and murmurs to himself, "I have to . . ." And then he trails off, but his hands rise in front of him for a fleeting second, facing each other, as though he can enlarge or shrink a sentence within his palms. After a moment, he drops his hands to the keyboard and begins to type.

Frankie's gestural listening starts as quiet reception, looking toward me, at the front of the room, with chin in hand while I give directions. As he continues to respond, however, his listening behaviors shift into those that register after the fact, as he motions with his hands and even briefly verbalizes his thoughts in an undertone. This, too, is gestural listening, flowing moment to moment between modes of reception and expression. In this instance, Frankie's gestural listening projects outward, something highly visible and readily legible in the context of our classroom. He acts out his thinking for me gesturally and even through his vocal response, showing, almost to the point

https://doi.org/10.7330/9781646428182.c002

of exaggeration, that he has listened and understood and that he is moving forward to follow instructions.

Such an overt performance of attention is relatively rare. In this case, it matches Frankie's personality: outgoing, enthusiastic, eager. Frankie's gestural listening is a type that many instructors might prefer, whether they realize it or not. After all, it is helpful for instructors to get visual and audible feedback from their students on a moment-to-moment basis. Frankie's gestural listening here reassures me, as the instructor, that he has heard and understood the directions, that he cares enough to think about them and take them seriously, and that he has even begun to act on them, rewriting his topic sentence. Per the listening tropes I outline in the last chapter, Frankie's listening conveys obedience, visibly reflecting the dynamics of authority that shape the classroom space. Through his listening, Frankie demonstrates respect for the usual practices of the classroom, instantiating the "preferred" call-and-response of class discussion. He is likely to be rewarded in classroom spaces for this type of "good" gestural listening.

But there's more to the story here. Frankie's overt gestural listening may win him my approval but at what cost? In the previous chapter, I noted how my Sunday school performance may have earned me my teacher's star of approval but certainly not the camaraderie of my peers—in fact, it may have even garnered a strike against me in the subtle social accounting of adolescents. Against the backdrop of a relatively quiet class, Frankie's is often a lone voice, unaided by the vocal support of classmates. In the front row, he jumps to answer the questions I pose to the class. His expressiveness is not always welcomed by his classmates. One day, Frankie has been speaking even more than usual, giving lengthy responses to questions intended to prompt discussion. As he speaks, his classmates begin to rustle: shifting backpacks, abruptly changing their posture or sitting position; the occasional sigh can be heard. Students gaze pointedly down at desktops and out the windows, as though simply waiting for Frankie to be done.

At first glance, the students' quiet, still listening seems respectful toward Frankie, but through their prolonged silences, rustling, and averted eyes, Frankie's classmates subtly disaffiliate him from their midst, punishing his deviation from the stoicism that the others in class demonstrate, especially the men. Wordlessly, they deploy their gestural listening to enact resistance. Through their classroom quietness, many of his male classmates in particular may be protecting a different aspect of their own identities in class, that of the impassive, unflappable male. Resisting the display of uncertainty that is encouraged, and may even be necessary in a first-year college writing course, they avoid the risk of being exposed for not knowing something, retaining a kind of quiet solidarity with each other. In fact, Frankie may sacrifice a certain construction of masculinity in order to succeed in the academic space.

So far, it seems that Frankie's gestural listening is a trade-off—a gestural listening way of being that wins approval within the authoritative hierarchy of the classroom but that comes with the sacrifice of his peers' affiliation, and possibly of his gender identity. But there is another dimension in play here, too: gesture's role in learning. Frankie also gesturally listens for himself, allowing his gestures to compel his thinking. His listening, especially in the moment where he uses his hands to "resize" his topic sentence, demonstrates how gesture is a crucial and generative part of cognition. Gesture theorist Susan Goldin-Meadow puts forward the idea of gestural "mismatches," moments when gestures momentarily outstrip a student's verbal capacity, when a student's movements "mismatch" with their words. Mismatches are important moments that signal a student's readiness to learn a new idea, and a "mismatch marks a child as being open to instruction, and thus on the precipice of learning" (40). This gestural conduit for learning may be an example of how students seem to "gather," or draw thoughts into existence, as the philosopher Gemma Corradi Fiumara suggests. So far, gestural listening moves outward from Frankie toward the instructor and to his classmates, bringing about certain responses, while it also circles inwardly upon himself as part of his learning process.

Finally, there is my own gestural listening as I take in Frankie's responses and confront the often long periods of silence from the rest of the class. When students do speak, I gesturally listen in a way that I hope encourages them, through nodding, vocalizing, turning in their direction, and making eye contact. I show my attention and interest visibly, an effort to draw them out, to let them know their contributions are taken seriously and appreciated. I also do it because the core ideas of the course are best arrived at collaboratively, through discussion, so it behooves us all for me to facilitate conversation. So while I "direct traffic" in discussion in a way that reflects my role of authority in the classroom, as the one who makes and carries out the lesson plan, my idiom of gestural listening still adheres to how women are generally socialized to listen: to "facilitate" in the sense of making something easier; to show encouragement, involvement, and care.

Gestural listening operates in scenes of instruction, like this one, in several ways at once. It is not limited to dyadic relationships between myself and one student at a time but, like the choral listening I describe in chapter 5, forms a crisscrossing network linking groups of students to each other, too. My gestural listening puts pressure on them just as theirs puts pressure on me, informing me of whether what I'm doing is resonating with them and sometimes making me change course—trying a different way of posing a question, or using a new image to help explain a concept—if I continue to face a "tough crowd." Frankie's classmates put pressure on him to fall in, while he affects the situation, too by disrupting their tacitly agreed-upon, collective way of being. At the same time, students' gestural listening may work inwardly upon themselves, contributing to their learning and further constructing them as students.

In the preceding chapter, I traced a rhetorical history of embodied listening, mapping some of the large contours of how listening has been conceptualized over time. With that groundwork, I will analyze instances of gestural listening through many of the concepts I moved through in that chapter: its valences of obedience and defiance, "correctness" and "incorrectness"; its dual expressive and impressive qualities; its generative capacities; and its special ability to be deployed tactically as a form of pressure alternative to more overt modes of influence. In my investigations of gestural listening and, in particular, through observation and study of classroom gestural listening behaviors, it's possible to find all of these concepts layered into listening moments, as well as others that I have not yet dwelled on: absorption, judgment, vigilance, and openness, for instance. In this chapter, though, I aim to show, as Frankie and his classmates do, how performances of respect and resistance—and the terse, dynamic currents between these poles of self-presentation—most often and most clearly characterize gestural listening in classroom environments. A third major dimension to classroom listening exists as well, in which students use gestural listening to assist in their own learning processes, as Frankie also does.

This chapter is informed in part by a pilot study I conducted based on two classes of students at a small liberal arts college. With the study, I wanted to develop ways of capturing and knowing about how students perceive the gestural listening of others, and how they think about embodying it themselves. The study involved a survey, filmed class sessions, and follow-up interviews with participants. While a small, pilot study will not provide generalizable findings, it nevertheless suggests possibilities for patterns in classroom gestural listening and allows me to locate larger phenomena in specific examples. To unpack the dynamics of gestural listening in this chapter, I also draw upon the thinking of teacher-scholars like Mary Reda, Stacey Waite, and S. Brooke Corfman, who attend carefully to authority in classroom spaces and offer alternative ways of investigating when students operate outside of listening performances that are considered "correct" or immediately legible. Later, Tina Campt's analysis of an unusual photo series helps bring into focus how students' self-regulatory behaviors operate both inwardly, upon themselves, and outwardly upon others.

Respect and resistance as a guiding principle come, I think, from the structures of authority that indelibly shape any classroom environment. In this chapter, I explore how those dynamics of authority give rise to a "gestural idiom" of the classroom that functions in unexpected ways, especially through nodding, note-taking, and other forms of embodied responsiveness. At the same time, authority in the classroom is not a monolith but rather always takes shape in the context of specific identities. For instance, gender has emerged immediately as a category of identity that comes to bear on gestural listening performances. I reserve the following chapter to narrow in on the question of whom a gestural idiom of the classroom truly serves and how instructors can respond to it.

Gestural Listening for Others

When I gave the students in two college courses an intake survey at the start of my study, their written responses raised an immediate and unexpected question: What is gestural listening really *for*, and, by the same token, *whom* is it for? The first question I asked students on the survey was as follows: Do you consider it important to "look like you are listening" while attending class? Twenty-three out of twenty-six students responded that they did indeed consider it important to look like they are listening. Already, by the majority of students answering yes, I get the sense that the appearance of listening, and being a "good" listener, is a topic that students find familiar and at least somewhat important to their overall success in the classroom. In answering this question overwhelmingly in the positive, students also show a remarkable confidence in their knowledge of what it means to look like they are listening. The college students in this classroom are aware of norms for listening behaviors; they have a strong sense of what "good" listening in the classroom should look like. That shared, felt sense came from somewhere—likely from earlier experiences in pedagogical, familial, or religious settings, which in turn are influenced by the cultural conceptions of listening that I identify in the previous chapter.

The reasons students gave for *why* they considered it important to look like they were listening, however, were surprising, and perhaps more interesting than the simple finding that they did consider it important to perform "good" gestural listening. In fact, many students who indicated they considered an appearance of listening to be important then wrote—unprompted, immediately in response to that initial question—that appearing to listen was not something they did for the sake of their own learning process. Rather, it was an effort they made for other people. Although the survey question did not specifically ask students to address this issue at all, fully fourteen out of twenty-three survey respondents volunteered that looking like they are listening is an effort directed toward others, for the benefit of others, especially as a display of respect or encouragement.

Some students focused on the presence of others quite generally in their efforts to show "good" listening, giving responses that could refer to classmates or the instructor: "I believe it is important," one wrote: "By at least 'looking like you are listening' it gives the person [speaking] more confidence." Another student focused further on helping others feel more assured and valued, writing: "I do think it's important because even if you are listening but don't look like it, the person speaking may not think what they said was important." This last student, in particular, formulates gestural listening—something visible, outward—primarily as a performance for others, not necessarily connected to listening for their own sake. This type of response conveys the sense that there is "performative" listening on the one hand and something like "real" listening on the other, which may be idiosyncratic, or simply not legible as part of respectful classroom listening directed toward others. As a sign of respect toward others, gestural listening is something these students see as undertaken above and beyond what it means to "just" listen for themselves.

Showing respect by "looking like you're listening" forms a notable thread through the survey responses to this first question. One student wrote: "I think it is important simply because you should respect the person speaking to the class," while another wrote: "Yes, I think it is rude if you don't." These students suggest that they think appearing to listen is just the right thing to do, as a manifestation of politeness. Showing respect for another person through listening is a value that transcends educational settings, of course, but one that takes on more complicated contours when dynamics of authority are in play. One survey response took both classmates and the instructor into consideration, writing: "Yes, as it engages fellow classmates while they are talking, while also displaying an interest to the teacher." Others focused specifically on the presence of the instructor in their displays of "correct" classroom listening. One writes: "Yes, it is important to me because I want my professors to know that I am paying attention, engaged in class, and interested in the material." Others write: "Yes, because you want the professor to know you are learning the material," and "Yes, it is important for whoever is giving instruction to feel respected."

According to these comments, and others like them, students extend themselves to enact gestural listening behaviors in large part to ensure that the instructor has a positive impression of them as students. They write about listening behaviors as though those actions—or lack of actions, the case of sitting still or not checking their phones—beam a steady, ongoing message to the instructor that their engagement as students is sustained and serious. Projecting that impression strikes many students as important, exemplified by one student, who writes: "Yes, I feel as though the perception of listening is important. If I don't look like I am listening, then my professors will think I am zoned out and do not care about the class." Here, the respondent indicates that being seen to *not* be listening is a negative thing, something to be avoided. The student fears that an absence of obvious listening could leave them vulnerable to the perception, by the instructor, of being "zoned out."

Indeed, the choice of the term "zoned out" is significant. The phrase carries connotations of being not just momentarily distracted but in a woefully out-of-touch state, not attending to the matters at hand but wandering, detached, in a world of one's own. Being zoned out goes hand in hand with not caring about the class, according to this student's survey response. For this student, performances of attention appear to be linked with caring, which in turn may bring about a positive perception of the student on the part of the instructor. So students must show that they care and that they care in the right ways—that their gestural listening is "correct" according to the expectations of the classroom.

When the student writes, "If I don't look like I am listening, then my professors will think I am zoned out," they imply that if gestural listening is stopped for any significant period of time, what inevitably fills its place is the appearance of being out of touch. As such, gestural listening emerges as something that requires constant vigilance and self-monitoring. Gestural listening is a dimension of students' classroom performance that they are, on the one hand, pretty fully in control of: students can use it to send the particular message they want to send about themselves and their engagement in class to others. But if gestural listening sends its messages of engagement or the lack thereof whether the student likes it or not, it no longer seems to be so under control, so able to be instrumentalized by the student. One student highlights this issue, writing, "Yes, but I don't always have the energy to do it—it makes me feel bad though, b/c I know it makes teaching harder." That is, the students convey the sense that gestural listening actually influences the instructor and class-mates. Correct and recognizable gestural listening sends positive signals of care, engagement, and seriousness, while incorrect (inattentive, or zoning out) or illegible listening behaviors (not having the energy) send a message of lack of care, detachment, and maybe "making things harder" for the instructor and other students. The embodiment of listening, apparently, is a rather power-ful force. Furthermore, without fairly constant self-monitoring, messages of detachment may quickly replace those of attention. When students are in class, they can't seem to "opt out" of projecting listening behaviors at any point—that projection continues ongoingly whether the student can keep up the appear-ances of caring the right way or not, even if they don't "have the energy" to do it. When they enter the classroom, students appear in one way or another—they are relentlessly "on" as soon as they step in the room.

In a similar vein, Mary Reda, the author of *Between Speaking and Silence: A Study of Quiet Students*, recounts a formative moment in her own education that illustrates the result of being "on" without meaning to be or wanting to be. Received at the end of a seminar in which she herself had been a quiet student, a note at the bottom of a paper from her professor read "For your paper, I give you an A. But because of your *refusal* to speak in class, I am forced to lower your grade." Reda continues: "My relative quietness in this large class broke an unspoken rule, apparently projecting an active, hostile resistance I had not actually felt" (60). The reaction of Reda's professor represents a similar fear the students in the survey recounted here might have—that if they allow a constant projection of attention to falter, their behavior may be interpreted as "zoning out," which might "make things harder." This passage reflects once again on the influence that gestural listening has on communicative situations. Further, I interpret it to mean that Reda is unwilling or unable to produce a legible, "correct" form of gestural listening for that particular classroom con-text. Other students either put more effort into that performance, or it comes more easily to them, perhaps springing from ways they have been socialized in the past. It's important to note that Reda refers to breaking an "unspoken rule," a rule assumed to be so natural and obvious an expectation that it goes unarticulated but is later assessed nevertheless as part of her performance. In the previous chapter, I discuss how developing the "correct" or preferred type of listening—often a particular blend of obedient and respectful yet also involved and interactive in appropriate ways—is a skill that is taught and learned, the result of a process of enculturation in specific contexts, rather than something that is effortless, natural, or intrinsic. Here, Reda has not passed muster, having not learned the preferred listening performance well enough, or in being unwilling or unable to enact it.

Reda goes on to elaborate on how she ended up having to adjust her in-class comportment to meet expectations for correct classroom listening, and her reflections here can clue instructors in to the types of adjustments many students have made over the years, and, perhaps, the adjustments we ourselves have made throughout our schooling:

> I began trying to anticipate where class discussion could go so I could be certain to have something "important" to say. Ultimately, I often could not genuinely engage in these conversations, because the sort of internal dialogue that comes most naturally to me would often leave me stumbling to articulate what I was thinking. I am disappointed to realize that being seen as successful as an academic meant I had to step away from the learning processes that are most productive to me so I could perform in the ways that others expect. (60)

Here, there is a clear trade-off for Reda, of the "learning processes that are most productive" to her for the necessity of performing "in the ways that others expect" (60). I think of Jacqueline Jones Royster once again, who is "compelled" into a "state of tolerance" that belies the emotion and energy within (30). The survey responses I have looked at so far corroborate the sense of effort and the potential for trade-off.

Based on these survey responses, gestural listening in the classroom gains definition as having a multifaceted audience: first, for classmates, helping them feel their comments are valuable; then, taking in the whole scene, for the presiding instructor, who is ostensibly sensitive to students' engagement with each other as well as with the instructor themselves. In a follow-up interview, another student said it's important to be "conscious that you're showing [yourself] to be participating," and, referring to small groups making in-class presentations, that you don't want to act like "once your group's done, you're not interested anymore." Instead, you should be "showing the teacher you're still engaged." The gestural choreographies of the classroom respond to and reinforce dynamics of power and authority, with students acutely aware of how their interactions, including interactions with each other, should adhere to a rubric of preferred behavior.

There is another dimension in play here, though—the dimension of self-interest. The effort that the survey participants reported putting into listening for the sake of others may have important kickbacks for the students, too.

Students likely want to be accepted and liked by their peers. As we begin to see in the preceding instructor-focused responses, they also want to stay in their professor's good graces, in order to reap the benefits of being a "good" student. In a follow-up interview with a student participating in the study, one student had this to say in response to the question "Do you think listening behaviors benefit students?": "When you do them they tell the professor that you are listening and you're getting the materials. If you would go to their office hours they would probably treat you differently if you were asking for help about a subject if they could tell that during class you were trying to pay attention, compared to someone who wasn't." According to this student's response, preferred gestural listening during class sessions can ease a subsequent office-hours interaction. So while gestural listening behaviors may initially seem to be really for the benefit of others, according to the survey responses, they may also be beneficial to the listeners themselves, albeit indirectly. Ongoing gestural listening behaviors in class act as a kind of insurance for this student, a continuous "payment" that could benefit the student at a time in the future when they need extra help. Gestural listening may be, at times, all about paying this type of "academic insurance." Students pay, in part, to protect themselves from possible consequences of being perceived as rude or disengaged.

In fact, "good" gestural listening comes to represent something that cuts much deeper than respect or correctness. Reda describes a student's balance between speaking and silence as a dance that "affords students citizenship" in their classroom (25). In this key moment in her book, Reda couches her statements in the language of silence, writing:

> I see two major kinds of silence in the classroom: those implemented by the teacher and those initiated by students. When teachers require silence, it is often for pedagogical purposes, for example, during tests, individual reading or writing, or while one person is speaking . . . When students are silent at these times, their behavior is interpreted (at least by the teacher) as respectful compliance (or, at the very least, the shrewd appearance of compliance). . . . In these ways, behaving appropriately—abiding by teacher-initiated silences—affords students citizenship in that classroom. (25)

In this passage, Reda outlines a useful distinction, between teacher-initiated silences, seen as crucial to the intellectual work of the class, and student-initiated silences, which Reda notes are often interpreted through the lens of failure—failure to participate, for instance, or failure to volunteer answers based on readings of course materials. This control of classroom silences—who gets to grant them?—highlights once again an element of the uneven power dynamic in classroom settings. Through her observations about silence, however, Reda points out something about gestural listening, more specifically, especially when she writes that respectful quietness during teacher-initiated silences may be a "shrewd appearance of compliance." Even if a student's respectful compliance is merely a "shrewd appearance," that appearance contributes to being afforded "citizenship in that classroom." That is, even if it is "just an act," it's an act with real consequences, one that comes with the protections of citizenship, of belonging. A student who can produce the "shrewd appearance" of compliance may receive better help in office hours later, or may otherwise benefit from coming across as a "good" student in the eyes of the instructor.

Thus far, I have focused almost entirely on the role of the student, when some readers may be thinking that the responsibility should truly lie with the instructor to reserve judgment about their students' listening comportment. In everything that I have read produced by teachers, however, the move beyond a rhetoric of failure, resistance, or noncompliance comes from a kind of default position of doubt, frustration, or more generally a self-assuredness about the aims of "productive" classroom conduct. Take, for instance, what Mary Reda, a champion of quiet students, writes about her initial impression of them: "Still, every semester I find a Frank, a Maggie, an Alice, a Steve—students whose silences overpower the voices that fill class discussions. And on rough days, I'm startled to realize that I've begun to resent these students and whatever it is that drives them into their silences" (2). In the next section, I dwell on Stacey Waite's notion of "queer participation," which focuses on one student, a student she initially describes like this: "Before Andy Dejka was my student there were things I took for granted—that class participation means talking in class, that participation is good, that the best students will participate in class, that the best model for teaching writing is a model in which students talk out loud to the group" (73). Dejka's in-class comportment, that is, would not have aligned with Waite's sense of "good" participation, or who the "best students" are. Paul Kameen, whose teaching of a graduate seminar forms the main material for his book *Writing/Teaching*, has a "gradual" realization about "tenaciously taciturn" students in this descriptive passage:

> Still, there were some students who were tenaciously taciturn, seeming to prefer silence no matter the expense. Gradually, I started to notice something about at least some of the students: when they were absent, discussion didn't go as well. When they returned, it perked up noticeably. Why? What I

finally realized is that these students, while they might not be great talkers, were wonderful listeners—to me and to their colleagues. They were right with us, paying close attention, nodding heads, raising eyebrows, smiling, looking puzzled. They were participating, with quite powerful effects. All of us were performing better because at least part of our audience was visibly, if not verbally, responsive, even supportive. (129–30)

Kameen "finally realizes" the impact the quiet students have, providing a brief illustration of their gestural listening behaviors. "They were participating." he writes, implying that he might not have thought they were previously. All in all, there is a clear sense of expectations that characterize the preferred, accepted norm in higher education classrooms. Even these highly self-aware instructors note a turning point when they broke from their prior, deeply ingrained expectations.

I asked similar questions in a follow-up interview with the instructor of the two courses I filmed, including "Which students would you say are listening, and how can you tell?"; "Which students would you say are demonstrating 'good' listening behaviors"; and "Do 'good' gestural listening behaviors benefit students?" The most high-frequency observations this professor makes about behaviors that indicate "good" gestural listening pertain to where the students' eyes and gaze are and how their heads are pivoting by extension. In doing so, he links listening to the gaze, a common trope in looking for listening that reads as obedient and focused in classroom settings—think of the primary school teacher's exhortation when calling the class to attention: "Eyes on me." He notes that while he is conversing with one student directly in class, "the person right next to him, turns and look at me; [then] turns and looks at him." He makes note of another student in the video clip, who, he says, "gaze-wise, [is] really fixed on me." When prompted to point out what he thinks might be recognizably "good" gestural listening behavior, he observes: "A good many folks had their eyes up and on the speaker." He also notes students' body positions and their relative amount of movement in their seats: two students are "forward on their desks, focused down in my direction." He repeatedly mentions the movement of eyes and heads even as he begins to question his own focus on those behaviors, already skeptical of listening that is "performative": "You can sort of see heads pivoting, tennis-match style," he says, "[which] suggests, performatively, at least, listening behavior." Although the term "performatively" casts doubt on the "authenticity" of students' listening, the students' behaviors nevertheless register. That is, they affect the professor's sense of the students' engagement, whether or not they truly reflect mastery of the course material. Here, listening behaviors move outward, just as the students suspect they do, to influence the professor and other students.

The professor I interviewed, unsurprisingly, has a high awareness that students can "fake" attentiveness and, on the flipside, can also look deceptively disengaged. "By the time students are in their twenties," he notes, "some of them have the skills of faking attention," but, he counters, "some people don't bother." He notes that some students seem to be more concerned about these types of performances than others: "Some students actively do things . . . because they recognize they suggest their engagement; other folks just do what feels natural to them, whether that signals engagement or not."

For this professor, "good" gestural listening tends to have a quality of feeling rewarding, a feeling he is then immediately suspicious of. Of students who listen in more overtly expressive ways, he observes, "they give that tighter feedback loop," which may ultimately be, as he jokes, "more about neediness on the part of the professor . . . [and] trying to assess the relative success of things short-term . . . versus longer-term opportunities for feedback." Indeed, beyond the rewarding feeling, he notes that overtly responsive gestural listening behaviors allow him to make adjustments to his teaching based on more immediate, moment-to-moment feedback. Aware of his possible partiality to students who gesturally listen rewardingly and who provide pedagogically helpful feedback, he says: "It can be beneficial for the student, but it's not necessarily in a good way . . . In teaching, we want a closer feedback loop . . . to find out what you're really learning." Further, "affective response encourages us to invest," he says, but the professor makes it clear to me that, again, it's "not necessarily in a good way," implying that differences in gestural listening behaviors could cause an instructor to invest in some students more than others. Throughout his responses to the interview questions, the professor notes the ways in which he is affected by students' gestural listening behaviors, and, immediately, how perhaps he shouldn't be. This instructor notes his "preferred" forms of listening even as he reminds himself not to be limited by them and, in doing so, risk writing off students who do not perform those preferred forms of listening.

We begin to get the sense of gestural listening as an embodied rhetoric that operates before and beneath the verbal or the conscious. It takes the shape of a fluid, ongoing matrix of embodied and verbal communication that is both performed and received in ways that often move beyond the intentional or the conscious. The question arises: Does influence need to be intentional to count as rhetorical? I don't think so, and many of the scholars I cite in the first chapter are likely not to, either—rather, I understand rhetoric more capaciously as diverse forms of influence that often contain a mix of the intentional and the unintentional. In speaking and writing about gestural listening, I have sometimes received another question, about the quality of performance in gestural listening, what the instructor I interview here refers to as "fake attentiveness": Does it matter if a student is, in fact, underneath their skillful performance of listening, not listening at all? My answer is of course and, also, not really. Of course I want students to be "really listening" in the classroom, because I want them to learn as much as they can. Students do seem to use gestural listening behaviors to help them do that, through its quality of self-regulation, which I will explain in detail in a later section of the chapter. But here, it is more important to note the simple fact that students do often enact gestural listening performances regardless of whether they are "truly" listening or not, and the implications of that performance are what I am most focused on here as a rhetorical phenomenon in classroom settings. That is, while "true listening" is difficult to measure on a moment-to-moment basis without relying on what students say, or write, that reflects their comprehension of the material, the performance of listening is important enough to keep up regardless of what is truly going on within students' minds. Gestural listening seems particularly important to understand, because, as I mentioned earlier, once students enter the classroom, they do not have the ability to opt out of being assessed, however subtly, on their gestural listening. Rather, its communicative qualities move outward toward others ongoingly, as long as the encounter lasts.

This complexity within the performance of gestural listening may be why the professor I interviewed notes repeatedly that knowing the students better, or in other capacities, helps him to form a fuller picture of their gestural listening behaviors in class, even compensating, at times, for a student's relative "lack of affect" in the classroom. For this professor, knowing students in other capacities could mean teaching the same students more than once, or working with students as an advisor. "You do get to learn some of how they do their body language," he notes. "[This student] here . . . who kind of is really leaned way back, and that's sort of her body language, but I also learned from seeing her work that she takes stuff in very well . . . Early in the term, I was like, I don't know what's going on here, but then by the time we had the first test and the first essay, I was like okay, she's picking up very much on what's happening." Teaching a student more than once or knowing them in another context aids in mediating the professor's impression of less "correct," or immediately rewarding, gestural listening behaviors in class. Of another student, for instance, he clarifies physical behaviors that might be hard to interpret: "I've also taught him a bunch of times, and he's kind of twitchy . . . does his hands through his hair a lot, and all that's just kind of part of twitchy behaviors he does . . . but he's doing them while he's thinking." The way he says this makes me realize that "twitchy" behaviors could also seem to convey distraction, but he wants me to know that for this student he's confident they happen during thinking, not as a result of distraction. He also mentions that students who perform "good" gestural listening, which he here refers to as "affective sensibility," tend to stick in his memory the quickest. "Students who are new to me, in that opening several weeks . . . I'm probably memorizing the names first of the people . . . giving some of that 'affective sensibility' back . . . I learn those people first, often." He also reflects on the benefits of knowing students better by interacting with them in different capacities: "Because we often get to teach people more than once," he says, "and sometimes we have people that we know as an advisee before we get around to teaching them . . . it's partly about investment." He continues: "Affective response encourages us to invest because they seem like they're investing in what we're all about." Especially for students who have nonnormative, or less immediately legible gestural listening habits, it can apparently be beneficial to have the same professor more than once, allowing the instructor to develop a deeper knowledge of that student's gestural ways of being. These responses also highlight the benefits of working with students in various capacities, both as an instructor and as an advisor, for instance.

Notably, the professor reformulates his interpretations of students' gestural listening behaviors in conjunction with their written work, turned in after the fact at intervals throughout the semester. This written input, too, can compensate for gestural listening behaviors that the professor notes he might otherwise perceive as "checked out" or disengaged. "I know from past experiences that some students . . . don't give you much affect of any kind," he says, "but then you see substantial evidence of engagement in work that they turn in later." He continues: "You don't have an accurate gauge of who's engaged . . . based just on the affect they give you in class or even what they say." He also refers to a deep knowledge of three other students, whose work he knows, perhaps in addition to knowing them as an academic advisor. They are

> three students [who are] outstanding at catching everything . . . they kind
> of have slightly different listening behaviors . . . hers is very quiet and very

focused, and the two of them kind of [are] kind of moving around, which could suggest listening or not, but deep experience with them, I tend to be highly confident that they're paying attention and taking things in.

Impressions of gestural listening behavior can be strongly inflected by written work that is turned in after the fact, a point I deal with in more detail in the following section.

The "How" of Gestural Listening

In my interview with the instructor, in the last section, we start to get a sense of how one professor observes gestural listening behaviors in his students. He catalogues elements of the gestural idiom of the classroom that I have been pointing out by noting eyes, heads, and postures; he also notes the affective power of students' gestural listening upon him, even as he indicates that he stays on his guard toward its subtle, nonverbal influence. His comments coalesce around what it means to know students—teaching them over more than one term, interacting with them as an advisor in addition to as a classroom instructor, and gaining a fuller picture of their class engagement through their written work in addition to their classroom comportment.

In my study, what I wanted to home in on next was how students felt listening should be shown. If appearing not to listen carries negative connotations in the classroom, as some of the students suggest in their survey responses, it seems important for students to learn to produce gestural listening that is the "preferred" or "correct" type, that is—a kind that's readily legible in classroom contexts according to a certain rubric. With that in mind, in the survey, I next invited students to write what they do and what they especially do *not* do to indicate listening. The question was phrased as follows: "What behaviors do you do (or not do, like checking your phone, for instance) to show that you are listening?"

One of the highest frequency items that students mentioned had to do with taking notes. Taking notes, according to many of the students, was an essential element to listening and the effort to show their listening in class. Looking into existing literature about note-taking in classrooms, I was curious to know: Are note-taking behaviors known by researchers to actually improve learning outcomes? That is, do they truly reflect the presence of listening? If so, perhaps they should be taught more explicitly as learning strategies. Once again, my findings surprised me.

At first glance, it may seem obvious how taking notes reflects listening. In a follow-up interview, one student identified students writing notes as demonstrating listening, and she put it succinctly: "As [the professor] was saying stuff, people were like writing them down, so they had to be paying attention to be able to write that stuff down." But as my study has shown up to this point, the rituals of the classroom are not always as straightforward as they appear, and the embodied idioms of classroom spaces have already been shown to operate on more than one level. So what is really going on when students take notes in class?

Existing literature on note-taking confirms its prevalence as a classroom practice, and its importance in students' perceptions of effective classroom behavior. While some of the first-known studies of college students' note-taking habits were done in 1924 and 1925 by J. A. Charters, a 1974 study by Robert Palmatier and Michael Bennett forms the baseline for more recent investigation into note-taking among college students. Palmatier and Bennett found that "when asked about their own note-taking on lectures (question 1) 220 of the 223 students (99 percent) replied in the affirmative" (216). Further, they found that "two hundred fourteen of the 223 respondents (96 percent) felt that notetaking was essential to success in college (question 3)" (216–17). Interestingly, they continue: "Of interest is the fact that apparently six students who did not place great value in the taking of notes felt compelled to do it any-how" (216–17). As far back as 1974, students laud note-taking as a crucial classroom behavior, so much so that even those who do not consider it important do it anyway.

It may be that *how* students take notes matters more than whether they take notes, however. Also part of the 1970s burst of attention to note-taking, Judith Fisher and Mary Harris put eighty-eight students into groups that listened to two lectures and used different combinations of note-taking and review. Their study confirmed the belief college students seemed to have in note-taking: when asked about their opinions on note-taking, "over 90 percent of the Ss stated that they believed note taking and reviewing notes aided recall" (292). After participating in different combinations of note-taking and review, the students in this study were then given a free recall test and a multiple choice test based on the content of the lecture. While the quantity of notes taken correlated with better recall on the post-tests (i.e., the more notes the better), no one combination of note-taking and review produced better results in the post-tests overall. In the end, student belief in the helpfulness of notes persists, but their belief seems outsized compared to the actual utility of the notes they take.

More recently, in the 2009 study "An Investigation of the SOAR Study Method," Kenneth Kiewra, one of the preeminent contemporary researchers on note-taking, confirms alongside Dharma Jairam that "note quantity is important; research confirms that the more notes students have available for study, the higher their achievement" (Jairam and Kiewra 608). However, they also remark that students commonly tend to employ weak study strategies, such as taking incomplete notes, organizing notes linearly in lists or outlines rather than hierarchies or sequences that highlight relationships, and employing redundant review strategies like rehearsal rather than self-testing and generating questions. Jairam and Kiewra suggest that one reason why students persist with ineffective study strategies is because "students seeking learning assistance are sometimes led astray. Some study skills books (e.g., Ellis, 1997) advocate popular practices like selective note taking, outlining, and rehearsal even though these practices lack empirical support" (606). In other words, some study skills have been adopted as academic "truisms," passed along to new generations of students and adopted without question. These practices seem to have become elements of academic culture, a kind of "preferred behavior" that may or may not truly facilitate better learning. Much of student note-taking may end up falling into this category.

As part of the follow-up interview, I had participants watch a clip of the filmed classroom observation. They were prompted with the questions (1) "Which students are listening and how can you tell?" and (2) "Which students are enacting 'good' listening behaviors?" In response, one student said: "As far as the group listening behaviors . . . looking in the direction, and sort of paying attention, and I think jotting things down things that are relevant." She continues: "Sometimes with listening . . . you can sort of feel when someone's sort of paying attention and listening . . . that sort of feeling you get of someone paying rather than just looking in the direction." Indicating three students in the video clip, she said, "Those three . . . showed signs of . . . having an ear or watching and jotting things down occasionally . . . that would lead me to think that they were paying some attention and listening to what's being said." In the follow-up interviews, none of the students who mentioned taking notes mentioned what *kind* of notes they considered important, or even any "type" of note at all. The closest thing to a mention of what kind of note he took was one student who referred to "jotting down" the "odd note." The "odd" note tends to refer to a type of note-taking that is not continuous, rather just every once in a while. To me, this implies that the student occasionally takes a note to jog his memory later, or to reinforce something just said, but especially that it's good to be *seen* to take a note. Here again, we see classroom behaviors geared not toward the best learning outcomes but toward a kind of social success in class, toward participation in the embodied idiom of the classroom.

Between the heavy emphasis students place on gesturally listening for others and the knowledge that note taking may be more of a "truism" than a reality, something new begins to take shape: the sense of a preferred embodied "idiom" of the classroom, based more on a particular set of behaviors accepted in academic spaces as polite and cooperative than on what would actually help students take in and engage with the course material. That is, in addition to helping students encode information and store it for later review, note-taking also functions importantly as an element of gestural classroom culture. As an accepted piece of gestural listening vocabulary, taking notes may be one way for students to present themselves as "good" students. Note-taking starts to emerge as a key component in a collective image held by US students and teachers of an ideally attentive, hardworking student. In a follow-up interview, one student illustrates this when she said that she focuses on "always taking notes":

> It's sort of like a fail-safe to always have something that's keeping me on track. I had a high school teacher say to be the kid in the front row of the lecture hall taking notes—be that kid on top getting hundreds; looking directions where people are, sometimes it's hard to turn around, but don't be staring off into space.

Note-taking emerges as a major way that listening is assessed by others, and as something that students identify in themselves as an important listening behavior. But to what extent are students taking notes to help themselves learn, and to what extent are students taking notes because it has been presented to them as a kind of "universal truth" that good students take notes? Are students taking notes that really work for them, either in process or in product, or are they largely taking notes to show respectful listening and take part in the embodied idiom of the classroom? Note-taking is a complex cognitive task—one that might, at times, be better defined as a social behavior or preference for "good" listening, rather than a behavior directly linked to the acquisition of new knowledge.

Often, it takes an experience with a particular student to bring about a change in instructors' perceptions of "good" participation. In *Teaching Queer*, for instance, Stacey Waite offers a striking example of when a student's in-class comportment diverged from Waite's own expectations for the classroom's gestural idiom, a student who only did in the classroom what was useful to him for his own learning. His in-class comportment initially puts him at odds, on two different levels, with Waite's sense of "good" participation. First, there are Waite's assumptions about participation, which she summarizes as a set of values that form a kind of contemporary academic "default" expectation for classroom behavior. She writes: "It's a normative university value often posed as a problem for teachers and programs to solve—often asking questions like, How can we *get participation* from students? or, How can we signal to students that participation is good for them, like eating their peas?" (75) It turns out that Waite's personal sense of "good" classroom comportment has additional dimensions. She then delves further into what, for her, motivates her sense of what good participation means, a line of self-reflection that connects participation norms to the role of identity in her particular historical moment. She writes:

> I was a teenager in the nineties. I attended a small liberal arts college in central Pennsylvania at a time when queer youth were gathering to encourage one another to "come out" or "be out." We considered it both a political responsibility and a personal triumph to speak out, to say who we were . . . We read feminist and queer authors as biblical. When Audre Lorde told us, in essays and on bumper stickers, *your silence will not protect you,* we took that to heart. Silence meant oppression . . . I think it sank in for many of us as reading out beyond the politics of oppression and into the politics of education, the politics of group participation, the politics of personal interaction. (78)

Between normative university values and Waite's own lived experience, Dejka certainly seems at risk for being misunderstood in his embodied classroom performance—still and quiet. What saves him from that misunderstanding, and brings about a new consciousness on Waite's part, are two things: (1) Dejka's ability to create a particular form of gestural listening that keeps him within the bracket of "preferred" behavior, and (2) sharing about himself, as a listener and as a student, in his writing.

Of Andy Dejka's gestural comportment in class, Waite writes: "Andy was, for the most part silent—though any look over to his corner of the room on any given day, and Andy was locked in. His eyes are a pale green-blue, reflective in a quite striking way, which is not surprising, given that this student is probably one of the most intensely reflective students I have had the gift of teaching in many years" (74). Even as Dejka does not conform to a more typical norm for classroom comportment, however, I notice that he is still notably able to transmit the sense of being "locked in," or intensely focused and alert, and Waite even lets the color of his eyes help suggest his quality of reflectiveness. That is, even though Dejka's listening is not "participatory" in the way his classmates' might be, and in the way Waite has been taught to value, his listening is still recognizable, legible, as adhering to other classroom values, such as holding still in a particular way, making eye contact, and of course being reflective, a prized quality in many learning environments. Already, Dejka shows his own way of adapting to classroom expectations, eschewing one code of conduct—like taking notes or participating verbally—but ably generating another aspect of it. He is still able to embody a form of gestural listening that falls within the bracket of "preferred" classroom behavior.

Waite seems to be aware of Dejka's unusual bearing even before reading his writing. But in the end, it is Dejka's writing that makes Waite more definitely aware of how she should interpret his gestural listening behaviors. Waite shares portions of Dejka's essays, including the following passage:

> Some students learn by thinking out loud, bouncing ideas off the professor and their fellow classmates, and find discussions vital to their understanding. Conversely, those students like myself, who often require more time to effectively articulate their ideas . . . will appreciate writing projects and discussion board posts. We tend to "soak in" the class discussion and spend time out of class processing or ruminating. (79)

Many instructors have likely had experiences when reading a student's work, or meeting with a student in a one-on-one setting, drastically changed their sense of that student's engagement. These experiences highlight the importance of creating different ways to hear from students, such as in small groups, individual conferences, and so on, as well as opportunities for students to reflect upon and write about who they are as listeners, observers, and more generally as students—as "good" students, perhaps.

Waite describes her course and course assignments as sites that explicitly encourage self-reflection and critique of social behavior, especially as regards public performances of gender. In that context, it makes sense that Dejka would share his sense of how he shows up in class within his writing. Nevertheless, a pattern emerges from the examples I've looked at in this chapter, of teachers learning to interpret their students' listening behaviors: a pattern where written work, turned in and read after the fact, serves to clarify students' in-class gestural listening in the eyes of their instructors. Instructors like Waite and the professor in the two courses where I filmed class sessions use student writing to form a fuller picture of what is going on within their students, how much class material they are really taking in. Perhaps, like the professor in my filmed observations states, these are simply two forms of feedback: the gestural being short-term and in the moment, and the written being a longer-term, after-the-fact form of feedback. The instructor notes that he has been wrong, at times, implying that he may have learned, as I did and as so many instructors do, to reserve judgment about a student's gestural listening until some of their written work comes in. Other times, as in the case of Andy Dejka, a student will end up "explaining" their in-class behavior in their writing assignments. In Waite's telling, Dejka not only writes about his own behavioral preferences but also speculates that they might come genetically from his family, relating a story about his younger brother that highlights the younger boy's persistent quietness and difficulties with speech and reading aloud. This dynamic on the one hand allows for a more holistic understanding of our students; it on the other hand concerns me in the sense that it seems to require student self-disclosure, a disclosure that may well be made to mediate an instructor's in-person impression of them, given the high awareness the students I surveyed had about the importance of looking like they're listening.

When we only have a student's moment-to-moment comportment, we have to accept that, as instructors, there's much we don't know and won't know. Some classes may not lend themselves to student self-disclosure or Dejka's style of self-explanation unless instructors intentionally encourage it in a writing assignment or survey response, for instance. S. Brook Corfman, also engaging with Waite's work in *Teaching Queer*, dwells on the paradigm of not knowing about aspects of our students, especially regarding their gender. Corfman notes that this is particularly important when one acknowledges the possibility trans people present in classroom spaces without identifying themselves as such: "How can we account for this kind of space," Corfman writes, "one in which we know trans people must engage but seem unwilling to identify themselves? How to do this without the violence of forced identification?" (263). On the one hand, writing assignments can provide opportunities for students to share about themselves in ways that then shape conditions of discourse in the classroom. On the other hand, instructors should not, and cannot, necessarily rely upon student disclosure, because of its ethical complications, and simply because of its own limitations. Corfman, for instance, understands students as being in a process of becoming that may be actively encouraged along by their work in college courses, writing: "While Waite's *Teaching Queer* does not explicitly address transgender students, it picks up on the possibilities of students' becoming beyond our ability to know by balancing a reading of Butler's 'becoming a gender' with the task of students to continually 'become' within their writing and as participants in a first-year writing course" (275). Seeing students as continually "becoming" brings about a different way of interacting with disclosures in student writing: as conditional, fluid, and subject to change. Student self-disclosure in writing is no guarantee of certainty, and it may or may not "explain" a student's habitual gestural listening. Further, with Corfman's sense of "becoming" in mind, when students self-disclose in writing, their comportment may not necessarily "match up" with what they've disclosed.

Waite locates Dejka's comportment in terms of disciplinary conversations about refusal and rethinking failure. She concludes that there could be something queer about listening but only "when it is employed in environments that require speech as a model of success" (82). Importantly, Waite's experiences with Dejka lead her to expand her sense of what she terms "queer participation," a phrase suggesting that elements of gender and sexuality can inflect classroom comportment and perceptions of it by both instructors and students. The idea of "queer participation" also asks us to think about how gestural elements may be deployed as forms of resistance and as forms of maintaining the self in the face of a rubric of good behavior that asks certain things of classroom participants. Corfman, further, reminds us that students in ongoing processes of becoming may dwell in or between forms of gestural listening that resist easy gender identification, or, alternatively, are used to afford the student the relative protection of gender legibility. Frankie, at the beginning of this chapter, hints at the risks involved in pushing the boundaries of legible gender performance in classroom spaces.

Readers may wonder at this point: Why focus on gestural listening as a phenomenon in the classroom when it can be so easily misinterpreted, and when it sometimes requires writing to "explain" it, something that can only happen after the fact? Here's why: as I hope to have shown, even if instructors misinterpret students' gestural listening, that interpretation still matters. In fact, because it is so easily misinterpreted makes it all the more urgent for those working with students to become aware of how it operates: slippery, constant, at times shielding even as it reveals. As I have pointed out, gestural listening behaviors "beam out" or project continuously, with students being "on" as soon as they enter the classroom. Students develop and internalize their classroom comportments in different ways, and some enter college classrooms having more successfully learned to transmit "good" listening behavior than others. Additionally, some students may have certain personality traits or aspects of their identity that align them more closely with academic expectations.

Gestural Listening as Self-Regulation

The next major idea springing from my study findings is an element that emerged later, with students almost "admitting" that perhaps their listening behaviors could be for themselves, too. This is the idea of gestural listening as self-regulation, as something done for oneself in addition to others—think here of Frankie's motioning in class to help himself learn, not just to show me that he is listening. Gestural listening of this kind takes shape as something that affects the listener (rhetor) as much as their co-participants (audience), in ways reminiscent of the generative listening of Carl Rogers, and of the participatory listening identified by Carol Harrison in early Christian contexts and Charles Hirschkind in Islamic sermon-listening. Another of the most frequently mentioned behaviors that students listed, when surveyed about what they do (or not do) to show that they are listening, was nodding. Here, nodding allows me to illustrate this dimension of how gestural listening works.

I want to return to the student whose response I quoted earlier in my discussion of note-taking. Looking at her words in a different way provides an insight into how gestural listening is also for herself. Again, she states:

> It's sort of like a fail-safe to always have something that's keeping me on track. I had a high school teacher say to be the kid in the front row of the lecture hall taking notes—be that kid on top getting hundreds; looking directions where people are, sometimes it's hard to turn around, but don't be staring off into space.

Taking notes and looking in the right directions, refraining from "staring off into space"—all these are things that the student feels "keep her on track." That is, these behaviors not only project out to instructor and classmates that this student is serious and engaged; they also serve as signals that she gives herself—a "fail-safe"—to guide her own attention. Further, the student recounts her high school teacher telling her to "be the kid in the front row of the lecture hall taking notes." The implication is that she should want to be "that kid": learning as much as possible, taking responsibility for class material, showing "good" engagement to the professor and to classmates. Enacting these behaviors are part of what might allow this survey respondent to become that student. That is, if she does those behaviors, she can make herself into the admirable college student her high school teacher encourages her to become.

In mentioning nodding throughout their survey responses, the students in the study made it clear that they see nodding as a kind of "self-shaping," or self-regulating behavior, too. In one of the classrooms I observe, a student keeps up intervals of nodding throughout class, mostly subtle, staccato micronods. It's a small, yet nearly continuous bobbing of his head as he takes in the class discussion, especially noticeable when speakers reach an "arrival point," finding an elusive word or rounding out a sentence. The student's nodding strikes me, as an observer, as an ongoing registering of what's being said. It indicates, on the one hand, a continuous engagement with the movement of conversation. On the other, the continuous quality of the nodding has the automaticity of a habit, ingrained virtually to the point of unconsciousness.

This student has taken in a particular embodied way of being in the classroom. He relies on nodding not only to show others his attention but also as a version of the first student's "fail-safe." That is, he comes across as respectful, indiscriminately affirming whatever is being said. In his gestural performance of listening, he can't be faulted, although it must be said that the ongoing nodding made me question whether all those nods really reflected understanding. Still, he comes across squarely within the bracket of legible, respectful classroom listening. At the same time, automatic nodding like the type demonstrated by this student may operate as an embodied reminder to himself to pay attention. In working both upon himself and upon others in the room with him, the student uses gestural listening as a way of adopting his role as a student, of becoming, in a thoroughly embodied sense, his student self.

In an interview focused on classroom listening behaviors, including nodding, one student elaborates on how this works:

> It's kind of like "fake it 'til you make it." So if a professor sees that you're nodding, they have a feeling that you're paying attention, even if it's going in one ear and coming out the other . . . when I fake it and try to pay attention, that kind of tricks my body into waking up more. (Student A)

Even if the content of what's being said goes "in one ear" and "out the other," nodding assures—maybe even convinces—the watchful professor of the student's alertness. She highlights the need to *appear* attentive as a kind of classroom imperative, as I discuss earlier—to adhere to the embodied idiom of the classroom. But while she first focuses on the "fakeness" of attentive behavior, perhaps like that of the continuously nodding student—were all those nods really "real?"—she also notes that when she fakes it, it actually "tricks" her body into "waking up more." This description once again encapsulates the dual nature of the nod's rhetoricity as a piece of gestural listening vocabulary:

it affects the self at the same time as it reaches out to affect others. Further, it is a conduit through which the nodder tries to shape herself into the kind of student she wants to be.

In a follow-up interview after the observation, another student picks up on the importance of the nod as a self-monitoring behavior, and its duality: "Having to show your engagement helps you re-enter and focus again," they say. It "can be a natural response to get you back into the focus," they continue, "or a genuine response to something you agree with." Here, the student again articulates a dual role for classroom nodding: showing engagement, as through nodding, can help the nodder "reenter" and regain focus in a classroom setting; and it can be a "genuine" response of agreement. With the use of 'or," the student implies that the two nodding functions may be mutually exclusive and that nodding to focus oneself may be less genuine, less of a "true nod" than nodding in agreement to something that has been said. Indeed, the student responses reveal a particular attitude toward the nod's different functions: the nod is recognized for its power to agree, conveying a meaning and shoring up social ties, but its function as a self-monitoring behavior seems to be one of its more "covert" or less-recognized functions. Mixed into the overt performance of gestural listening that students direct toward others, they also nod as a way of quietly shaping themselves.

Through gestural listening as a form of self-regulation, individuals in class work to make themselves into their "student selves," the person who is "that kid," or who "fakes it 'til she makes it," or who makes himself "re-enter and focus again." Here, we begin to see how gestural listening is something that works inwardly to affect the rhetor—the listener—even as it simultaneously moves outward to affect others. In *Listening to Images*, Tina Campt notices a similar quality in the subjects of the Gulu Real Art photo series, and her observations about these striking images enrich an understanding of gestural listening as a uniquely "inward-and-outward" rhetorical force. The portrait subjects' efforts to shape themselves and self-regulate ultimately emanate outward to the viewer. That is, their self-directed, self-regulating behavior, or what I might also call "self-composing" behavior, also communicates to others, even without words. Further, Campt describes these self-presentational choices as a type of refusal—the refusal to be erased, flattened, or decontextualized. Campt's understanding of the portrait subjects in this photo series as enacting refusal through their self-composing choices, and through their embodiment of "stasis," provides a way of viewing students' listening that acknowledges its effortful, intentional qualities.

In this unusual photo series collected by Martina Bacigalupo, the faces of the portrait-subjects are fully cut out, an empty rectangle in place of a face. The cut-out portions of the photographs—the faces—become ID photos, used on passports, university IDs, bank accounts, or job applications. What remains is the rest of the seated portrait. These "leftover" photographs draw our attention to how people compose themselves through their embodied choices, like how to sit, how to arrange their hands, how to dress, what to carry with them—in short, the rest of the portrait contains much of the sitters' gesturally expressive being. Some women wear traditional dress that establishes them as well to do, for instance. A man poses in a camo-printed uniform, his fingers laced neatly on his lap in a thoughtful bearing at odds with his military dress. In the case of one photograph, a small child kneels on the floor, head resting on the sitter's lap, well outside the frame of the smaller, facial photo. These forms of self-fashioning through clothing, posture, and the sharing of space with others are parts of a fuller, embodied repertoire of how people expect to be received and interpreted by others. With that in mind, one way to interpret these photos would be through a sense of loss, necessary for a different type of gain. The ID photo cuts away much of its subject's full self—and yet, it provides the opportunity for education, financial advancement, and mobility. That is, the ID photos are a bid for citizenship that come at a cost. That "bid for citizenship" hearkens back to Mary Reda, who articulates how students are sometimes required to gain "citizenship" in the classroom at the cost of their own idiosyncratic—or less-preferred—ways of learning and being. Students may also end up trying to "cut away," or at least strategically separate, parts of themselves to gain that citizenship, especially through neutralizing their gestural listening. As I will show in the next chapter, it is an effort that affects some students more than others.

Campt's interpretation of the Gulu Real Art photos is different, however. She shows readers, by contrast, how the photograph subjects work to refuse the overt "flattening" of government identification, both through their self-composing choices in dress and especially through particular embodied aspects of their bearing. At first, it may not seem obvious what gestural or embodied qualities can be found in photograph portraits like these—after all, the subjects are just sitting. But Campt notes a certain physical quality that the portrait-subjects demonstrate: "In and around their strength and vulnerability," she writes, "I see, as well, what most viewers take for granted: their stillness" (50). With this, Campt brings our attention to the effort that goes into holding still, of collecting oneself to sit for a photograph. This type of stillness contains a special kind of application, the energy of gathering and stilling oneself from within. In this sense, the exercise of stillness itself becomes a gestural dimension present in the photographs—an intentional stillness, a tension, a stasis. Writing about the subjects in the photo series, Campt describes it this way:

> We must engage them instead as tension—a tense self-fashioning of/in stasis. These are not women frozen in time or by the camera. Their taut demeanor is an active, tense, and expressive practice of both restraint and constraint. Each of them appears to hold back, hold in, or keep something in reserve—in preparation or anticipation of something to come. The muscular tension they display is an effortful balancing of compulsion, constraint, and refusal that vibrates invisibly. (57)

Describing the sitters' "active, tense" gestural way of being, negotiating the boundary between "restraint and constraint," Campt helps us see how the embodied presence of the whole self, its "muscular tension" and "effortful balancing," is more than just a lack of motion (57). It is a gestural choice, and it requires its own measure of effort. What's more, while the official image-making process implies that only the face signifies, the full body inevitably comes to bear on the face. This way, through their tense, gestural stasis, the portrait subjects refuse the "cutting away" that comes with the government ID photo.

From Campt, we gain two ideas that come to bear on how we view students' gestural listening in classroom spaces. First, stillness can be understood as a gestural quality when it is an intentional lack of movement, or, as Campt describes it, a "tense stasis." Holding still requires energy and focus. Further, in the enactment of "stasis," we see how self-composing, or self-regulating behavior, serves the individual enacting it while also communicating outwardly to others. In the classroom, students also engage in "self-fashioning of/in stasis" (57). In their self-regulating nods or note-taking, for instance, they shape themselves as students inwardly, managing focus and energy, in a way that then also subtly communicates outwardly toward those around them. Second, intentional stasis, as well as forms of gestural expressiveness like dress, can be leveraged by those in a position of lesser power to refuse forces that may "cut away" their wholeness. Like the portrait-subjects who both participate in and resist the act of documentation, students appear in an environment of unequal power relations, meaning that in their comportment, they must negotiate a performance of respect and resistance. But in the ways that they create themselves as students through self-regulating behaviors, students too exhibit a kind of tense stasis: it is neither totally acquiescent, nor, to use Campt's words, is it really an "inherently transgressive [enactment] of resistance" (59). Through this "third thing" they gesturally listen for themselves, in addition to performing respect and resistance toward others.

The implications of the Gulu photos are thrown into particularly sharp relief when considered in their cultural and historical context, which has seen the residents of Gulu dealing with political upheaval and displacement. Nevertheless, the gestural dynamics of self-fashioning that Campt brings to our attention are helpful for understanding how the students I interviewed describe using the gestural regime of the classroom, including nodding, as a form of self-fashioning—both in their own eyes, and in the eyes of others, as they become their embodied, classroom selves.

Toward Difference in Gestural Listening

In their responses to my inquiries, the students in this chapter convey a sense that listening behaviors are forceful, affecting the communicative situation. They conceptualize behaviors of listening as though they reach beyond themselves, beyond their own "actual" listening processes—what it takes to perceive and understand language—to ultimately register with the instructor in complex social ways. Listening—a seemingly quiet and receptive process—actually moves outward to shape the rhetorical situation and its conditions of engagement. Further, the contradictions between how students often present in the classroom and what they actually need or want to best engage in learning reveal what I am calling a "gestural idiom" of the classroom, a delimited set of embodied expressions in classroom spaces that both afford and deny citizenship.

In this chapter, listening emerges as a site of contradiction and subtle maneuvering, as participants in classroom spaces negotiate the dynamics of respect and resistance through their embodied behaviors. For educators and those engaged in communicative work, it is important to resist, or at least suspend, the idea that there is one "right way" to listen, or that listening is a monolith aimed only at obedience. An awareness of gestural listening creates an opportunity for students and instructors both to see their classrooms in a new way, with an expanded rubric of what "good" listening can look like. Reda instructs us again when she urges instructors to consider "how limited a model of the 'good student' we have created . . . This becomes even more problematic for me when I consider the ways that this model of the highly vocal student as 'good student' is often gender-, class-, and culture-bound" (29). In the next chapter, I focus in more detail on aspects of identity and ways of being in the classroom, especially instances of classroom comportments that challenge the status quo.

The results of my small study also revealed another dimension to gestural listening—students recognized how gestural listening also works upon them inwardly, playing a role in how they shape their student selves. Here we begin to see gestural listening's potential as a particular form of sensory rhetoric, operating both inwardly and outwardly, expressively and impressively, flowing modally between semantic and nonverbal manifestations in ways that defy a rigid understanding of the sensorium and that disallow the conceptualization of a hard dividing line between the communicative roles of speaker and listener. As I illustrated in chapter, listening has been conceptualized in more and less capacious ways over time. What else might listening be capable of if freed from a limiting gestural idiom in pedagogical settings?

Readers may be wondering, at this point, about another major issue when it comes to how students take notes and gesturally listen: the role of devices like laptops and phones. The presence of devices adds important dimensions to what I have argued for here, a gestural idiom of the classroom. I return to my survey data and handle the presence of devices further, also in the context of COVID-19's expansion of the role of digital technologies, in chapter 4. In the meantime, I offer the following questions as a starting point for encouraging students to reflect on their own ways of showing up and engaging in class. What students write or say in response to these questions may also help instructors better understand and more accurately interpret their students' in-class comportment, in an effort to transcend a more limited, inherited gestural idiom of the classroom and make way for the recognition of a new embodied vocabulary for listening.

Early-Semester Survey Questions for Students

The following questions are intended for students in a classroom setting, providing them with prompts to reflect on how they perceive listening—especially what we might call "good" listening—in themselves and others. The results of a survey along these lines, or asking students to turn in an informal reflection on one or more of the questions that follow, could help instructors gain insight into their students' listening behaviors.

- Who are you as a listener? As an observer?
- What has made you who you are as a listener in classroom spaces? Did you "learn" to become a certain type of listener in class?
- How do you tend to enact your listening? Nodding, taking notes, etc.? What does listening look like for you?
- Is it important to enact listening in the ways you listed above? Why or why not?
- What does it mean for you to show up as a "good" student?
- What does it mean to "participate" in class?
- How do you show that you are listening in class? That is, how do you embody your listening in class?
- What does it look like for you to be engaged in class?

3

Gestural Listening across Identity

In an installation called *Game of Skill 2.0*, designed by artist Christine Sun Kim, visitors enter a museum exhibition room, nearly bare, with white walls and a wooden floor. Attached to the walls are three long, thin strips of blue Velcro that stretch high across the room like telephone wires, attaching again to the opposite wall. The Velcro gridlines cast sparse, weblike shadows.

Visitors are given a device with a long, thin metal rod extending upward. Their task is to walk underneath the Velcro lines, keeping the tip of the rod in contact with the line. Only then can they hear a recording play, which features the voice of the artist's intern reading a text written by the artist herself. If visitors go faster, the recording plays faster. If they falter backward, likewise, the recording plays backward. Only certain, controlled movements allow for the recording to be intelligible. Mostly, visitors walk with their eyes up, carefully keeping the rod tip in contact with the line, frequently wavering and slipping on and off, starting and stopping, making their way forward with slow, tentative steps, sometimes laughing at themselves. It is truly a game of skill to listen in this way.

Christine Sun Kim is a Deaf artist who creates art with and about sound. This installation, in particular, defamiliarizes the act of listening: visitors are made to work hard, to use their bodies in unusual ways, in order to listen. It

https://doi.org/10.7330/9781646428182.c003

likely makes many visitors reflect on how their normative hearing allows them to take their listening abilities for granted, while others, like those who are d/Deaf, who are hard of hearing, or whose listening is impacted in other ways, may struggle to slide the metal rod along the wires overhead. It may seem that, in contrast to the laborious listening in Kim's exhibition, our everyday gestural enactments of listening—at work, at school, or in conversation with others, for example—simply come naturally. But in fact, as I have aimed to show in the prior chapters, people learn to gesturally show their listening in particular ways throughout their lives. People may gesturally listen differently in different spaces. Further, gestural listening behaviors may be more or less correct, legible, or impactful depending on the particular listener and the particular environment.

In an ideal world, each person would have the ability to flow easily between a wide range of listening behaviors, adopting gestural listening "vocabulary" suited to any environment they find themselves in. In reality, however, many powerful social factors come to bear on how listeners present themselves, shaping—and, at times, delimiting—their gestural listening repertoire. Here, I work through several examples of how layered, intersecting dimensions of identity come to bear on gestural listening in the classroom. In doing so, I hope to show how the gestural idiom of the classroom, which I illustrated in the last chapter, serves some participants more than others, rendering certain students vulnerable to being perceived as incorrect, or illegible listeners. In my discussion of neurodifference, I note the findings of several researchers focused on autism and disability, but especially Shannon Walters and Melanie Yergeau, who work to reinterpret gestural aspects of disability and autism, allowing us to see them newly through the lens of rhetorical agency and meaning. The research and editorial work of Krista Ratcliffe and Cheryl Glenn provide anchors for my exploration of gestural listening as it is inflected by elements of gender, while a cluster of theorists including Perry Gilmore, Vershawn Ashanti Young, and Jennifer Lin LeMesurier enrich and complicate my reading of race as it intersects with gender in performances of gestural listening, especially in how they are delineated by expectations for performances of Black masculinity. Ultimately, I call for an expansion of the rubric that has defined "good" gestural listening, allowing educators to recognize a wider range of listening "ways-of-being" in classroom spaces.

Gestural Listening and Neurodiversity

Many of the students I surveyed indicated that looking like they are listening was important for them while in class. That importance may vary across individuals, however. In an interview, one student made note of differences in how students display their attentiveness, possibly depending on how their "brain is wired":

> It feels good to pay attention and not get distracted by something else if I can help it, but my brain isn't wired to—I don't think anyone's brain is wired to act like you're listening on purpose—that's an odd thing. It's a sign of respect, a sign of like, yes, I care about what you're saying. It's more natural for some people than others, depending on how your brain works.

This student suggests that nodding to perform attentiveness is a learned behavior done to show respect, not a natural impulse—it's an "odd thing." Acting like "you're listening on purpose" strikes the student as unnatural, or learned for the sake of strategy; she implies that nodding in genuine agreement, by contrast, occurs more naturally and is not "acting." Nodding or "listening on purpose," can be a sign of care or respect, the student acknowledges, but she suggests that it should be optional, as doing that is "more natural for some people than others," depending, in her own words, on "how your brain works." In the survey responses that I received and follow-up interviews I conducted, some students self-identified with aspects of neurodifference. Here, I focus on their responses, which while few in number, nevertheless suggest possibilities for many other students with nonnormative ways of being in the classroom.

Students identifying as neurodivergent face particular challenges as they navigate self-presentation in the classroom. Question 1 in my study's intake survey was as follows: Do you consider it important to "look like you are listening" while attending class? By contrast to the majority of students who answered yes, one student—I'll call her Casey—answered: "I consider it unimportant. You should look like it sometimes, but as a person who is neurodivergent, it is easier for me to listen and retain info by keeping my hands busy with something else." Immediately, Casey's response seems full of contradiction. "I consider it unimportant," she begins by declaring, but then immediately concedes that "you should look like it sometimes." While she does not elaborate in her survey response about when a student should "sometimes look like it," it is easy to imagine that an appearance of respect is what she is referring to here. Casey, like so many of her classmates, is fully awake to the need to appear respectful according to a certain rubric. Right away, however, the need for Casey to look like she's listening out of respect seems to chafe against her clear initial statement that she considers it "unimportant."

In the next sentence, Casey, like many of the student respondents, draws a distinction between, on the one hand, "looking like it" with her listening and, on the other hand, listening to really "retain info." She appears to put her own learning process first, subordinating the need to "look like it sometimes" to what it takes for her to best retain what she's hearing: it is "easier" for her to "listen and retain" if she intentionally utilizes another sensory channel, keeping her "hands busy." However, she also indicates, through that distinction, an understanding that "keeping her hands busy" is unlikely to correspond to what it means to "look like" she is listening in the eyes of others. As a reader, I get the sense that this awareness may be hard won, the result of being written off as inattentive in the past, or being impatiently told to pay attention in ways that struck educators as the right ways. Further, this disconnect between what really helps Casey retain information and what she knows "looks like it" to others is something that she connects to her neurodivergence. A particular self-awareness is required of Casey: she needs to do what works best for her learning in the classroom, which may be different from that of her classmates, while also negotiating a behavioral expectation that may be at odds with her most effective learning process. For Casey, the preferred gestural idiom of the classroom creates an additional burden.

Casey describes her preferred way of listening as "keeping her hands busy," a phrase that contains interesting value connotations. "Keeping one's hands busy" conveys the sense of industry, of constant "doing." It's the direct opposite of other phrases that come to mind, in the same breath, that carry overt moral valences: that "idle hands are the devil's workshop," or "the devil finds work for idle hands," for example. With that in mind, one would think that keeping the hands busy would be looked upon favorably. At the same time, that type of busy industry is usually not considered part of the "correct" gestural vocabulary, or gestural idiom, of most higher education classrooms. Rather, students should either take notes, as I discuss in the last chapter, or essentially sit still, with only particular flashes of movement like nodding, hand raising, or joining verbally into discussion. All this should be embedded into an overall bearing of quiet attentiveness, similar to what Tina Campt might call a "tense stasis." A hum of productive industry does not really align with this vision for classroom comportment.

Here I want to illustrate a progression that many readers will recognize from their own schooled lives, or perhaps those of their children. Early grades of schooling largely focus on shaping the playful movements of childhood into the embodied expectations for schooling and work. Children are taught to sit nicely in a circle or in rows during morning meeting, to sit upright at their carefully spaced desks or tables, to stay seated even when something exciting happens—all in all, to rein in erratic movements that seem unsuited to the crucial early learning of reading and writing. Young students learn not to "call out," not to wander around the classroom without permission, to form lines, and so forth. Dealing with crowded classrooms, teachers understandably call for a manageable order. As time goes on, students are taught more specific embodied ways of being in the classroom: not to slouch, for instance, or rock backward in one's chair.

But the paradigm seems to fully shift by the time students reach higher education settings. As Stacey Waite summarizes in *Teaching Queer* (which I quote in the last chapter), in college classrooms instructors are largely faced with the opposite problem: the problem of getting students to break their stillness and silence to participate in class, take part in discussion, or engage fully with classmates in small groups, for instance. A common theme among first-time instructors of classes that depend on discussion is how to get the conversation going, often approached with a million "ice-breakers," activities intended to thaw the apparently frozen barriers between students and each other, and between students and instructor. So the problem at the college level becomes the need to make students move or engage visibly more, rather than less. As the last chapter shows, however, the preferred gestural regime of the higher education classroom also, ultimately, welcomes certain types of movements and not others.

In the midst of this, I return to Casey. She negotiates the changing behavioral demands of classroom environments with the added dimension of her neurodiverse perceptions and preferences. It may be that "keeping her hands busy" was allowed in her primary and secondary schooling environments but that she discovered it was frowned upon in college. She may have even worked to channel her energy into hand tasks because they were considered appropriate in certain classrooms (in my own grade school, students were encouraged to draw or handle a kneaded eraser when they needed help focusing, for instance), only to find that even this was not the type of busyness preferred in other classrooms. With this in mind, Casey's response to Question 2 showed many of the same inner tensions as her first response did. Question 2 read as follows: Do you make an effort to enact listening behaviors, or act attentive, while in class? Casey responded: "Even though I do look like I am focusing on another topic, I always try to make eye contact while the professor is talking to make sure they know I am attentive." Even though she is sure that she looks distracted, or rather that she is "focusing on another topic," she "always tries to make eye contact" to convey attentiveness. So her awareness that she tends to look inattentive prompts her to "always try" to mitigate that by using a gesture strongly associated with listening and attentiveness: eye contact.

Few gestural listening behaviors are as powerful as eye contact, or as imbued with an almost mystical force; research even suggests that it may be crucial for normal cognitive development in infants (Senju et al.). But preferences for eye contact, while seemingly important the world over, tend to be culturally shaped, playing out in culturally specific ways, and deviations from cultural expectations for eye contact can lead to significant misunderstandings. Studies have shown that sustained eye contact is viewed more positively by those of European descent, for instance, while refraining from excessive eye contact and looking down is viewed as more respectful by Japanese people (McCarthy et al.). The social imperative to make eye contact while listening may be at odds, furthermore, with the realities of mental bandwidth. For example, a Japanese study found that maintaining eye contact impeded study participants' ability to perform a cognitive task, such as naming the color in which a word is written (Kajimura and Nomura). Right away, eye contact emerges as a behavior that carries tremendous social weight, even though its cognitive functions may not align with those social imperatives.

Eye contact is notoriously hard for some neurodivergent individuals, especially those with autism spectrum disorder. With the idea of "bandwidth" in mind, autism researcher Debra Bercovici (who also voluntarily discloses her own diagnosis of autism) writes that for many autistic people, eye contact can "often cause distress," because "the majority of autistics experience eye contact as a form of hyperarousal." Instead, she notes, autistic individuals often "make eye contact when talking, but not when listening," in an effort to reduce the cognitive load of the encounter. In a study of adults and teens with self-declared ASD, Dominic Trevisan et al. find that the experience of eye contact is qualitatively different for autistic individuals and can bring about adverse reactions like fear or anxiety, a sense of being violated or overly intimate, sensorially overloaded, and socially awkward. The authors go on to note that this can pose problems for autistic people in social interactions, as making eye contact is a particularly strong social expectation during periods of listening. The authors suggest that "this may stem from an inability to concentrate on auditory (verbal) information while looking at someone else's eyes, which may represent sensory overload, i.e., difficulties simultaneously integrating visual and auditory information." Neurodivergent students may have trouble presenting themselves in class as gesturally correct in their listening, as they balance the need to mitigate possible cognitive overload with the need to appear attentive according to a normative rubric.

In other words, neurodiverse students may not have access—or at least not to the same extent, at all times—to the same set of gestural listening tools with which to present themselves rhetorically in classroom spaces. In *Rhetorical Touch: Disability, Identification, Haptics*, Shannon Walters looks for elements of rhetoric that can be leveraged by disabled and neurodiverse rhetors. People living with disabilities, Walter argues, are often individuals for whom the usual ways of harnessing logos, pathos, and ethos, for example, are not available, or are compromised by the fact of their disability and the way narratives of disability are mostly funneled into one of three categories: the inspirational "overcoming obstacles" narrative, the pity narrative, or a narrative of disgust and its resulting isolation for the disabled individual. Her focus, in a sea of scholars studying vision and hearing, is touch. Touch emerges as a uniquely useful modality for these individuals as they find ways to use rhetoric that serve their needs. As Walters puts it, looking at touch rhetorically allows for "persuasion beyond explicit verbal and linguistic means" (42). The students Casey and Adam, discussed next, use their hands as conduits to show their effort at attentive listening. In doing so, they highlight the hands' tactile primacy, as though their hands, in the act of touching through craft, they are "in touch" with the unfolding learning process in the classroom.

Adam gave a response that highlights these issues with the expectation of eye contact. He responded to Question 1 this way:

> I try not to look like I'm *not* listening, if that makes sense—I'm not on my phone/laptop or anything like that. But I find eye contact hard and focus best if I'm crocheting while listening, so to some extent I am limited in this respect. That said, I picked up crocheting specifically b/c it is not seen as being as inattentive as other forms of stimming, so I guess I've put thought into this.

At first, Adam focuses on the negative space of gestural listening. That is, he does not focus on taking notes, nodding, or speaking up in class, the "positive" signs of listening, as Casey does, but rather tries to avoid the appearance of *not* listening. This approach implies that there are certain behaviors that can make it look like a student is not listening—or "zoning out," as a student in the last chapter called it. Adam mentions being "on his phone/laptop" as one of those behaviors, according to him, that is a sure sign of a lack of listening. The presence of devices like laptops and cell phones forms an important throughline in the data I collected about gestural listening in my study, one important enough to warrant its own chapter, connected as it is to broader issues regarding perceptions of technology and, of course, the explosion of remote teaching technologies like Zoom in light of the COVID-19 pandemic. For now, I want to point out simply that Adam intentionally avoids being on his phone or laptop, in order to avoid what he believes to be signs of a lack of attention. With the phrase "anything like that," Adam seems to gather all interactions with mobile devices as behaviors that are questionable in class, pointing to a kind of general, societal agreement on that issue, something "everyone knows."

Next, Adam notes in passing that he finds eye contact "hard," a phrase indicating that he knows eye contact is one of the positive signals that tends to convey listening and attention, just as Casey does, and as many students are taught. Eye contact is hard, and he knows about himself that he "focuses best" if he is crocheting, and these are things Adam notes as being "limiting" to his ability to show gestural listening, or, at least, gestural listening that adheres to the rubric of correctness and legibility that I have been pointing out in many classroom settings. Adam forms another in a line of individuals we have heard from so far whose preferred way of listening is at odds with preferred gestural regime, or idiom, of the classroom. He strikes a compromise, choosing crocheting as something that is "not seen as being as inattentive as other forms of stimming." With the mention of eye contact being "hard" and of "forms of stimming," Adam shows that he is conversant in the vocabulary of neurodifference and of his own neurodifference: in his survey responsive here, he implies that he'd like to stim in other ways but that those other ways would be even less acceptable than crocheting, even less positively perceived by others. And with good reason: Melanie Yergeau, in *Authoring Autism*, outlines how stimming—like other outward signs of autism—carries a brutal history of institutionalization, surveillance, and violence in the way it has been treated. As someone who enacts a nonnormative gestural idiom, Adam understandably has developed ways to redirect his stimming; likely, as he mentions, from ways deemed less acceptable in classrooms settings to those more acceptable. Yergeau helps us understand how much accommodation there may be in Adam's adoption of crocheting in place of "other forms of stimming." While stimming is generally discouraged in majority-allistic spaces due to its qualities of excess when seen through neurotypical eyes, Yergeau maintains that for autists, it may in fact be a form of embodied invention, a site of possibility that may communicate or allow for autistic ways of knowing while it at the same time resists essentialized meanings. Continually pushing back against prior scholarship and widespread beliefs in autistic people's essential arhetoricity, Yergeau proposes that stimming understood as part of a "sensorimotoric schema" can "work as a counter to those theories that so ardently deny the autistic's capacity for rhetoric" (200). Exemplified in the work of Ralph Savarese, sensorimotoric approaches to autism see the disorder as "sensorimotoric divergence" that "resist[s] spectra and diagnostic fixity" (200). Sensorimotoric approaches allow autists to "author the conditions of their rhetoricity," too, as Yergeau writes: "Autistic people have long been claiming that they have theories of mind, much like they've long been claiming that autism is a fully embodied experiential, much like they've been claiming that autism is a motoric culture of flaps and echoes and bodily disobedience" (200). Adam chooses crocheting as a kind of middle ground between "other forms of stimming," which would be even less legible in the classroom's motoric culture, and adopting the preferred gestural idiom of the classroom, which may not be possible for him and which would most likely be ineffective for his learning. He needs instructors to recognize his highly intentional motoric choices, however apparently "disobedient."

Autism advocate Erin Felepchuk notes a tendency for the disobedient, seemingly excessive motions of stimming to be spoken of using sound-focused language. For instance, she writes: "Industrial education systems demand silence from deviant bodies, and school-aged autistic children are silenced through the practical usage of the special education adage 'quiet hands.'" The term "quiet hands" also puts me in mind of Casey, who listens best when she "keeps her hands busy," though she knows that busy hands may also be "noisy." Here, the body is talked about in terms of noise, as if a body moving in ways deemed inappropriate to the context it finds itself in is something that causes the distraction or excess of audible noise. The idea that a body can be "noisy" without actually producing sound lends itself to the idea of gestural listening as a force that moves outward to affect others in a communicative situation as sound does, and to the idea that classroom spaces require a "quiet" gestural idiom, with the exception of certain, approved types of movement or vocal production. Indeed, the term "noise" carries valences of the disruptive, the inappropriate, the excessive—connotations explored by scholars of sound like Brandon LaBelle, Steve Goodman, and Jacques Attali. In "Embodied Semiosis: Autistic

'Stimming' as Sensory Practice," Jason Nolan and Melanie McBride further identify the link between "noisy" bodies and what has coalesced over time as "correct" comportment in educational settings. They write: "Even so-called progressive classroom management is characterized by an ableist discourse of engagement, attention and participation that is socially and cognitively overwhelming for the autistic" (1070). My research findings suggest that gestural listening plays an outsized role in how behavior like "engagement, attention, and participation" is perceived and that gestural listening deemed "correct" in the classroom falls within a narrow range of physical expression. The authors highlight the implicit privileging of "quiet bodies" when they write: "Words like 'disengaged', 'distracted' and 'disruptive' are used to describe individuals whose bodies or sensory responses disrupt the outdated and alienating performativity of engagement defined by behaviourist norms and values" (1070).

Alongside these scholars of autism in classroom spaces, Casey and Adam begin to teach us an important lesson: that gestural listening can take on a range of embodied manifestations beyond what educators often presume to be "good" listening behaviors. They teach instructors to suspend internalized rubrics of what correct listening looks like in academic spaces, becoming aware of the embodied traditions of the classroom and how they may put some students at a disadvantage who are unable to perform an embodied norm. Expanding our vision of what "good" listening looks like can help us welcome students whose embodied ways of being have been historically penalized in classroom environments.

Some readers may note that crocheting, like other handcrafts using yarn or needlework, tends to be a gendered activity, coded as feminine in its role as part of the domestic sphere. And indeed, the story of gestural listening across identity categories in classroom spaces gets more complicated when taking gender into account. Their neurodifferences are only one aspect of Casey and Adam's identities, which intersect with other categories carrying their own considerations for rhetorical presence in the classroom.

Elements of Gender in Gestural Listening

Molly is a first-semester student in my First Year Composition class. In the midst of class discussion, a period of silence ensues. After thinking for a while, Molly lifts her head suddenly in a sharp, sparrow-like movement, making eye contact with me at the front of the room. I call on her, but she declines to comment. These quick movements out of rest are characteristic for Molly, and throughout the semester I notice that they sometimes indicate she has something to say, but other times she's "just listening" or, possibly, just not ready to speak yet.

Molly's gestural profile is notable for being at once active and restrained: the mental processes of her listening and thinking seem to be visible in her occasional, darting movements, but, as I touch on in the previous chapter through the ideas of Tina Campt, she also exercises stillness. In fact, her movements emerge as all the more noticeable because of the way they take place against a backdrop of relative stillness. At times, when I call on her, she refuses to comply with the gentle request to speak. She navigates the classroom dynamic of respect and resistance gracefully, arriving at a kind of "respectfully resistant" compromise. I call on her, with an instructor's hope of facilitating discussion, in part because she conveys the appearance of listening, but often she chooses to keep her inner life or mental processes to herself. I am reminded of a passage from Colm Tóibín's *House of Names*, in which Ianthe, observed by Orestes, establishes an authoritative presence through her detailed household and societal knowledge and through her cultivation of a particular appearance of listening and deliberation:

> Ianthe spent her day in the room where there was the most activity. She knew each messenger by name and noted what time each one left and was expected to return. She also remembered what had been decided or on what matters the various elders had asked to be consulted. Usually she said little. She had a way, Orestes noticed, of listening and then seeming to be about to speak and thinking better of it. She gave the impression that she was wrapped up in her own thoughts while also paying close attention to everything. (260)

Ianthe's gestural way of being allows her to move into a more authoritative role in her high-ranking family, and in more recent historical context it is no accident that this balance between movement and stillness, subtly conveying expertise and thoughtfulness, builds Ianthe's credibility in the eyes of observers. Questions of citizenship, as Mary Reda mentions, and the kind of comportment that allows people to claim citizenship in classrooms warrant a turn to feminist and historical rhetorics, an area that contends explicitly with the forced absence of women from rhetorical traditions. In *Silence and Listening as Rhetorical Arts*, coedited by Krista Ratcliffe and Cheryl Glenn, several authors seek to reread rhetorical traditions from the perspective of women's participation, reframing aspects of that tradition through the lens of rhetorical agency under duress, forms of persuasion that emerge when rhetors do not have recourse to the full rhetorical toolbox. The interplay of respect and resistance in students' gestural choices takes on greater depth in historical context, especially the history of women's participation in rhetorical arts and public life.

Taking Lisa Suter's perspective on the American Delsartist movement into account, it may be particularly important for women, even today, to negotiate a balance between stillness and movement, as well as speech and silence. In "Living Pictures, Living Memory: Women's Rhetorical Silence within the American Delsarte Movement," Suter examines the rhetoricity of silence and the body in regard to the American Delsartist movement. Among other forms, the Delsarteans revived genres such as statue posing and *tableaux mouvants* (or "moving pictures"). Suter writes: "At the end of the century, as women continued to fight for the franchise, women's education, labor reform, and temperance (among other causes), it became common to refer to female activists speaking their minds in public as 'freedom shriekers' (Johnson 64), 'shrieking sisters,' or 'screaming viragos'" (Jorgensen Earp 96) (105). "In this climate," she continues, "the voice that male rhetors could take for granted was for women a dangerous means of expression: a rhetorical medium likely to backfire. Small wonder, then, in this historical context, that many American Delsartists began to study the rhetoricity of silence" (105). This historical perspective on women's choices around silence and vocalizing can help broadly contextualize certain choices that students make in the classroom even now. In an effort to gain an audience, according to Suter, women often inadvertently alienated potential listeners by speaking out what was considered "too boldly." The voice was something to be held in reserve, in order not to dull its effect when used. An attitude like this is unlikely to disappear quickly: to some extent, the notion of vocal women as "freedom shriekers" persists. A felt sense of these constrictions on speech is an attitude that may come to bear on Molly's comportment, as a student who feels she may render her voice ignorable by using it too much or too loudly.

Molly may also be unwilling to share thoughts that are not yet fully formed, because of the risks involved. Delsarte art forms were self-conscious modes of performance, rehearsed and then performed onstage. Being in a classroom, on the other hand, is less often considered a real mode of performance in the same sense of theater or music, except in pedagogical situations that assess a student's "performance in class," a term that often refers not just to participation in the classroom but also more generally the student's writing or exam results. Nevertheless, there is a quality of performance in discussion-based classrooms, in the sense that being prompted to speak in class could reveal the quality of a student's preparation, or a lack of familiarity with disciplinary norms.

With this in mind, students often use the performance of gestural listening strategically. Nancy Myers, also examining silence and listening in the context of women's rhetorical agency in the *Silence and Listening as Rhetorical Arts* volume, takes a perspective on listening and silence that frames them both as tools for negotiating a complex and often unfriendly social climate as well as "acts of learning." She writes that "purposeful silence (based on a woman's deliberate restraint and choice) and perceptive listening (based on a woman's processes of reasoning and reflecting are ongoing acts of learning). Contingent and negotiated, purposeful silence and perceptive listening ensure the possibility of cooperation and influence when a woman chooses to speak or write" (59). According to Myers, purposeful silence and perceptive listening allow for the 'social perception of conformity and submission while offering women the opportunity to make deliberate choices about when to be silent and when to speak" (59). Molly avails herself of this complex rhetorical strategy. She demonstrates a gestural idiom that conveys the appearance of listening to me and her classmates—I even go so far as to call on her when she has not raised her hand. In doing so, she creates an environment for herself within the class that will be friendly to her when she chooses to speak. Further, she declines to speak at times even when I have prompted her, showing a careful selectiveness with her spoken contributions. She primes the room for her contributions, and shows explicitly that she will not speak until she is ready and feels she has something fully formed to contribute.

It is not only women who use strategies like these to leverage rhetorical force. Mary Reda writes about a quiet male student who made a rare and impactful comment midsemester: "I suspect that part of the power of Jon's question came from his relative silence. His question had more power and weight because he so rarely spoke, thus we knew it mattered a great deal. We listened," she concludes (68). This student leverages his usual quietness, in order to ensure close listening when he finally chooses to speak. In this, he demonstrates what Nancy Myers describes as the techniques women have used in climates unfriendly to their contributions: choosing the quietness of listening until the opportune moment arrives. The question remains, however: How are men perceived when they sit quietly, and how are women perceived when they do the same?

Gendered norms for gestural listening come to bear on how those judgments are made in classroom spaces. As part of her discussion of gender and listening, Krista Ratcliffe makes note of linguist Deborah Tannen, who claims that in US culture, "speaking is gendered as masculine and valued positively in

a public forum while listening is gendered as feminine and valued negatively"
(129). She goes on to point out specific ways in which men and women vocally
and gesturally manifest the act of listening differently:

> Tannen further argues that U.S. culture socializes men and women to lis-
> ten differently: Men often listen by challenging speakers to a verbal duel to
> determine who knows more and who is quicker on his feet; women often
> listen by smiling, nodding, asking questions, and providing encouraging
> verbal cues (yes, uh huh, is that right?, hmmm) (142). In other words, men
> are socialized to play the listening game via the questions "Have I won?" and
> "Do you respect me" while women are socialized to play it via the questions
> "Have I been helpful?" and "Do you like me?" (129)

The idea of "likeability," and the specter of sexism that accompanies it, looms
large; the act of listening emerges as one of the sites in which a person's "likeability" factor takes shape. Gestural listening that may seem "correct" for a man
may strike an observer as aggressive or "unlikeable" when enacted by a woman.
If a woman sits listening, making no outward indication of responsiveness, she
may be more likely to be perceived as inattentive, passive-aggressive, or slow
on the uptake, whereas a man may simply be perceived more neutrally, perhaps
as being calm and collected.

Further, gender also intersects with preferences within different ethnic
groups for the successful handling of silence, interruption, and interactivity.
Definite, if not often articulated, preferences exist around the ratio of silence to
speech that are culturally and contextually specific. Tannen explores this phenomenon in a piece called "Silence: Anything but," in which she compares the
preferred silence-to-speech ratio to two groups of people sharing a Thanksgiv-
ing meal. Three of the participants in the dinner identify as Jewish with family
based in New York City, while the other three are Californians and not Jewish.
Based on an audio recording and subsequent transcription of the conversation
at dinner, Tannen argues that different groups have preferred pause-lengths
between the end of what one speaker says and the beginning of a respondent's
reply. Furthermore, these differing preferences for pause-lengths also result
in differing tolerance toward and perception of interruption, or overlap,
between conversation participants. Perceptions of pause-length and overlap
affect whether silence is seen, Tannen writes, as a "chance for personal exploration vs. failure of language" (100). Perceptions of gestural listening that shape
communicative situations, that is, are inflected not just by gender but also
by cultural understandings of the meanings of speech and silence. Cultures

that tend to prefer displays of involvement and warmth, or that value verbal performances of wit or repartee, may perceive the silence of listening after a verbal contribution of a conversation partner to be a sign of detachment or a "failure of language." In an arena like school, where those preferences collide with expectations for "good" listening as defined by obedience and quiet respect, there is likely to be friction.

In an illustration of the resulting friction, Götz Aly's investigation of the prehistory of the Holocaust called *Why the Germans? Why the Jews?* includes evidence of how Jewish girls were received in school during the second half of the nineteenth century, a period that saw increasing integration of German Jewish students into mainstream German schools. Synthesizing the findings of a statistical researcher named Arthur Ruppin, who investigated the "demographic and social life of German Jews" in a series of publications at the turn of the twentieth century, Aly writes: "Depending on their ages, [Jewish girls] often behaved in 'unruly and precocious fashion' and received middling marks for diligence and conduct. Many teachers complained that their Jewish pupils were too interested in 'social diversions.' But they studied hard and ended up with excellent marks" (23). Jewish students, at this time, were relative newcomers to mainstream German secondary and university schooling. Due to what Aly refers to as the "intellectual legacy" of Jewish communities, emphasizing literacy and study of religious texts, Jewish students were able to rapidly improve their social and economic standing by taking advantage of higher levels of schooling (19). Aly makes the point that the girls' academic achievement reflects cultural norms for literacy and text-based inquiry in Jewish communities; by the same token, their embodied and vocal presence in class is also likely to be shaped by their community. Between a cultural preference for warmth, verbal involvement, and volubility in personality, pointed to by Tannen's study, and their relative newness, the girls' comportment is at odds with the expectations for in-class comportment in the greater European school system—their behavior is considered to be "unruly" and overly "social."

It is easy to see how the girls may have been vulnerable to gendered valuations of their conduct in class, with "unruly" and "social" sliding easily into stereotypes of feminine communication as chatty, trivial, or gossipy. However, the tendency toward "unruly" behavior does not seem to be limited to Jewish girls, and not just to Germany. Aly goes on to cite the work of Ottokar Němeček, an Austrian researcher, who during the 1913–14 school year focused on the relative performance of Jewish and Christian students. Aly writes: "Jewish students excelled at the tests, while their marks for conduct were below average. The reason for this, Němeček concluded, resided in 'the greater liveliness of the Jews, who, as every teacher will attest, are much more prone than Christian pupils to chatter and cause disturbance'" (26). What we learn from this report is that categories of identity layer together in complex ways to bring about a student's embodied presence in class. Here, there are cultural preferences for expressiveness and conversational involvement springing from Jewish communities that seem to span the genders. In other situations where the group being observed all come from the same cultural and/or ethnic background, gendered differences in communication styles may overtake differences in cultural subgroups in their importance to an analysis of gestural listening. Intersecting elements of identity inflect gestural listening performances. Molly, for example, presents socially as a young woman, and she is also of East Asian descent. Her listening strikes me as recognizable and perhaps even preferred, or "correct" in our classroom environment, but she gently reminds me that I cannot make assumptions about what listening looks like, and certainly not without consideration to constructions of race.

Gestural Listening through Raced and Gendered Identities

Amid rows of more gesturally restrained classmates, Katherine makes eye contact with me boldly in our composition classroom, moving forward to the edge of her desk seat when the conversation especially interests her. At times, she seems about ready to leap up from her chair. Throughout class, Katherine actively responds to my questions and to her classmates' contributions, with her facial expressions and her posture. Her embodied way of being is so overtly active and involved that often it's as though she is speaking, commenting, when she has not actually spoken.

It is easy to see how Katherine's listening acts as a rhetorical force here, reaching beyond herself to help create a more flowing, responsive discussion dynamic. With such noticeable and legible listening behaviors, Katherine's is a type of gestural listening that she, especially as a white woman, has probably benefited from throughout her schooling. She is perceived as a visibly "active" participant and, in that way, as a "good" student. She has probably been described by some teachers as having a "good attitude." As an early-career instructor at the time, I felt relieved to have a student like Katherine in my class—someone who would likely be willing to speak up in moments of silence that I interpreted, at the time, as many instructors do, as a form of failure. In short, Katherine demonstrated a type of "preferred" listening behavior.

I would like to revisit my observations about David here, a student I also mention in the introduction to this book. David is a young Black man starting his first year of college. In our class of nineteen, he is the only Black man. David introduces himself on the first day of class, when everyone is asked to say a few words about themselves. He then assumes a persistent silence, becoming what Paul Kameen may have described as "tenaciously taciturn" (129). As the weeks go by, David's silence begins to feel stony. Throughout the semester, he shows little on his face, taking on a statue-like stillness. Even in small groups, although I see him conferring with his classmates from across the room, I can't find an opportunity to actually hear him say anything. This goes on for some weeks.

Here, too, David's listening reaches beyond himself and has an impact on the discursive situation but quite a different one. Initially, I interpreted David's still, quiet behavior as a stony silence, one that might indicate he did not like the class or think it worth his while. I worried that I wasn't reaching David, that my lesson plans were lackluster, or that our class texts struck students as irrelevant. Other times, I interpreted his behavior as a lack of engagement. My impression was overturned a few weeks later, however, in a one-on-one conversation with David during my office hours. There, David offered observations and asked questions in a way that reflected a deep, lively engagement with our main course text. He had, in fact, been listening, but I had not perceived his listening behaviors to be legible according to the limited rubric that I brought with me into the classroom.

To help me understand the way Katherine and David came across to me, I turn first to Perry Gilmore in her three-year study of a predominantly low-income, Black urban community and elementary school, "Silence and Sulking: Emotional Displays in the Classroom." In it, Gilmore looks primarily at children in grades 4–6, but her observations nevertheless shed light on what children learn about the performance of listening in their classrooms. Her observations begin to explain how Katherine and David may have come to perform their listening so differently and what the danger is in only recognizing and rewarding some listening behaviors to the exclusion of others. "Many of the most crucial social interactions in school settings are highly charged with emotion and regularly interpreted with regard to 'attitude,'" Gilmore writes (140). "Attitude," however, takes on particular dimensions of meaning. "In talking to many of the staff, and in the initial phases of general observation in this school and community, it became apparent that 'attitude' was delicately woven into a broader context of what might be labelled 'propriety,'" or "proper standards of what is socially acceptable in conduct or speech" (140–41). Gilmore observes, in talking with faculty and staff, that students with "good attitudes" were also the ones who were deemed, much more generally, "good kids." The problems with this association between attitude and a student's overall character become clear when Gilmore goes on to write: "Yet when the behaviors subsumed under the label 'attitude' were examined, the data indicate that they consist largely of a set of paralinguistic and kinesic communicative adornments which are associated with a particular ethnic style of socioeconomic class, rather than a set of character traits reflective of the nature of individuals" (141). With this, Gilmore shows that there is danger in collapsing "kinesic communicative adornments … associated with a particular ethnic style of socioeconomic class" with a much more generalized statement about "attitude." What Gilmore is showing us, or reminding us, is that embodied ways of being are part of how students are socialized and are brought into the classroom with them, a space that rewards some of those embodied ways of being more than others.

These connections between comportment and the perceived value of individuals, furthermore, do not seem to be limited just to primary school education. In a study called "Psychological Correlates of Silence and Sound in Conversational Interaction," Cynthia L. Crown and Stanley Feldstein examine responses to patterns of interruption in conversations between white and Black college students, both male and female. In their findings, they first confirm the effect of gender, among white study participants, on how responsive listening is enacted: it is, on the one hand, more visible and responsive from women, a quality they describe as "interruptive," and, on the other hand, less "interruptive" on the parts of the men, in general. They then speculate about why that may be, writing: "That noninterruptive speech of the white men and interruptive speech of the white women were viewed as positive seems somewhat counterintuitive" (46). They continue: "It may be that the white women who engaged in such interruptive speech were thought to be assertive rather than impolite, and that the assertiveness of white females may be a quality of which college students approve. For white men, however, noninterruptive simultaneous speech may be viewed as supportive and as expressing interest and, therefore, worthy of approbation" (46). Next, they compare their findings between the white and Black study participants, noting "that the blacks, whether male or female, only tended to be viewed positively by other blacks and whites when the former refrained from interruptions of any kind is open to several imaginable interpretations" (46). One of the "imaginable interpretations" is that different standards for the attentive behavior of Black and white people are still held, consciously or unconsciously. More investigation is necessary into how and why students of different racial backgrounds come into classrooms performing their listening differently.

I turn again to Gilmore, especially her extended description of what she calls sulking, a description that, importantly, also layers in elements of gender that coincide with the students' racial identities:

> Girls will frequently pose with their chins up, closing their eyelids for elongated periods and casting downward sideways glances, and often markedly turning their heads sidewards as well as upwards. Girls will also rest their chins on their hand with an elbow support on their desks. Striking or getting into the pose is usually with an abrupt movement that will sometimes be marked with a sound like the elbow striking the desk or a verbal marker like "humpf." . . . It is necessary to draw attention to the silence, and with the girls it seems to be primarily with a flourish of getting into the pose.
>
> Boys usually display somewhat differently. Their "stylized sulking" is usually characterized by head downward, arms crossed at the chest, legs spread wide and usually desk pushed away. Often they will mark the silence by knocking over a chair or pushing loudly on their desk, assuring that others hear and see the performance. Another noticeable characteristic of the boys' performance is that they sit down, deeply slumped in their chairs. This is a clear violation of the constant reminder in classrooms to "sit up" and "sit up tall." . . . The silence displays go against all the body idiom rules of the classroom. (149)

The kind of sulking that Gilmore illustrates here can be understood as a particular performance of listening. Sulking students are listening "resistantly." Another way to view this would be to see sulking students as purposely *not* listening, making a performance of how they're *not* open to what's happening. At the same time, this raises the question of whether the opposite of listening is actually talking, or simply inattention. Sulking students, on the other hand, seem to be paying close attention. They're engaged enough, after all, to maintain a physical performance based on a perceived slight.

Gilmore goes on to discuss the responses of teachers to student sulking, including how the teachers in the observed school interpret the behavior. She notes that "a black teacher was more likely to discipline a dramatic sulking display, sending the child to the office, calling the parent, or in some way immediately chastising the student" (157). To a white teacher, on the other hand, stylized sulking was seen as a cultural variation of expression: "Sulking," Gilmore writes, "in the highly stylized way it is performed by many of the students, was viewed by both black and white teachers as part of a stereotypic communicative style of blacks. Much the way Jewish or Italian gestural style might be characterized, so too this behavior might easily be interpreted as a black gestural performance" (157). The performance of resistant listening through sulking, according to Gilmore's study, then, appears to be influenced by a student's race. Black children, performing that resistance through sulking, are likely to experience more disciplinary action, interestingly coming mostly from Black teachers. This realization brings Gilmore to articulate the question: "Is there a trade of blackness for success in the study site?" (160).

Gilmore, in her essay, does not interrogate her use of the term "sulking" or the implications of mobilizing that term in his examination of behaviors that, she notes, may be characteristic of some Black communities of a particular socioeconomic class. The word "sulking" has negative connotations. Even the sulker knows full well that being accused of this comportment is undesirable. Others, usually adults, seem to retain the right to accuse a child of sulking. Doubtless, sulking can be an immature form of passive resistance. Nevertheless, sulking, in the context of Gilmore's study of fourth-to-sixth grade students, is a form of self-expression, even rhetorical agency, on the part of the student, who may not have recourse to other forms of asserting themselves. Sulking can be a powerful tool available to a student who feels wronged, ignored, or misunderstood.

What I take from these vignettes of Katherine and David, with help from Perry Gilmore's analysis, is that some performances of gestural listening tend to be rewarded in classroom spaces, while others are not. Importantly, those performances are often shaped by aspects of identity, especially race and gender. In *Your Average Nigga: Performing Race, Literacy, and Masculinity*, Vershawn Ashanti Young articulates how performances of Black masculinity are often further infused with a compulsory heterosexuality and that this mixture is often at odds with success in classroom spaces. Reflecting on his upbringing, during which his success in school was often perceived by others to be linked to his "insufficient" masculinity, he writes:

> Because some boys see school as a site of effeminacy and school language (WEV) as a discourse for girls, white and black boys resist some forms of language instruction, which in turn causes them to fail literacy classes. But the difference between black boys and white boys is that black boys not only feel coerced to give up their masculinity if they do well in school, but they also feel forced to abandon their race—the ultimate impossibility. (90)

Race, gender, and literacy bundle tightly together here, with White English Vernacular (WEV) being the problematic key to socioeconomic mobility but only if traded for race and gender identities. In one particularly dramatic moment, Young illustrates how his Blackness, his masculinity, and his middle-class status are challenged because of the very way they are on display and how they are still, nevertheless, misread by others. He recounts giving a talk to a mostly white audience of university colleagues about his research on code meshing, arguing that students' language blending Black English Vernacular (BEV) with formal English should be welcomed in writing assignments and in classroom settings. With this stance, Young pushes back against many who believe that Black students must produce a formal, standard English in order to succeed professionally. Young is surprised when a colleague, Diane, espouses that same opinion, in direct opposition to Young's argument: "She was the only other black teacher in the room," Young writes. "I had noticed that she sat unusually stiff backed and stone faced during my presentation. Her unemotional expression surprised me, since we had been generally friendly toward one another the few times we'd met before. As she spoke, however, it became evident that she had been masking her fuming discontent" (106–07). Here, Diane signals her resistance to what she's hearing by sitting "unusually stiff backed and stone faced," "unemotional," conveying a stoniness that turns out to be "masking" a "fuming discontent." In this instance, Diane's resistant listening takes the shape of refraining from what Young would expect to be a more comfortable, friendly responsiveness. She embodies a tensely contained, reeled-in energy, giving away nothing, as though refusing Young's views through her physical refusal to engage. From that state of gathered energy, she stands and delivers a strong rebuttal of the argument he had made in his presentation.

Simultaneously, Young tried to "listen back" gesturally in kind. Young writes that he "stood in the front of the room, trying unsuccessfully to don the same stony disposition that Diane had displayed earlier" (107). With this description of a moment in the "hot-seat," Young struggles to contain his responses as Diane has, to remain within the type of "professional" role that she assumes he wants to occupy but that he, even in that moment, does not want to be forced to inhabit. "I managed to hear Diane without getting too hot," he continues, until she wraps up her comment with the kind of painful misconstrual of Young's own presence that his book is populated with: "She finished her rant with an example of someone whom she thought best showed why we shouldn't code mesh—me! 'Look at you,' she pointed, 'a well-dressed, well-rehearsed, polished, articulate, black male college professor—how'd you get here?'" (107). Diane literally points to Young as an example of where standard English can get Black men—out of the ghetto and into middle-class privilege and stability. In fact, Diane assumes that Young is, and that Young wants to be, a certain kind of white professional, while in that very moment he struggles with a performance that he is uncomfortable with and, as he has just argued, that he does not want to be forced to master.

Diane assumes that Young has, in fact, been able to achieve a stable professional life through his mastery of WEV, that he is a prime example of what switching to WEV, and other white-coded performances of literacy, can bring about. But this is far from the case—in fact, Young details how challenging it is for him to keep jobs where he must negotiate his complex role, at once Black enough and white enough, and that he does not truly feel that he has a deep comfort with WEV or middle-class life. He conveys this by recounting conversations with a Black friend whose whiteness he feels is more "authentic" than his: "I used to see her as whiter than I could ever be," he writes, "because she never slipped into the blackness I know. I used to see her whiteness as authentic and mine as made-up, since I had to mold myself so that I could sound and act white proficiently, whereas she just grew up that way, in Tacoma, Washington, in an area heavily populated by white people" (41). Young lives under the pressure of continually needing to act man enough in Black environments like the hometown he visits, yet nonthreatening enough to be welcome in predominantly white school and even simply to avoid arrest while walking to his job on campus. Instead, in Diane's response to Young, we see a tendency to flatten Black men in academic spaces into unrealistically stagnant, monolithic roles, such as young men who successfully "got out" of the ghetto, as Diane believes Young represents—a story he believes is much more complicated—or young Black men who can't quite trade their Black masculinity for success in the school site, as both Young himself and Gilmore suggest is often the case.

The discomfort Young experiences moving through home, school, and other spaces while carrying the embodiment of his interrelated socioeconomic, racial, and professional identities is a theme taken up by other artists and scholars who have noticed the difficult "trades" Black men often must make. Throughout Childish Gambino's music video for the song "This is America," for instance, forms of dance alternate suddenly with provocative acts of violence. In the first few seconds of the video, Gambino dances, oriented toward the camera, then suddenly turns and shoots a hooded Black man who is playing the guitar nearby. In "Winking at Excess: Racist Kinesiologies in Childish

Gambino's 'This Is America,'" Jennifer Lin LeMesurier interprets the video as a critique of the way Black men are so often framed either as entertainers and athletes, performing spectacular embodied feats, or as associated with violence, either as perpetrators or as victims. "The repetition of this structure," she writes, of "dancing bleeding into violence, is a metacognitive questioning of common narrative structures and available roles for Black bodies" (147). Either through acts of violence or through spectacular entertainment, LeMesurier notes, "expectations for Black male behavior are based on a deep assumption of the Black body as naturally always in motion" (140). LeMesurier contextualizes these "archetypal Black kinesiologies" through a longer history of racialized performance in the United States, arguing that "this caricature of Black embodiment is indebted to minstrelsy, an extremely popular entertainment form in the mid-nineteenth century that was based on refracted performances of blackness" (141). Within that historical context, she goes on, "Gambino's performance demonstrates how racial progress is still stunted by normalized expectations of racial embodiment, specifically that a still Black body will never be enough to satisfy white audiences" (141). Gambino's jarring shifts from spectacular performance to violence, a heightened binary that apparently bars Black men, in particular, from a huge range of quotidian states and actions, resonate with Young's difficulty in finding a comfortable and legible-to-others embodied way of being in the world. While LeMesurier focuses on Black bodies as they are perceived mainly by "white audiences," Young adds layers to the issue in that he also confronts the way he, as a Black man, must perform sufficient maleness and Blackness to other Black folks in his life.

In his quietness and restrained facial expressions, my student David affirmed certain visions that I carried about straight masculinity as stoic, impassive, and unflappable. In some contexts, such as earlier years of primary and secondary schooling, this highly controlled, quiet listening may read as receptive obedience and thus be rewarded in the classroom space. In a discussion-based college classroom, though, as I have shown earlier, a very particular combination of vocal and embodied participation is the preferred gestural idiom. Like Casey, David may have become successful at producing the preferred embodiment of school in grades K–12, only to find that in college, the same way of being in class was regarded as insufficient. At the very same time, in his stillness, David defied a deeply set societal expectation that Black bodies should appear "always in motion."

But there are many other possibilities for how Black men appear in classrooms. Perhaps David was, in fact, composed yet relaxed, a version of Tina

Campt's idea of "stasis." Perhaps he felt comfortable enough in class to just be quiet and still, to be absorbed. As Young teaches us, he likely moved through many embodied and mental states from day to day. In my observations, I flattened David's affect according to raced and gendered expectations that I carry with me, feeling defensive and reacting to the frustration of confusion, of not knowing.

Toward New Possibilities in Listening: Game of Skill, Revisited

As an early-career educator, I needed to do what I hope this book will help all those in our field to do: to expand our vision of what "good" listening looks like, becoming hospitable to a wider range of embodied ways of being in classroom settings. This chapter is intended to illustrate many of the identity categories that come to bear on gestural listening performances, as well as their intersections, which in turn affect educators' perceptions of students, students' perceptions of other students, and even students' perceptions of themselves.

In her *Game of Skill 2.0* exhibition, Christine Sun Kim challenges visitors to enact an unusual form of embodied listening, calling us to question expected norms for listening behavior and invite a different form of gestural listening into view. She reminds us, as I have explored in this chapter, that who you are affects how you listen. Unlike in this playful exhibition, however, how gestural listening is inflected by identity and perceived by others has real stakes in the classroom. We need to ask: Who are those really served by the normative idiom for gestural listening? What else might listening be capable of if only a wider range of listening behaviors were acceptable? Kim teaches us that listening should not only belong to one disciplined, embodied regime. I point again to Tina Campt's formulation of "stasis," which I explored in the last chapter, recognizing stillness that requires the energy of composure, of refraining from extraneous or erratic movements. In a similar vein, Kevin Quashie—a writer I will revisit in chapter 5—develops the idea of "quiet" in *Beyond Resistance*, moments when outer stillness conveys the presence of, even as it veils, a listener's interiority.

But Kim's provocation to defamiliarize the act of listening asks us to continually reconceptualize listening itself, and those it belongs to. In fact, listening may not only belong to the hearing. A 1988 *Washington Post* article by Molly Sinclair describes a scene unfolding at Gallaudet University, a university primarily for d/Deaf and hard of hearing students, in which what is meant by listening—especially the kind of gathered, demanding gestural listening that sometimes coalesces in moments of public protest—must be redefined from its usual terms. On March 8, 1988, Gallaudet students demonstrated against the election of a hearing person, Elizabeth Ann Zinser, to the role of university president, after their organized efforts to bring about the election of the university's first Deaf president (Sinclair). Board Chairman Jane Bassett Spilman faced a crowd of students at a meeting on the day of the election results announcement. Against the backdrop of outrage about the election of a hearing president over a Deaf candidate—I. King Jordan—according to Sinclair, Spilman "also drew criticism from the crowd for complaining about the loud sound of the fire alarm, which was set off in the fieldhouse shortly after the meeting got under way":

> "We aren't going to hear you if you scream so loudly that we can't have a dialogue," Spilman told the deaf students, who had interpreters translating for them and for the hearing board members. She also said, "It's very difficult to be heard over the noise of the fire alarm."
>
> "What noise?" some students shouted or signed back. "Why not sign?" asked one deaf student. "If you could sign, we could hear you."

Spilman assumes that with the noise of the fire alarm in the air, no one would be able to listen, or "have a dialogue." In fact, the Deaf students would be perfectly capable of "listening" to her, if she were able to meet them on their own literal terms, by using sign language—with "If you could sign, we could hear you," the Deaf student in just a few words redefines what it means to "hear" for Deaf people who communicate via sign. What Spilman really meant was that she, as a hearing person, would not be able to listen to the Deaf students as a part of that dialogue, a scenario that seems to reflect the ideological disconnect between the students' conviction that their Deaf university was ready to have a Deaf leader, and the board's decision to continue its paternalistic, caretaker approach to university leadership. While it may look, at first glance, like the noisy students foreclosed dialogue, they ended up simply calling further attention to deep assumptions, springing in part from the expectation of normative perceptual abilities, that shape what are usually seen as acceptable listening behaviors. In gathering with noise and expressive anger, the students' style of listening actually influences what gets said, provoking interactions that continue to starkly reveal the very conflict they seek to address with the election of a "Deaf Prez Now." Taking ownership of their listening, the Gallaudet students listen in a way that is active and resistant, nonneutral, shaping the conditions of discourse in new and powerful ways.

Student protest is a place where we see the expectations and idioms of student behavior collide, react, and overlap with idioms of protest—resistance writ large, larger than classroom displays of disobedience or refusal. In the final chapter of the book, I examine how gestural listening behaviors transfer into sites of public gathering, how its dynamics have the ability to shape conditions of discourses in areas outside of school, too. There, in the spirit of the Gallaudet students of 1988, I begin by examining two sites of student protest.

First, though, I stay in the classroom for a little longer. In the next chapter, I attend to the presence of personal mobile devices in the classroom, and how the private yet differently public bubbles of personal space they engender inflect the dynamics of gestural listening. The prevalence, the sheer ubiquity, of phones, laptops, and tablets in classroom spaces mandates this attention, certainly. But further, the way gestural listening operates alongside and through technologies, like the frames of our pandemic-era Zoom windows, sheds light on its connective functions and its remarkable persistence across digital boundaries.

Approaches to Listening and Engagement in Pedagogical Materials

This chapter prompts readers, especially teachers, to consider how it may be possible to incorporate an expanded vision for acceptable gestural listening into classroom spaces. Not all students will demonstrate gestural listening that is legible according to long-standing rubrics for "good" classroom listening, as I have shown. With that in mind, it becomes increasingly important for instructors to create alternative ways for students to show engagement. Implementing an understanding of the range of listening behaviors that may take shape in the classroom could take many shapes, including but not limited to

1. Developing syllabus policies that detail distinctions between attendance, engagement, and participation in class. Participation through speaking up in class is often a taken-for-granted value in many classrooms. It is important for students to know how or if they will be graded on their vocal participation in class; or if, on the other hand, there will be other forms of assessing engagement like a daily attendance grade, or other forms of engagement like those listed in #2.

2. Creating opportunities for students to demonstrate engagement across modalities—not just through speaking up or demonstrating "correct" gestural listening in class but also, for instance, through posting on an online discussion board after class; turning in a brief, informal written

response at the end of class; or taking part in different forms of in-class participation like group or partner work.

3. Administering an early-semester survey or reflective writing prompt (such as the ones I offer at the end of chapter 2) that asks students about how they best listen and take in class materials, so instructors can learn and be aware of, what students know about themselves as listeners. Student responses to these prompts may help instructors see students' gestural listening in a new light—especially students who may listen gesturally in a way that might not be readily recognizable.

4. Initiating a class discussion early in the semester about how forms of student comportment in the classroom might be perceived by the instructor and by fellow students. For instance, an instructor might note that students in the past have positively used handcrafts (like the crocheting student) to help themselves stay focused in class, and generate a discussion among the students about how they perceive attentive listening in themselves and others. Please see chapter 4 for a discussion of laptops and cell phones.

4
Listening with Technology

In a class meeting, I'm directing a discussion about maps as humanities documents—what can we learn about the values and worldviews maps convey by noticing what is fully centered and what clings to the edges? What warrants marking, and what spaces, on the other hand, are depicted as empty? A student in the front row, normally quiet both verbally and in his gestural comportment, suddenly makes a face of surprised outrage at the laptop open on the desk in front of him, spread hands raised in exasperation, like the wrong team just scored.

I asked him if that's what happened. He admitted that in fact he had been playing a game, which he'd suddenly lost. It was the week before spring break; I played it off with an exaggerated, long-suffering sigh and shake of the head, looking up toward the ceiling as though to say—"Kids these days . . . what can you do?" While moments like this can feel undermining to an instructor, enough other students were listening "well" and engaging in discussion that day that there was a sense of most of the class being with me. The gestural displays of respect in the class on the whole were friendly, a collective mood for which I'm grateful.

In this class, many students have laptops open on the desks in front of them. While I sometimes walk around to gauge the progress of students responding

https://doi.org/10.7330/9781646428182.c004

to a writing prompt, I largely do not know what they are doing on their devices. I direct them to resources on our course webpage where they can refer to class readings and follow along with discussion questions or lesson plans, and I'm sure some of them are using their devices for these purposes, at least some of the time. But there is a sense, shared by many college and university instructors, I'm sure, that students could be doing almost anything and that students are most likely engaging in more than one thing at once. Students who can see each other's screens know more than I do, in truth, about what else is happening in class while I hope students are listening.

The presence of devices like laptops and cell phones in the classroom gives rise to a thick layer of additional considerations when it comes to gestural listening behaviors. Their presence creates doubt, requires trust, and places ever-greater demands on students' self-regulation efforts. The small movements of hands and eyes on screens and keyboards join the choreography of gestural listening as a rhetorical force. The student reaction that I have recounted is an unusually overt response to screenic activity—usually, students deploy a much more subtle combination of appearing to pay respectful attention with whatever they are doing on their devices, much the same balancing act that I myself have used in many a work meeting.

Since the day I mentioned, I have seen the same hands-up shock gesture almost exactly from another student with a laptop out on the desk, but as usual in the subtle landscape of gestural listening the majority of students negotiate their embodied presences within a much more restrained bracket of respect, resistance, and self-regulation. Nevertheless, personal mobile devices like laptops and cell phones inflect the gestural listening idiom of the classroom, complicating the communicational tableau of the classroom with added dimensions of networked connection. The roles of digital technologies and personal devices require special attention, especially the ways that they interact with and, at times, even shape gestural listening as a rhetorical force. This chapter fills that gap by addressing listening with technology in two ways: first, investigating how personal devices like phones and laptops fit into perceptions of classroom listening behaviors, and then by exploring the ways in which listening behaviors in online environments can be understood in light of the explosion of remote, synchronous learning since the start of the COVID-19 pandemic.

To do this, I draw first, once again, upon the results of the study I conducted that informs chapters 2 and 3, with the responses of students and instructors shaping my findings about how students and teachers perceive listening to be happening—or not happening, or not happening in the "right way"—with the use of mobile phones and laptops in class. In their survey responses, students almost unanimously noted that "not checking phones" was one of their most intentional ways of showing that they were listening in class, for instance. Multiple responses noted uncertainty about what a classmate might be doing on their laptop during class, giving rise to the sense that personal devices "decenter," or create new, ambiguous patterns of attention within classroom spaces. Suspicions about the rightful place of personal, digital devices in class point to the presence of overarching cultural ideas about industriousness, obedience, and engagement—all key in prevailing ideas about what it means to be a student. It may seem like listening with devices unduly emphasizes gestural listening's impression-making functions, to the exclusion of its other capacities. But in our moment, students and instructors often show up in class as combined "person-plus-device" entities; with this in mind, I hope to illustrate here how they reinforce, and in some ways also complicate, the patterns of respect, resistance, and self-regulation that I have explored in the last two chapters. This discussion, which I begin with the warnings of Sherry Turkle, then moves to synthesize a group of researchers working to understand the effects of personal devices on social perceptions, especially Takashi Nakamura. Ultimately, it leads us to become curious about what Derek Mueller calls the "digital underlife" of the classroom, when students use devices to create various communicative channels outside the "official" channels of the classroom (241).

Next, I expand my arguments about gestural listening into digital and online environments, considering how gestural listening behaviors—and what it means to show "good" listening—have been shaped in unexpected ways by video-conferencing technologies, especially in the post-2020 move toward hybrid education alongside heightened public conversations about mental health issues such as burnout and emotional labor. Drawing on the interdisciplinary field of critical interface studies, I introduce the term "interface thinking," through which I aim to show how technologies like Zoom create new options for listening behaviors—like the self-protective (or self-effacing) move of turning off one's camera—while it also circumscribes gestural listening's possibilities by limiting listeners to interface-enabled responses, such as laptop-embedded camera framing. "Interface thinking" is inspired by scholars like Johanna Drucker, Lori Emerson, and Michael L. Black, who apply insights from art and media studies to illuminate how computers variously intersect with and influence reading, writing, and design. In particular, I argue that the concept of "Zoom fatigue," used generally here to refer to fatigue associated with synchronous, online video-conferencing software (VCS), can be readily explained in terms of gestural listening as a rhetorical force. Here, I am in conversation with scholars working on aspects of virtual experience, especially Jeremy Bailenson and Robby Nadler. This chapter completes my inquiry into gestural listening across a variety of classroom sites, arguing that the dynamics of listening remain a vital rhetorical force even—and especially—in contemporary online environments.

Gestural Listening in the Classroom amidst Personal Mobile Devices

In a follow-up interview from my study, one student shared his thoughts about the ambiguity produced by student laptop use in the classroom. Here, "he" is the professor. The student observes:

> When you've laptops on your desk, you could be writing notes on your laptop, but for all he knows, it could be anything on the laptop—it could be BuzzFeed quizzes or it could be a Word document. When you have just a notebook and pen, it's really useful, because then he knows that your focus is just on the work, unless there's an online source that we need for class.

While this student frames his comment in terms of what the professor might perceive, implied, too, is the interviewee's own inability to know what his classmates are up to. Of a laptop, the student continues: "It's a blank screen almost, you can't interpret."

It's intriguing that this student uses the term "blank screen" in this moment. In fact, perhaps the only thing he can be sure of is that the student using their laptop is not looking at a blank screen—they are looking at a populated screen, which could show almost anything. But what happens when looking at a content-filled screen is that the laptop user themselves becomes a kind of embodied "blank screen" to any co-present people. In particular, as the interviewee notes, the professor cannot know what the laptop screen contains, and most of the other students can't either, except perhaps those sitting directly next to the user. "You can't interpret," the student says, a comment that encapsulates the resulting feeling: of a puzzled shoulder shrug, a mild, mundane alienation from a classmate in their own personal, screen-induced bubble of unreadability.

The student mentions BuzzFeed and a Word document as examples of why one can't interpret the blank screen of a laptop user in class: BuzzFeed stands in as an example of something trivial one might do instead of paying attention and engaging with the "serious stuff" of class, while a Word doc represents, in the student's framing, a use of the computer that could be legitimate in the classroom context, an extension of the intellectual work of class. Two ideas emerge: (1) there are sanctioned and unsanctioned uses for personal devices in classroom spaces (like Word and BuzzFeed, respectively), and the puzzling corollary that (2) no matter which type of material is on the device screen, co-present others can't be sure of it anyway. That's part of why a "notebook and pen" are "really useful" in showing one's intention to focus on schoolwork in class, as the student says, allowing the professor to know that "your focus is just on the work." A notebook naturally delimits the type of things its user might be up to, making it superior, in this student's eyes, for showing the type of correct, focused listening valued in classroom settings. And yet, doubt creeps back in once again at the end of the same sentence, as the student admits that there may at times be an "online source that we need for class," in which case "good" attention and listening may actually require the pandora's box of a personal computer screen.

Right away, this student's interview response highlights the competing roles that personal devices can play in classroom environments: they can be tools to enhance learning and access resources, and in contrast they can represent a seemingly unlimited source of alternative activity, both course-related and non-course-related. Other students, too, made note of ambiguity in their perceptions of their classmates' listening behaviors in the presence of devices. One says: "I usually like to take notes with a notebook, because that shows I'm listening [more] than on a computer, because you can never tell what someone's doing on their computer." Another student says a listening behavior that is "super hard to get a 'read on' is when other[s] get on their laptops." As they do in the responses I quote in my prior chapters, students show a high awareness of how they appear in class and of how their use of personal devices may impact perceptions of their engagement and productivity. Of their classmates, another notes the value of legible in-class behaviors: the student prefers making "eye contact, [and] taking paper notes (just because you can tell compared to a laptop)." Based on this response, it is unclear whether the student finds it easier or more convenient to take notes on a device. What comes forward, rather, is the sense that this is what the student believes "good" listening looks like: the elimination of a screen's potential for distraction and off-task activity. Another describes a personal code of conduct in the classroom that includes the use of a laptop but that limits its presence—and its potential for ambiguity—during group discussion: "When the task involved researching or taking notes on my laptop before, I often close my laptop when we begin discussing." Judging group discussion to be an important time for listening, the student removes possibilities for distraction, and the appearance of distraction, using laptop-free gestural listening as a form of self-accountability. In these comments, the students can be seen to manage their perceptions of others, and make purposeful choices about their own comportment, aimed at keeping their gestural listening behaviors legible within the rubric of "correct" and respectful classroom listening. Throughout, they negotiate the appearances of presence and absence, and often, as we have seen in prior chapters, too, utilize the embodied behaviors of listening to help them do the work of self-regulation in the classroom.

Dynamics of presence and absence link gestural listening amidst personal devices in the classroom with a longer discourse, one in which Sherry Turkle's is an important voice. Turkle writes extensively about human interaction with different types of "sociable robots," from Furby, Tomagotchis, and My Real Baby dolls to robots like Nursebot, intended to help with aspects of senior care. In her 2017 book *Alone Together: Why We Expect More from Technology and Less from Each Other*, she explores human-robot relationships in conjunction with the impact of personal mobile devices on relationships both close and casual. Throughout, she sounds a warning note about the results of the proliferation of technologies that lead to users being marked as "absent" even when physically present in public spaces. She writes: "When people have phone conversations in public spaces," for instance, "their sense of privacy is sustained by the presumption that those around them will treat them not only as anonymous but as absent" (155). She continues, lamenting what results, in real time, from absent presence: "It is those on the phone that mark themselves as absent . . . What is a place if those who are physically present have their attention on the absent?" (155–56). When the students in my study prefer notebooks to laptops to signal respectful gestural listening, they point to the ability of a laptop user to mark themselves as absent even when physically present in the room, in much the same way as Turkle describes here. Marking oneself as absent is the "blank screen" mentioned by the student at the start of this section. Students, as Turkle is, are sensitive to how the device user implicitly links themselves to a massive conduit of other types of information and interactions.

Being connected to that conduit comes with distinct attentional consequences. Building on the nature of the "present absent" way of being, Turkle later writes of an interviewee who monitors multiple emails, social networking platforms, and even online avatars in Second Life, that he can be said to be continually "cycling through" different forms of digital engagement; further, more rapid and continuous "cycling-through" then "stabilizes into a sense of continual copresence. Even a simple cell phone brings us into a world of continual partial attention" (161). Even if the classroom laptop or phone user is not doing many different things on their device, on-task or off, the fact is that they could if they wanted to, and networked devices lend themselves to a kind of constant monitoring for notifications, updates, and other forms of input. These potentialities, and the way devices ask us to use them in these constantly receiving and ever-updating ways, add to the ambiguity that devices create in the sense of a classmate's attention.

Another in Turkle's camp is Kenneth Gergen, who reaches back to Jacques Derrida for the roots of the term "absent presence" and looks for its "21st-century expansion" (227). He argues that "in the case of monologic technologies we find a relatively low degree of transformative power, but an increasing potential for immersing people in private as opposed to collective worlds" (230). Here, Gergen writes about device-induced "private worlds" like personally curated chambers that individuals access, which he places in opposition to the "collective worlds," which should take shape among gathered, co-present people. In this sense, his sensibility is a bit different from Turkle's: Gergen posits separate, public versus private worlds, while Turkle positions the interviewee in the prior example of "cycling through" as accessing not necessarily a private world; rather, it is a different, alternative collective that he chooses and exercises great control over but that is only available online and that is overlaid, or superimposed upon, his regular, daily life. They arrive at a similar warning, though, with Gergen prophesying: "The erosion of face-to-face community, a coherent and centered sense of self, moral bearings, depth of relationship, and the uprooting of meaning from material context: such are the repercussions of absent presence" (236). While some may chafe at the doomsday tone of Turkle and Gergen's cautions, aspects of their concerns do seem to be borne out by subsequent research, some of which I will summarize in the discussion that follows, and their words here serve as a kind of baseline, commonplace stance that many hold about the deleterious effects of personal mobile technology use. I suspect many of the students who participated in my survey in fact hold more complicated views about device use in public settings, but in their survey and interview responses they can often be seen to reproduce the cautionary stance exemplified by Turkle and Gergen.

Regardless of whether the use of personal devices in classrooms may provide important learning resources, as a student notes earlier, or whether it results in the absent-present erosion of self and community, device use is folded into gestural listening, complicating its contours. Because this book focuses on gestural listening as a rhetorical force that moves outward to affect others while it also shapes the self in certain ways, what's more important to me here, in the context of my investigation of gestural listening, is not students' or instructors' "true" attention, largely difficult to quantify on a moment-to-moment basis, but rather the perception of the quality or nature of their listening, in their own eyes and in the eyes of others.

So what do we know about those perceptions? Worryingly, results of many recent studies affirm Turkle's findings about how the presence of personal computing devices affects co-present interactions. For instance, in a widely cited study published in 2012, Andrew K. Przybylski and Netta Weinstein find that "the mere presence of mobile communication technology might interfere with human relationship formation" (244). That is, a device's visible presence during a co-present conversation—implying the potential for interruption and the conduit to other people and information—could negatively affect relationship formation. In an article entitled "The iPhone Effect," Shalini Misra et al. go further to gauge how exactly the quality of conversation fares during face-to-face conversations happening in the presence of a smartphone. Echoing Turkle's concerns, they find that

> if either participant placed a mobile communication device (e.g., smartphone or a cell phone) on the table or held it in their hand during the course of the 10-min conversation, the quality of the conversation was rated to be less fulfilling compared with conversations that took place in the absence of mobile devices. The same participants who conversed in the presence of mobile communication devices also reported experiencing lower empathetic concern compared with participants who interacted without distracting digital stimuli in their visual field.

In other words, just the presence of a cell phone, even if it is not actively being used, has an impact on the quality of interactions between co-present people. In their survey and interview responses, participants in my study consistently mentioned cell phones in this spirit. For instance, when prompted to say which classmates in a video clip looked like they were listening and which didn't, one participant said: "The student that asked the question, she forgot her notebook so she told him [the professor] that she would be taking notes on her phone. But if I didn't know that, I would say that she wasn't paying attention." In fact, one student who was known to take notes on her phone felt compelled to actively manage her reputation in class by verbally informing others about what she was doing with her phone. As a result, another respondent suspended judgment about that classmate's gestural listening, saying: "And I know she's on her phone, but she takes notes on her phone. She says, 'I'm not texting, I'm taking notes.'" The student continues: "She did get a little bit defensive about it at the beginning of the semester, but we're all kind of adjusted to it now." The cell phone user knows that the presence of her phone may lead to perceptions that she is simply texting, an activity that links her to people and places outside the classroom space, an activity generally considered to be distracted, off-task, or non-course-related. Aware of those perceptions about the possible quality of her attention and engagement, she actively pushes back against them, asking others to suspend judgment and see her more as she sees herself. She resists strong, automatic perceptions that assign absent presence to cell phone users in class.

The student's reputation management, as she explains her gestural listening behaviors, is an understandable effort. In terms of social perceptions of others' device usage, the news from recent research is aligned with Turkle and Gergen's fears, with Mariek Abeele et al. finding that "phone users were perceived as less polite and less attentive. Apparently, checking a mobile message during a conversation damages the impression that other people form of you" (565). Like Przybylski and Weinstein, they hypothesize that smartphone use will "have a negative impact on perceived conversation quality because this behavior likely causes the user to cognitively withdraw from the conversation, thereby hampering the natural flow of the conversation" (567). Indeed, that proves to be true according to their study, too, and the authors also nod to the warnings of Turkle: "The findings of our experiment support this hypothesis, and thus lend support to Turkle's (2012) claim that smartphone use during face-to-face interactions makes persons less involved in the conversation, thereby decreasing the quality of the conversation" (567). This may be why one student stated, when she wanted to show that she is listening in class, "I made sure my phone was all the way away; I wasn't on my computer."

Refraining from interacting with her device is not enough—this student uses the term "all the way away," a phrase that likely reflects the way cell phone presence has been closely monitored in earlier years of schooling. She has probably been told, or heard others be told, to put devices "all the way away." Indeed, cell phone use comes to college classrooms with a long, contested record in students' lives. It is something that is heavily controlled by classroom policies throughout primary and secondary schooling, strategically withheld and perhaps judiciously meted out by parents and teachers, and an activity with contested meanings in public spaces. On the one hand, a networked cell phone can be a membership card into society, a necessity for twenty-first-century life; on the other hand, it comes dogged with negative connotations—of addiction, of "kids these days glued to their phones," and all the rest. Students are subject to those social mores regarding cell phone use, and, as the results of my survey and follow-up interviews suggest, they also reinforce some of those norms among themselves.

Of the many issues in play when it comes to public use of personal devices, Elyssa Barrick et al. help explain why people may continue to use mobile devices while in the company of others in spite of how devices affect relationship formation: in short, we tend to overestimate ourselves and underestimate others. That is, a lack of awareness to the effects of our own behaviors develops, while our impressions of others, and their device use, continue to take shape. The authors state that "people may not fully appreciate the negative impact of their own phone use, even while acknowledging the negative impact of others' phone use" (6). This may be because, as the authors suggest, "people attribute their own phone use to different reasons than they attribute others' phone use" (11). When it comes to our own use of devices, in other words, we know what we are looking at our devices for—to scan for emergencies or to find something that might enhance the conversation—but we cannot know that about others. We judge ourselves based on our inner knowledge of our own motives, while not tending to give others the same benefit of the doubt. In this vein, one survey respondent made note of another possibility for screenic activity in the classroom: "Computers are always hard, because I feel like it makes it hard to tell. You could be listening and taking notes, or you could be doing online shopping. You could literally be doing whatever," she remarks, "and it's a lot harder to tell." When she states that "computers are hard," the student encapsulates the difficulty in judging listening behaviors of laptop users in class. It's "hard" because we tend to assume others are using their devices for off-task reasons. Like the BuzzFeed quizzes mentioned earlier, "online shopping" stands in for an activity at odds with the ethos of the classroom. But at times, as with the cell-phone notetaker above, observers may need to work against their own habitual perceptions or assumptions and suspend judgment about what others are doing. They are asked to tolerate more uncertainty as far as knowing what their classmates are doing on their devices in class. When it comes to a classmate using a computer, many things are possible. This is part of the message that device users end up sending in class.

Building upon the sense of a "blind spot" toward the consequences of our own device-checking behaviors, Juliana Pattermann et al. suggest further that many students may only have part of the picture when it comes to device use, especially non-course-related (NCR) use of devices. Their findings suggest that students may realize device use is distracting to themselves in class but that they remain unaware of any additional impact on others co-present in the space. They write: "Students have an inaccurate impression of their own interrupting behavior, and . . . they are not capable of fully estimating the consequences of their behavior" (4). They continue:

> While the majority of the participants are aware of the interruptive impact that NCR activities conducted on their computers have on their learning, . . . 25.69% of them are convinced that NCR activities have no impact on their own learning when on campus, whereas only 15.34% see no impact during webinars. The effect of their computer use for NCR activities on others seems to be a blind spot, with 70.8% of students not perceiving its impact during the on-campus sessions on others at all. (11)

Overall, we can see again the tendency to overestimate our own abilities to navigate distraction, while remaining unaware of how the presence of our devices may affect others. This, in spite of what the authors also find, which is that "almost one-quarter of students indicated that they felt disrupted by others using their laptops in class (23.7%)" (11). So the presence of personal devices in learning environments impacts others, but while participants felt distracted by the devices of others, they tended to feel that their own device use was an exception to that rule. The findings of this study suggest that students may not be fully aware of how laptop use in class contributes to the overall gestural listening impressions they make on those around them, a finding that is at odds with the high level of awareness students show in their responses to my survey and interview questions.

Nevertheless, personal device-use as a part of the gestural listening repertoire clearly continues to move outward to affect others. Listening amid personal devices follows many of the expected patterns of gestural listening that I have explored in earlier parts of the book, but the presence of personal devices also adds particular contours of ambiguity to gestural listening dynamics. A picture starts to take shape here of how mobile device use impacts the user's own quality of attention and how one person's device use also moves outward to affect those around them. The ambiguity that personal devices create—each user nautilus-like in their device posture, looking at once at and through their screen—leads to new expressions of familiar gestural listening dynamics: respect, resistance, and self-regulation.

Negotiating "Good" Listening within Contextual Multiplicity

"Absent presence" takes on particular meanings and implications when personal devices are present in the classroom. In the past, not paying attention, or even a conscious choice to spend the class time doing something else, was more limitedly the realm of writing or doodling in a notebook, passing notes, or simply daydreaming. And yet, to say that a student could have spent class time "simply daydreaming" is an oversimplification, an underestimation of the alternative states of mind possible in classroom settings. In his study of human attention and perception as reflected in, and shaped by, late nineteenth-century art, *Suspensions of Perception: Attention, Spectacle, and Modern Culture*, Jonathan Crary writes: "Though its history will never be formally written, the daydream is nonetheless a domain of resistance internal to any system of routinization or coercion. Similarly, institutional models of attention based on imperatives of recognition, identity, and stabilization are never fully separate from nomadic models of attention that generate novelty, difference, and instability" (77). The daydream, according to Crary, signifies more than just a wandering mind. Among other things, it is a capacity for resistance within imperatives of "recognition, identity, or coercion" (77). What does this mean for personal devices? On the one hand, it may be that the presence of mobile devices represents a variation on the theme of "nomadic models of attention" that Crary describes here, providing another conduit for students to exercise resistance to the "routinization" of school. After all, Takashi Nakamura will teach us, later in this section, how students may leverage devices to retain social advantage, possibly allowing them to maintain autonomy and exercise agency within the restrained, "correct" gestural idiom of the classroom. This move to retain agency and personal choice within the classroom aligns with the "domain of resistance" Crary refers to. On the other hand, the information architecture and attentional regimes instantiated by devices may have unintended consequences for student attention, channeling students' imaginations and daydreams into certain preferred or preestablished patterns. In the nature of their networked messaging and social media apps, for instance, devices lend themselves to checking for new notifications or posts. In their overall objective to monetize, device users may find themselves idly shopping, simply because that is one of the main activities toward which internet browsing channels users. So from this perspective, the presence of devices may create a different "institutional model of attention," one that has the effect of standardizing into predictable shapes the diffused attention of daydreams that may otherwise take on different patterns altogether. Daydreaming has fewer of the immersive, urgent qualities that personal computing devices have, and more flexibility.

Handling a device in class, then, does not really imply free daydreaming on the part of its user—it more strongly implies energies channeled toward absent others or, possibly, other tasks. In this sense, using a device oscillates between the implication of trivial, off-task distraction, like doing BuzzFeed quizzes or shopping online, and the implication of productivity: on-task activities like taking notes and looking at course materials, or even non-course-related activities that are nevertheless industrious, like completing an assignment for another class, ordering groceries, or booking a dog walker. A student could always be "doing something" on their device. While a student with no device who is daydreaming is unlikely to be deemed productive or industrious, simultaneously the daydreamer cannot be accused of, or even perceived to be, online shopping during class. So the presence of a phone or laptop can connote productivity and industriousness and, by the same token, the potential for mindless, off-task activities.

A set of scholars I turn to now develop a vocabulary for this paradigm of classroom devices, a vocabulary that is important for articulating their effect on gestural listening. What the following descriptions have in common is the quality networked devices have to destabilize, decenter, and create multiplicity within classroom spaces. In "The iPhone Effect," Misra et al. capture their unique potential for both sanctioned and unsanctioned use in class, writing that mobile devices act as "social nuclei—symbols of individuals' relational networks—diverting their attention and orienting their thoughts to other people and places outside the immediate spatial context." They continue:

> Even when they are not in active use or buzzing, beeping, ringing, or flashing, they are representative of people's wider social network and a portal to an immense compendium of information . . . Their mere presence in a socio-physical milieu, therefore, has the potential to divide consciousness between the proximate and immediate setting and the physically distant and invisible networks and contexts.

What results, they argue, are "permeable and micro-fragmented contexts," in which people are "in a constant state of poly-consciousness in which multiple relationships and settings can be the focus of one's attention at any given time regardless of location or context." Derek Mueller describes this space-transcending phenomenon as "digital packets of discourse that are no longer confined by the physical space of a singular institutional scene" (241). Takashi Nakamura calls this way of being in the classroom a quality of "contextual multiplicity," wherein a person looking at their device can be assumed to be present not just in their physical space but also in multiple contexts that exceed their current milieu and location (71). It's important to note that the multiple contexts these writers refer to tend to be outwardly oriented, geared toward interests and contacts outside the immediate classroom environment. This outward orientation contrasts with the vision of daydreaming Crary conveys earlier, which suggests a more ambiguous flow between internal and external consciousness.

With contextual multiplicity in mind, Nakamura develops a different take on the impact of looking at one's phone in public, one that has the quality of a defensive tactic and in which we can find gestural listening dynamics. He finds that "motivations to look at a mobile phone display based on the surrounding context can be classified as follows:

> 3-A: To avoid engagement with the surroundings.
>
> 3-B: To express the user's contextual multiplicity." (71)

Avoiding engagement with one's surroundings reduces the chance for awkward or unwanted social encounters. But even further, Nakamura's interpretation of what results from a person looking at their phone in public has more to do with the device user's cultivation of social capital, a sense of their being "in demand" elsewhere. "Society has learned to accept public mobile use despite having insufficient information to understand the actor's motivations or feelings at the moment of use," he writes (73). He continues: "Consequently, we must wait for the actor's next action. Anticipating respect from observers, mobile phone users intentionally exploit social norms to maintain their advantage and adjust relationships with surrounding individuals during face-to-face communication" (73). Keeping those co-present around them "on hold" while busy tending to their contextual multiplicity, the mobile phone user retains and manages a subtle social advantage. The phone user exudes a kind of mystique, the implication of their importance in a digital "elsewhere." Looking at one's phone, or by extension at one's laptop in class, is something the device user enacts as a self-protective measure that allows one to avoid engaging with co-present others and retain a social advantage. Unlike the findings in the Pattermann study cited earlier, Nakamura makes a case for the intentional, strategic use of device-screen gazing as a gestural listening technique that moves outward to affect others.

Ultimately, the difference in Nakamura's interpretation of looking at one's mobile phone in public, compared to the apparent obliviousness of participants in the Pattermann study, highlights the reality that the use of devices in public contains a wide range of possible meanings, some of which run counter to the commonplaces voiced by Turkle, Gergen, and their ilk. In fact, in the Pattermann study, the authors note first how laptops are distracting to others and then suggest that some students may actually "stick to their phones as an act of social nicety to avoid distracting others" (11). This interpretation of device use shows the phone note-taker's behavior in my earlier classroom observation in a different light: rather than it being a form of rudeness to be using her phone, it may in fact be an intentional choice not to bring her laptop into class and thus an act of consideration toward others. Readings of students' gestural listening along these lines requires the suspension of commonplace perceptions of personal device-use in the classroom and a greater tolerance for the uncertainty those devices create in our perceptions of each other. For example, one student interviewee speculates that there may be intricate, age-related elements guiding the way she looks at her phone in public. Of herself and her classmates, she says: "But that may be a generational thing . . . When you go into a room, you look at your phone rather than looking at people." In light of Nakamura's research, we can read several possibilities in this student's comment. For a younger generation (as of the mid-2020s), looking at one's phone upon going into a room may be a way of retaining social advantage and indicating one's own contextual multiplicity. Alternatively, it could be a form of politely taking pressure off co-present others to socialize. It could also serve as a form of self-regulation as students compose their classroom selves at the beginning of a class session. It is likely to be a simultaneous combination of these possibilities.

In the same vein as these more favorable readings of device use in public, while much of the research on device use in the company of others bears out Turkle's concerns, some authors challenge Turkle's warnings about mobile technologies and add nuance to what the presence of devices may mean in classrooms. McKinley Green, for instance, argues for more nuance in perceptions of smartphone use in classrooms, positing that "not all smartphone use is distracted smartphone use" (92). He writes: "Pedagogies that configure all smartphone interactions as evidence of distraction—creating, for example, a technology policy that penalizes students for using their smartphones during class—fail to recognize that many students use smartphones as forms of course participation, to access course readings and materials or to learn more about a topic covered in class" (92). Green reminds us here that technology policies may not be keeping up with the ways in which students use their phones in class. While I would avoid looking at class materials on my phone screen, even in class—I prefer a laptop screen when reading extensively—many younger students do not share that preference. Going beyond mere preferences, students may in fact be operating within different value systems, some of which may compete with Turkle's sensibilities. Jenae Cohn's 2016 essay about the use of addiction tropes to describe technology use highlights these potential conflicts, noting that today's is a "generation of students being simultaneously rewarded and chastised for digital technology use" (81). Further, she argues that in the face of commonplace attitudes toward technology-as-distraction, "there is an imaginary relation at play between the embodied and virtual, one that suggests that the embodied is more persistent, dominant, and normative than the virtual" (81). Ultimately, according to Cohn, "the predominant narrative emerging from the addiction trope is the investment in keeping 'virtual' and 'real' lives as separated from each other as possible" (85). Cohn suggests that the insistent separation of the "virtual" from the "real" is a manifestation of normativity that warrants our skepticism, and one that younger generations may not accept as a given.

Formulating another vision of the mixed, virtual-and-real classroom that acknowledges its potential for constructive, alternative attentional pathways, Mueller acknowledges the presence of a "digital underlife," particularly in writing classrooms. He writes: "Digital underlife encompasses both an ulterior field for illicit communication and the elusive, underground discursive activities proliferated therein with the aid of digital technologies; it evokes an inexact sphere for extraneous, hyper-threaded interchanges—between pairs of individuals or among crowds of users, as often asynchronous as transpiring in real time" (241). While the digital underlife teems, however, on the surface of student's faces and comportments in class is what Mueller evocatively calls a "managed opacity" (242). This "managed opacity" characterizes students' gestural listening when in a classroom space with personal devices. They may participate in digital underlife, but they do so beneath a surface of opacity that usually conforms to the preferred gestural listening idiom of the classroom. Should they falter in that performance, or refuse to execute it, they may come under the scrutiny of instructors, or even other students, who respond in predictable ways to the potential for contextual multiplicity, multitasking, or simply "off-tasking." In the case of the students I mention in the opening of this chapter, playing games or watching sports for entertainment during class, this suspicion is warranted. But Mueller, Cohn, Green, and Crary together caution the appropriateness of that suspicion in every case. One student, for instance, who self-identified as neurodivergent, made the following comment in an interview with me in which she described one such experience:

> I've had professors call on me because it looked like I was zoning out, but I could answer the question . . . "I see you looking at your computer. What's x, y, z?": And I could answer it . . . It's not really fair, but if you look like a good student, you get treated like a good student. That holds true for every level of education. They look like what an attentive student is supposed to look like. Doing the right thing.

This student's comment aligns with Mueller when he argues that the digital underlife "calls into question default approaches to verifying attentiveness that have long privileged visual verification" (245). In this instance, visual verification of "correct" gestural listening behaviors is insufficient to gauge the student's true level of receptivity. As Mueller continues: "The inadequacy of the 'gaze' as a standalone metric for assessing attention has, with the development of digital underlife, grown more conspicuous" (245). A note of frustration rings in this student's telling of being singled out with suspicion due to the way she was conveying her attention. She states: "If you look like a good student, you get treated like a good student." Implied is the idea that looking at her computer did not fit the instructor's rubric for correct attentiveness, or "what an attentive student is supposed to look like." As such, she does not get treated with the respect and approval that a "good student" might receive. A "good" student is an attentive student, who conspicuously appears to be "doing the right thing." The student also makes the connection between looking at her computer and appearing to be "zoning out," a term we have already seen contains particularly fraught valences for students. In her telling, the potential for contextual multiplicity, multitasking, and off-tasking brought about by her laptop makes it easy for an observer to code her laptop-directed gaze as zoning out. Once again, we can see how deeply ingrained expectations for "good" gestural listening have uneven consequences for real students.

And yet, as Crary reminds us by pointing to the daydream-as-resistance, notions of "good attention" in classroom spaces may need to be questioned, freshly examined altogether. Green pushes back against any nostalgia about pre-device classrooms, noting that "distraction narratives often fail to allow space for these mental breaks; instructors' critiques of student distractibility often present utopic visions of a classroom in which students direct unwavering focus on instructors as alternatives to distracted and disinterested students on their cell phones" (101). Like Green, Mueller acknowledges the role of the digital underlife in how student self-regulate and manage their attention when he notes that the difficulty of knowing what is really going on during class is "a predicament that re-emphasizes that there are many varieties of meaningful attentiveness" (245). Another student makes note of an alternative nuance to what counts as a "good" or "correct" display of attention. Here, the student brings together expectations for attention with social etiquette, saying: "Not everyone is 100% focused on [the student who is speaking] at all times, because that would be kind of creepy if we just sat there and looked at him. But we're all kind of glancing around and coming back to the speaker." This student notes that paying intense, unbroken attention to the speaking class-mate through eye contact, for instance, would be not only unrealistic but even "creepy." Extreme attention, after all, can carry threatening connotations of aggression or being targeted. The diffusion of attention, then, need not always be categorized as distraction but a necessary and appropriate self-modulating in response to social cues.

Gestural listening behaviors projected outward can serve a protective role, hiding the digital underlife and its many functions for students from the scrutiny of an authority figure. Once, in a conversation with a former student after our course together had ended, I found out that students in our class had often texted each other about the class, in class, responding and adding to class discussion through their own private backchannel. At the time, I had no idea. That is, I often saw students typing on their laptops during class discussion, but I could not know what they were up to. On the "surface," they generally performed a correct, respectful listening according to typical expectations for a university seminar in the United States. This incident serves as an example of digital underlife within a classroom being protected by the managed opacity of the students' gestural listening.

Admittedly, none of the students who responded to my survey or follow-up interviews spoke about using their personal devices in many of the ways that Cohn, Green, Mueller, or my seminar students describe here. That may be because they did not use their devices to create "underlife" dimensions to the classroom. Cohn reminds readers, however, to be alert to the ways that students' true attitudes toward aspects of their classroom lives could be more complicated than what they express on surveys or in interviews, noting that "losses expressed" in student narratives about personal computing devices in the classroom "could result from inauthentic expression; students could very well be reproducing a narrative that they think their writing teachers will want to read" (85). Alternatively, it may be that they have internalized many of the expectations for "good" listening and classroom engagement and, with that in mind, did not want to speak about resistant or subversive ways they may have been using their devices in class. Cohn observes that syllabus policies coming from institutions and/or individual instructors regarding cell phones and laptops in the classroom may signal to students that a college instructor, as I identified myself while conducting this research, would not want to hear about smartphone or laptop use in the classroom. She writes: "Especially in an era when students often see class syllabi explicitly banning smartphones in the classroom, some students may expect teachers to want to see negative critique of digital writing technologies in their digital literacy narratives" (85). What might be valuable for students and instructors would be an assignment or exercise that calls students' attention to their habitual uses of personal computing technology, asking them to describe the ways in which they use mobile technology in different settings and then prompting students to articulate—and question—the values that guide their technology use and how they write and speak about it. As I mention earlier, most of the students I surveyed and interviewed reproduced certain prevailing ideas about technology use in classroom, likely echoing the voices of parents and prior instructors. It may be illuminating for students themselves to bring their habits and patterns of thinking about technology into focus and for instructors wanting to get a better sense of what is happening inside the contextual multiplicity generated by students with phones and laptops out in class. At the end of this chapter, I outline a sample activity to this end.

At this point, several new questions come up for me: What other possibilities are there for listening amid technology in classroom environments? How might students use devices differently—to gesturally listen in a way that connects, rather than separates; or that brings about a spirit of playfulness and openness? What might it take for a student's phone, tablet, or laptop to signal a willingness to engage with their fellow classmates, rather than signaling, by default, being closed or otherwise occupied? The positive implications for "digital underlife" in the classroom suggest that instructors may want to encourage it. It remains to be seen how that may be possible, however, without an instructor inadvertently imposing their authority within underlife channels, an imposition that may cause those channels to lose their value.

Thus far in this chapter, I have discussed how gestural listening in the class is inflected by the presence of mobile computing devices. But what about listening amidst technology in a different way—what about gestural listening through VCS like Zoom and its like, now so ubiquitously used to facilitate remote classes and meetings? In the second half of this chapter, I move to examine how gestural listening fares when it encounters the digital infrastructure of video-conferencing interfaces. While a full discussion of this topic is outside the scope of this book project, I nevertheless hope to convey a sense of how this technology compromises and disrupts gestural listening on the one hand, while heightening and placing new demands on gestural listening behaviors, on the other.

Interface Thinking and Listening through Zoom

In chapter 2, I examined the Gulu Real Art Studio–based photo series curated by Martina Bacigalupo and analyzed by Tina Campt in *Listening to Images*. In it, the photograph subjects' faces are missing, excised from their full seated portraits to create documents like passports and ID cards. What remains is everything else: the intricate signifiers of posture, clothing, hands, and even, in the case of one portrait, a child. The photo series brings attention to just how much these elements communicate—especially in the absence of the subject's face. In VCS, conversely, we experience the opposite. Users exist on the screen as a face within a rectangular box, with almost everything else cut away by the self-facing video camera frame. The photo series helps convey what a loss that is to the communicative dimensions of visible, physically present bodies.

In the early-pandemic explosion of VCS use, mostly via Zoom, the software provided a crucial means of continuation for formerly co-present activities like meetings and classes. It was presented, informally, as a better, richer experience than being on a telephone line with others, and better by far than moving to asynchronous modes of meeting and teaching like email. And yet, what followed closely thereafter was the rise of a new term, in spite of the continuity that VCS had heroically allowed for: Zoom fatigue. Alongside the many changes within the working world that tipped into motion with the sudden, wider adoption of remote work, there arose a collective sense that a Zoom meetings were somehow more tiring than in-person meetings, in spite of the time and energy they saved in eliminating the need to commute to work, and in spite of the other forms of flexibility they provided working parents or those living in rural areas. The impact of VCS on school and work is complex. But Zoom fatigue provides one lens, so to speak, through which to investigate what happens to gestural listening dynamics of respect, resistance, and self-regulation when they are moved into the synchronous, online environments facilitated by software programs like Zoom.

Here, I want to suggest that Zoom fatigue can be readily explained in terms of gestural listening. To get at this, we need to apply what I call "interface thinking," which I define as a critical approach to computer-mediated communication that focuses on analyzing elements of software and hardware interface. Further, interface thinking must exceed a simple taxonomy of interface features and reach to articulate the ways that communicative behaviors in digital and nondigital settings interanimate and inform each other, creating and then delimiting each other in turns. Ultimately, applying interface thinking to the way gestural listening both shapes, and is shaped by, VCS creates new insights about gestural listening in all environments, especially as it is leveraged by students.

In my approach to the idea of interface, I am particularly indebted to Johanna Drucker, who has examined the role of interfaces on humanities research from many angles. In her 2011 piece "Humanities Approaches to Interface Theory," Drucker focuses in particular on how digital interfaces affect the act of reading. She reminds readers that an interface is not a neutral conduit through which knowledge is accessed, defining interface as a "dynamic space of relations, rather than as a 'thing'" (3). Rather, an interface is something that shapes knowledge through the way it guides user behavior. She explains that "interface is not a thing, but a *zone of affordances* organized to support and provoke activities and behaviors probabilistically, rather than mechanically" (7–8; emphasis mine). With her description of "dynamic space, a zone in which reading takes place," Drucker adjusts the way we see and interact with interfaces; she writes: "We do not look rather through it (in spite of the overwhelming force of the 'windows' metaphor) or past it" (9). Here, Drucker refers to a piece of the dominant vocabulary used for software—the notion of a "window," implying something the user looks *through*, not *at*, something not in and of itself requiring critical engagement but that simply reveals what is already there. Drucker, along with the many other scholars—such as Anne Friedberg, Lori Emerson, and Michael L. Black—who examine interface through critical lenses, suggests that a computer window, among other common interface features, should in fact not be understood as invisible, or as an a priori "given" for how we organize information and experiences in digital environments. Drucker and other critical interface scholars call us to examine the interfaces that populate our daily digital lives, rather than ascribing to a regime that encourages us to simply look through them, or past them.

So what can interfaces bring about for environments of teaching and learning? What can we observe when we look *at* interfaces, rather than through them? Here, I give two brief examples, in which I use interface thinking to analyze elements of interface that are in play, and their implications for teaching and learning. In 2018, I published research about Writing Centers using VCS to conduct one-on-one writing tutorials. I noted at that time that while Writing Center pedagogy strongly encourages tutor and tutee to sit side by side, which I called "proxemic arrangement which reflects the non-agonistic, non-hierarchical power dynamic that writing centers strive to construct," most VCS effectively creates an arrangement where the tutor and tutee face each other, as though across a table (Feibush). This comes from aspects of interface hardware and software that are taken for granted, that are built in, that are "givens," in this case the way video is usually enabled by the self-facing cameras mounted in laptops or desktop computers. In a situation like this, we can see how the digital interface is designed to try to capture and convey complex audiovisual information but that it also ends up circumscribing, delimiting, and shaping the way the writing conference then takes place. Another example of how video-conferencing interfaces affects online teaching and learning environments comes from a pre-pandemic time when I used a VCS program called BlueJeans to conduct a first-year writing course. While conducting a discussion, I called on students I could see within the frame of the BlueJeans camera. As far as I was concerned, they were the only ones there. Suddenly, a hand rose directly in front of the camera, huge on my monitor. There were laughs. A student had been sitting toward the edge of the classroom, hand patiently raised, just outside the camera frame. I never called on him, because I couldn't see him, so he finally went straight to the camera and raised his hand inches away, an Alice-in-Wonderland giant. I wondered what else I had been missing. In this instance, the interface that enabled the class to continue or, as I healed from an injury that prevented me from traveling to campus, also hid participants from me, creating a dynamic in the physical classroom space that I could not even be fully aware of. It took a break from classroom norms, with the student approaching the camera to get my attention, to overcome the way this interface had shaped the classroom environment.

Some readers may be thinking to themselves at this point that, well, this is simply how the software works. What other options do we have? But the sense of inevitability, of "this is just how it is," of VCS interfaces is important to notice and question. The "invisibility" of the interface, or the way many users simply take it for granted, is not a given but rather a historically situated sensibility.

In particular, Lori Emerson and Michael L. Black, two scholars I mention earlier, show us how we are encouraged by a culture of ubiquitous computing to regard many common aspects of digital interfaces as invisible, or transparent, referring to the quality of intuitiveness or naturalness that many contemporary devices and applications possess for new users. Emerson locates the origins of this concept in the writings of Mark Weiser beginning in the late 1980s and argues that invisible interfaces gradually move users away from critical awareness of the way they interact with devices, and how those devices work. She warns that "the seamlessness of ubiquitous computing devices will make even choice itself recede into the background" and that "in this imagined near future, things will simply happen and we will simply do" (3). She adds: "We need not know how it works, or how it works on us rather than us on it" (6). A closely related term for this quality of invisibility in computer interfaces is the idea of "user-friendliness," widely accepted as a tech-industry standard for the design and use of new products. In *Transparent Designs*, Black similarly warns readers to stay alert to how "just as transparency conceals the mechanics of computation from us, so too does user-friendliness direct our attention away from the role that Big Tech's designers have in shaping the cultural, social, and political contexts of computer use" (44). Emerson and Black ask us to imagine that there may be different ways to do video conferencing or to manage remote meetings. While most VCS programs offer a predetermined set of built-in choices and orientations, these need not be the only choices. While transparent, invisible, or user-friendly interfaces lend themselves to the quick uptake of new programs and devices, they may also impose a regime of use that warrants our skeptical attention.

Since the start of the COVID-19 pandemic, theorists and researchers in fields beyond cultural studies have also published new writings focused on interface, weighing in, in particular, to speculate about and understand the causes of Zoom fatigue. While this research is of course in early days, we can nevertheless see the patterns of thought and modes of investigation that are emergent in understanding this phenomenon. All the sources I introduce here, for instance, have in common with Drucker's work a focus on the impact of computer interface features on aspects of nonverbal communication. Jeremy Bailenson, director of the Virtual Human Interaction Lab at Stanford University, demonstrates this interface-based approach to understanding Zoom fatigue when he suggests that the main causes of Zoom fatigue are "excessive amounts of close-up eye gaze, cognitive load, increased self evaluation from staring at video of oneself, and constraints on physical mobility" (1). First, in terms of their size and distance from the computer user, Bailenson notes, faces on the Zoom screen take up roughly the space in one's visual field as someone sitting intimately close to the user. He writes: "In one-on-one meetings conducted over Zoom, coworkers and friends are maintaining an interpersonal distance reserved for loved ones" (2). Additionally, the gridded Zoom screen full of boxed faces distorts the felt experience of the gaze. While in face-to-face conversational situations, people often reduce eye contact by angling their bodies in different ways or intermittently shifting their gaze to other things, Bailenson states, "Zoom effectively transforms listeners into speakers and smothers everyone with eye gaze" (2). That is, on Zoom, listeners are given equal amount of gaze as speakers are, as the grid affords all users an equal "spread" of gaze attention. In face-to-face scenarios, on the other hand, the group's attention usually focuses primarily on one speaker at a time, while listeners enjoy periods of "reprieve" where they are not receiving the full gaze of others. This type of organic flow of visual attention is channeled quite aggressively on Zoom, where, Bailenson notes, "all people get the front-on views of all other people nonstop" (2). Here, Bailenson draws attention to the perceived distance between users, the way people organically position their bodies in conversation, and the play of the gaze. These can both be readily recognized as gestural listening behaviors, and we can see how Zoom fatigue begins to highlight the juncture at which gestural listening meets user interaction with personal devices such as computers, tablets, and cell phones.

Indeed, Zoom fatigue seems to flow from how the software changes, reroutes, and distorts gestural listening behaviors, amplifying some elements while minimizing others. Bailenson goes on to acknowledge how VCS leads to an increased cognitive load on users, noting that "dedicating cognitive resources to managing the various technological aspects of a videoconference is a likely cause, for example, image and audio latency" (3). Image and audio latency, in essence, are ways that listening behaviors, as a part of a whole ensemble of communicative tools, get disjointed, glitchy, and fragmented. Once again, the importance of gestural listening, with all its communicative dimensions, stands out most in its importance when it is compromised by something like the digital mediation of VCS software. Illustrating the surprising accretion of cognitive load that VCS brings about, Bailenson continues:

> On Zoom, one source of load relates to sending extra cues. Users are forced to consciously monitor nonverbal behavior and to send cues to others that are intentionally generated. Examples include centering oneself in the camera's

field of view, nodding in an exaggerated way for a few extra seconds to signal agreement, or looking directly into the camera (as opposed to the faces on the screen) to try and make direct eye contact when speaking. This constant monitoring of behavior adds up. (3)

Applying interface thinking, we can analyze how aspects of the interface work in this type of situation, as Bailenson does, and consider its implications for teaching and learning. In VCS software, elements of interface aim to capture and convey listening behaviors that help form the gestural idiom of the classroom, such as the use of the built-in, self-facing camera. Simultaneously, the very real limits of those interface features—audiovisual lag time, the limits of the frame, the loss of detail—create a need for those self-same gestural listening behaviors to be exaggerated, or otherwise altered, in order for users to come across as they intend: as signaling agreement, or as participants in the complex dance of eye contact, as Bailenson mentions. In the prior chapters of this book, I have detailed the importance of all of those subtle elements of embodiment to students and instructors as they negotiate their classroom roles. The paradox of VCS interfaces, as we know them now, seems to necessarily bring about fatigue, or the "load" Bailenson refers to.

Applying interface thinking to other salient features of VCS, there is still more to consider with regard to how it simultaneously enables gestural listening even as it creates new gestural listening demands. Of the default inclusion of the self-facing camera view, which each user confronts when logging into Zoom, for instance, Bailenson notes a conflicting phenomenon: "While [seeing oneself] can lead to more prosocial behavior, the self evaluation can be stressful" (4). Again, the self-facing camera interface feature both enables the user to ensure they look the way they want to (visible, and centered in the frame, for instance) and at the same time creates a new demand on users to constantly monitor and evaluate their own image. Importantly, dealing with this aspect of the VCS interface may not "add up" the same way for all users. After all, user interfaces do not wipe clean aspects of identity that make for an uneven distribution of cognitive and emotional load. In fact, Geraldine Fauville et al. find that "consistent with psychological research on self-focused attention and negative affect, women experienced more mirror anxiety associated with the self-view in video conferencing than men, and mirror anxiety was a primary mediator for the gender effect on fatigue" (11). In other words, the self-facing camera view that has more or less become an interface "genre expectation" in many VCS programs sparks "mirror anxiety," which women tend to experience more strongly than men, leading to greater Zoom fatigue in women. Earlier in this book, I explored how gestural listening expectations for women often include more overtly visible displays of expressive caring and warmth. Here, we see how that becomes relevant in online listening environments. When gestural listening conduits are disrupted and compromised by the digital "in-betweens" of software and hardware, gestural listening ironically becomes all the more necessary to cohere communicative ruptures like audiovisual lag or lack of fully embodied information. As Bailenson mentions earlier, gestural listening must also be amplified in order to be fully conveyed by the limited VCS interface, much like a stage actor exaggerating their facial expressions in order to be seen from the back row of the theater. What results is fatigue, of course, especially for those already managing uneven expectations for gestural listening as it refracts along aspects of identity like race, gender, and ability.

Earlier, I described a time when I used a BlueJeans-enabled classroom to teach when an injury prevented me from appearing physically on campus. Temporarily disabled, I and my students had to navigate a pre-pandemic remote, synchronous learning environment. While I was lucky to be able to continue teaching at all, and grateful for the resources of the university where I worked at the time, it is important to notice how the burden of coordinating the specially equipped room and adapting my teaching to the remote, synchronous environment, to say nothing of Zoom fatigue, fell largely on me. Instances like this begin to show us how interfaces often reflect default expectations of normativity and how unintended interface consequences, like Zoom fatigue, are likely to disproportionately affect people affiliating with non-normative identity categories. This is especially important to bear in mind in light of prevailing discourses about user friendliness and transparent design that I touch on earlier, in which interface features come to seem so natural as to become almost invisible, inevitable.

Looking at what happens when gestural listening meets a hardware and software interface not only provides a new way to understand Zoom fatigue; it also enriches our understanding of gestural listening as a form of sensory rhetoric. Gestural listening depends on an understanding of listening as fully embodied, and as rooted in a full sensory spectrum, rather than in five separate, distinct sensory channels. It asks us to take seriously the roles of spatiality and texture in any given rhetorical situation. In fact, one of the proposed causes of Zoom fatigue in Robby Nadler's "Understanding 'Zoom Fatigue': Theorizing Spatial Dynamics as Third Skins in Computer-Mediated Communication" has to do with the filling in of, or compensating for, three-dimensionally embodied information that gets compressed in VCS environments. In his research, Nadler focuses on the idea of "third skin" that VCS, or what he calls computer-mediated communication (CMC), brings about, this flattening of complex sensory and social dimensions of face-to-face communication. Nadler applies his own interface thinking to explain how nonverbal communicative elements like the spatial quality of sound, for instance, fare when meeting software and hardware used for teaching and learning. He observes: "While hearing a voice in CMC may produce an identical utterance from an FtF exchange, the spatial dynamics between speaker and listener do not carry over" (7). So while it may seem that the most important information in a verbal utterance is successfully conveyed by the software, dimensions of auditory meaning like distance and direction "do not carry over," as Nadler puts it (7). Drawing on Bruno Latour's Actor-Network Theory (ANT), Nadler then goes further to argue that the flattening of sensory information actually reconfigures the rhetorical situation that takes shape when users communicate through VCS, writing:

> Rhetorically, the immediate audience in CMC is easy to identify: the party you interact with. But ANT challenges that assertion: the technological actant is your immediate audience. Remember, the interacted party in CMC functionally is not an audience but a tool . . . While I have hypothesized many elements contributing to CMC exhaustion, I argue this switch in audience is the most critical in generating our exhaustion because it triggers a disconnect between how our minds desire to interact with our party and how our bodies engage CMC. (13)

Nadler suggests here that while we see ourselves as interacting rhetorically with the person shown on our Zoom screen, the more immediate material reality is that we are interacting with a tool: our computer, tablet, or phone. While our minds "desire to interact" with the person on the screen, a disconnect is triggered because our bodies are in fact interacting with what Nadler refers to as a third skin. What is a third skin? The idea of a third skin becomes clear when we realize that the person we are communicating with through Zoom takes on the same materiality, on the screen, as the background behind them, and anything else in the frame with them for that matter. From a more holistically embodied perspective, the other person that we seek to interact with, as well as anything else in the frame with them, and anything else on our desktops surrounding their image, is simply an array of pixels—all the same. Nadler puts it this way: "While the viewer knows a human is not a background, in terms of interaction—the hundreds of thousands of years our genes are encoded with to sociologically interact with others on top of billions of physical interactions we accrue in our lives—there is no human-defining element that separates the party from tool" (13). He continues: "Compare this to the way that the physical human in a FtF exchange demands an interactive spatial reciprocity that a tool does not. Such is why, ultimately, we work our cognitive abilities past their limits in trying to make human that which the third skin renders a projection" (13–14). When humans interact with a third skin as though it is a fully presenced person, the flattening of person into third skin leads to fatigue.

In addition to gestural listening's particular sensorial mix and materiality, the rise of Zoom fatigue as a phenomenon further confirms that gestural listening is effortful, that it draws upon internal resources even as it moves outward to affect others. Whereas in face-to-face settings the "interactive spatial reciprocity" that Nadler mentions may help to constantly replenish a listener's energy, in digital settings, in which gestural listening may not be forthcoming from one's audience, as I will discuss in the next section, it can be unusually fatiguing to speak.

Respect, Resistance, and Self-Regulation through the Interface, or, Cameras On and Off

I have argued that Zoom fatigue can be explained by what happens when gestural listening as a rhetorical force meets the structures of VCS. But with that in mind, what are the consequences, for students and instructors, of interface thinking as applied to the VCS commonly used in online teaching? To begin, one thing instructors must consider are new contours for the display of respect and resistance, shown nowhere as strongly, perhaps, as in the choice of whether to keep one's camera on or off. Here, I focus only on the self-facing camera, but an examination of many other interface features would undoubtedly lead to insights about how listening refracts through the prism of software and hardware.

As most readers will be aware, a paradigmatic feature of Zoom's interface, or "zone of affordances," is the ability of users to turn their cameras on or off. With cameras on, participants convey significant visual information, confirming their presence, making themselves accessible to others in a way that at least somewhat resembles an in-person classroom. But as I have argued throughout this book, classroom participants are generally "on" whether they like it or not—that is, gestural listening and its various communicative implications continue to project outward to co-present others whether or not the student is actively monitoring their appearance or not. This dynamic carries over into the VCS interface when it comes to on-or-off cameras. In other words, a turned-off Zoom camera is in fact not a "neutral" presence, even if the user intends it to be so. If a person is in the Zoom room, there is no real way to go invisible. Rather, a turned-off camera box carries with it a range of rhetorical possibilities. For better or worse, even if a student has turned off their camera for an understandable reason, a turned-off Zoom camera is often read by instructors, and by other classmates, as a form of disengagement, just as a student in an in-person class may be written off as "zoning out" when they are simply not performing "correct" listening according to the unspoken classroom rubric.

Naturally, some students may indeed turn their cameras off as a form of resistance. Similarly to the ways students exercise agency in various way in in-person classrooms, students avail themselves of the turned-off camera to show their engagement in contextual multiplicity, to show their dissatisfaction, boredom, or disengagement. At the same time, early in the pandemic, turning cameras off in an online class meeting carried different valences. At the institution where I worked at the time, some classes had to be canceled due to overloaded internet capacity. Students were encouraged to turn their cameras off during class to put less strain on the campus Wi-Fi connection. From this perspective, a turned-off camera was a sign of cooperation. Given the experience that Bailenson describes as all VCS users being "smothered" in eye gaze, turning cameras off sometimes serves as a way to reduce pressure on a speaker, instructor, or fellow classmates. It has the same flavor of consideration that we see earlier when students speak about looking at their phones as they assemble for class to reduce the social strain or obligation classmates might feel to make conversation.

And yet, the picture becomes more complicated as the paradoxes of interface come into play. While keeping cameras off may in some ways reduce strain on both speakers and listeners, it simultaneously creates a different kind of strain. As I am sure many readers have experienced, it is highly taxing, as an instructor (or any kind of speaker), to address a screen gridded solidly with only named, black boxes. In "Understanding 'Zoom Fatigue': A Mixed Method," Hadar Shoshan and Wilken Wehrt find that employees interviewed for their study articulate this feeling of "talking blindly" to "silent others":

> Several participants mentioned the *"silent others"*: (i.e., participants that mute themselves and do not open their cameras) as a source of exhaustion: "It can be very exhausting, as you cannot see the facial expressions of the others, nor

their reaction … the 'silent' crowd is hard to read …," "… it is super frustrating to talk blindly to people, without knowing if they are even there." (841)

This response highlights several aspects of gestural listening through VCS interface. First, it is true that others are silent when attending a meeting with their camera off and mute button activated. But more than being auditorily silent, they are gesturally silent, without even the nonverbal cues of dress or posture coming through. Types of embodied information like clothing are often written off as trivial; for instance, the men and women sitting for portraits at the Gulu Real Art Studio illustrate how these nonverbal aspects of self-presentation convey multitudes of complex cultural information and are crucial for orienting ourselves in any given rhetorical situation. The lack of any gestural listening—or otherwise embodied—information leads speakers to "talk blindly" to people, or more specifically to talk without visual cues. In the respondent's comment here, we see a fluid overlap between sensory channels—technically, one should not need to see in order to talk, and yet the respondent here refers to "talking blindly," or talking without any visual information from the audience, confirming the sensory flow that characterizes so many communicative settings. While in-person communication involves a meshed ensemble of sensory information, over VCS visual and auditory information are literally separated into different channels of digital information. When the silent crowd is "hard to read," the speaker implies that in a more optimal communicative setting, they actually adopt a more reciprocal relationship to their audience. When we mute and turn our cameras off, we self-efface and remove the opportunity for casual reciprocity in a way that is simply not possible in a face-to-face interaction.

There is an additional quality of self-preservation in some Zoom-camera choices. Especially in the pandemic's early days, users "Zoomed in" from makeshift at-home workspaces, sometimes surrounded by kids, clutter, pets, or just a general disarray. In keeping their cameras off, students may have been shielding their own privacy, or that of others in the room, like siblings or roommates. They may have preferred not to have their living space visible to others for any number of privacy reasons. Students may choose to attend class with cameras off to lessen the surveillance-like feeling of being visible through Zoom's visual apparatus. In doing so, they may create space for themselves to engage in the class in idiosyncratic ways. Turning off the camera often feels like a self-protective move, releasing students from the self-scrutiny of the mirroring camera, the artificially intense gazes of other participants. In Shoshan and Wehrt's study, the authors make note of contradictions in VCS camera use, stemming from the push and pull between a desire for fuller connection through audiovisual information and a need to preserve energy. "Interestingly," they write,

> There seems to be a tension, between what people expect of others (e.g., rich cues, open cameras, participation), as one participant mentioned: "open your cameras, guys!" and how they experience the same social demands. Several participants mentioned that they feel "high awareness because my face is on the screen" as a source of exhaustion and "only listen" as a possible way to reduce exhaustion. (841)

In this sense, turning the camera off relieves some of the necessity to self-regulate in the ways that in-person classrooms demand. After all, we have seen how the Zoom interface brings about an exaggeration of gestural listening behaviors that can be fatiguing. In fact, with cameras on, VCS classrooms are highly physically constrained in ways that are different from in-person classroom settings. Bailenson describes this dimension of physical self-regulation, referring to the concept of a "frustum," or the pyramidal cone of visual space captured by most video cameras, writing: "The cultural norms are to stay centered within the camera's view frustum and to keep one's face large enough for others to see. In essence users are stuck in a very small physical cone, and most of the time this equates to sitting down and staring straight ahead" (4). Even the subtle choreographies of the in-person classroom, adjusting postures and changing the cross of the legs, for instance, are not subject to the discipline of the frustum.

Another important aspect of self-regulation in online, synchronous learning environments has to do with the devices that enable them, which make it so that the number one object of focus is not necessarily the other people involved in a meeting. Video-conferencing software students use for class is embedded into the same devices that allow for the contextual multiplicity that I discuss earlier. There is very little preventing student from engaging in the range of tasks that they may undertake on their devices in class, and without the co-presence of others they may feel even less inhibited in what outside tasks they engage in during remote class meetings. While it may seem that this relative freedom would release students from the need to perform a classroom self, it also means that students' efforts to self-regulate are taxed even further. That is, when separated in time and space during remote, synchronous classes, students' gestural listening is not being monitored by others. With that in mind, there is little external pressure for a student to remain in the gestural idiom of the classroom. In the sense that this flexibility releases students from the often too-narrow rubric for correct in-class listening, this can be a good thing. But as I have argued earlier, the gestural idiom of the classroom also serves a self-regulating function for students, helping them to create their classroom selves, a self that attends and learns, a self that shows up as a member of the classroom community. With no co-present others, the organic impetus to create that embodied self falls away. I think one of the outcomes for many students is a greater difficulty in staying focused on class activities or remaining on task when multiple other digital contexts are so readily available, many of which may be more immediately gratifying than the deliberately slower, step-by-step processes of classroom learning.

To return to Turkle's term, a feeling of absent presence on Zoom arises from the combination of turned-off cameras and the awareness of contextual multiplicity taking place within students' devices, the same ones they use to log into their online class. The uncertainty in our sense of students' attention is particularly high in light of the presence of personal devices, because, as Mueller explains, the nature of what students can be attending to during class exceeds what has been possible in the past. As he puts it, "Students' economies of attention encompass generative fields of activity—as often as not, giving way to distributed, fragmentary consciousness, attuned in a complex orchestration across highly varied attractions and playing at once across conceptual, material, and digital orders" (246). As instructors running a class online, we have a sense of being only one of many "highly varied attractions" students may be engaging with on their devices. Again, I do not want to idealize the quality of students' attention that may have characterized a pre-personal device and pre-internet classroom. I do want to point out that with internet-enabled personal devices, students' "economies of attention" can be channeled in device-specific ways that were not previously present when the daydream or the notebook was the main alternative to class content. Absent presence in an online classroom can cut both ways, too, with instructors needing to manage their own contextual multiplicity and "fragmentary consciousness." From an instructor's perspective, Nadler describes it this way, writing in early pandemic days: "Whereas a physical classroom space previously encoded the environment as a specific context for me, my laptop has become the site of my current teaching. However, it is simultaneously my network for this article, cat memes, and a work-in-progress Y/A novel" (9). Teaching online is different because, as Nadler continues, "the spaces for possibilities are different" (9).

Using web-enabled devices, Drucker further highlights the unique form of attention that attending a VCS-enabled class online brings about, focusing on the quality of "shifting" that our devices make possible. She, too, refers to the kind of "conceptual, material, and digital orders" that Mueller mentions. She writes: "We shift from editorial text to advertisement, from personal communication to social networking, from embedded video to text, audio to image, and often, in the process, from one domain of activity to a radically different sphere of activity" (4). "We are constantly offered alternatives," she continues, "not so much a garden of forking paths but a hopscotch of hotspots, launch pads, and sinkholes through which our attention runs at whim and will" (4). The implications that these alternative movements and directions have for education begin to emerge when she later adds that "in a digital environment, those relations are loosened from their condition of fixity and can be reorganized and rearranged according to shifting hierarchies of authority and priority" (7). With devices in the classroom, much becomes possible, including "shifting hierarchies of authority" that have already begun to push and pull on conventional structures of authority in the classroom.

Conclusion and Sample Class Activities for Cultivating Presence in the Classroom

The release from gestural listening brings about what may be unprecedented demands on students' abilities to focus and prioritize, even as it brings about what may be a generative "loosening" of fixity, the "shifting hierarchies of authority" in classroom spaces that Drucker refers to. The paradoxes of how gestural listening is inflected through VCS interfaces leave us with no easy answers about how to fix Zoom fatigue or to curricular decisions about how to incorporate remote, synchronous learning. Some writers suggest ways of altering VCS to reduce Zoom fatigue, such as when Fauville et al. conclude that their findings can "contribute to the design process of video conference platforms companies, for example the default should be that the self-view is hidden" (13). Drucker, on the other hand, imagines a constructive delimiting of online resources, writing that "the graphic environment of the web is often a scene of infinite distractions, unless we are inside a controlled environment—a library collection or single resource" (4). I expect to see many more iterations of "digital underlife" in my classrooms going forward, and I expect to see my students navigate and create new norms, at times both reifying and subverting common assumptions about the use of personal devices in classroom spaces. It will be interesting on the one hand, to observe the extent to which academic policies on an institutional level work to limit, or rein in, device use, perhaps in ways like Drucker suggests here, creating "controlled environments"; and on the other hand, to see how institutions, and individual instructors within them, will continue to incorporate students' personal devices skillfully into their classrooms, perhaps harnessing aspects of the "shifting" and "complex orchestration" that Drucker and Mueller describe, respectively. Respect, resistance, and self-regulation will undoubtedly play out in ways both expected and unexpected. An awareness of gestural listening dynamics amidst personal devices should enable instructors to continue to see their classrooms in constructive ways, looking for how students negotiate the various valences of absent presence and the architecture of interfaces. For the moment, I offer two sample activities that help instructors—or group facilitators in a variety of other contexts—enact the ideas in this chapter about (1) how gestural listening as a rhetorical force is affected by the presence of personal mobile devices in face-to-face classrooms, and (2) how students can respond to the ways video-conferencing software delimits gestural listening in virtual classrooms. Both activities are intended to cultivate a stronger sense of community presence in these educational settings.

SAMPLE ACTIVITY 1: CULTIVATING PRESENCE IN THE CLASSROOM WITH TECHNOLOGY GUIDELINES

The first half of this chapter moved through examples of how the presence of personal mobile devices in the classroom contributes to a sense of "absent presence." Recent research has suggested, too, that people may have a block with regard to the effects of their own device use on co-present others.

With those ideas in mind, the goals of this activity are (1) to reduce a sense of absent presence in the classroom, and (2) to increase self-awareness about the effects of personal devices on classroom perceptions and interactions. It takes shape in three steps: first, students brainstorm, independently or in small groups, while taking notes about their ideas; second, a whole-class discussion takes place in which students share thoughts from, and build upon, their brainstorming; third, the students and instructor work together to generate guidelines for classroom engagement and a rubric for how engagement and participation will be graded. This activity would be best implemented at the beginning of the semester, so that participation and engagement throughout the term may be guided by the student-generated rubric, and so that students may reflect on their engagement in the end-of semester self-assessment piece, described in the following outline.

Brainstorm

- What type of environment do we want to create in this class? What type of environment would we benefit from?
- What does it feel like when others are using devices in class? What effect(s) do devices have on classroom interactions? Does the use of devices change people's body language, or gestures, in class? What impact does that have on the classroom environment?
- Based on your thoughts about the questions so far, how *should* we show our attention to each other? What would that look like, exactly? That is, what might we do and/or not do to show attention and regard for one another, especially in our use of personal devices? How can we use the "body language of listening," or gestural listening, to show attention to each other?

Discuss

- Invite students to share their thoughts from the "brainstorm" questions.
- Ask: What are some things we should bear in mind as we decide how to "show up" for others in our class, and when thinking about how others "show up" for us? How should we interpret the body language, or gestures, of others?
- Based on what has been shared and discussed, ask students to put together a set of class-discussion guidelines. During the conversation, instructors may write ideas on the board, helping to consolidate similar ideas, summarize, identify patterns, or create categories.

Enact

- Working together in class discussion or in a collaborative document, generate a rubric for how participation and engagement will be graded in the course.
- Have students write a self-reflection at the end of the semester about whether, or how, they have followed the rubric. Instructors may also have students suggest and include a rationale for what grade they should receive for engagement and participation.

SAMPLE ACTIVITY 2: BUILDING COMMUNITY PRESENCE THROUGH GESTURAL LISTENING IN ONLINE CLASSROOM ENVIRONMENTS

The second half of this chapter outlines the challenges and limitations that arise when trying to create gestural responsivity in synchronous online environments. Taking those issues into account, this activity is intended for courses that are fully online or that contain substantial online elements. The goals of this activity are to (1) increase a sense of community presence in virtual classroom environments, and (2) increase self-awareness about aspects of embodiment that affect learning in in-person versus online settings. This activity also has three steps, which similarly culminate in having students generate a set of community guidelines for the classroom.

First, students brainstorm, independently or in small groups (consider using breakout rooms on Zoom or similar software) while taking notes about their ideas; second, an opportunity is provided for a whole-class discussion in which students share thoughts from, and build upon, their brainstorming; third, the students and instructor work together to generate guidelines for the classroom community that emphasize peer presence and how to show listening behaviors in the virtual classroom environment. Similarly to the first activity, this activity would be best implemented at the beginning of the semester, so that the student-generated guidelines can be used throughout the term.

Brainstorm

- What does a Zoom class (or any similar video-conferencing software used to facilitate a class) feel like compared to an in-person class? What specific aspects of the experience make it feel that way? Do you find it easier to learn or pay attention in one or the other? Why might that be?

- Building upon the last questions: In particular, what aspects of your embodiment change between online and in-person learning environments? For instance, do you find it easier or harder to sit still in online or in-person classes? Do you find yourself nodding, taking notes, or checking other devices or apps more in one environment than the other? Why might this be?

- How are interactions with your classmates different in an online class compared to an in-person class?

- Thinking about your responses to the prior questions, what effect(s) does the embodied presence of classmates have on your learning? During an in-person class, does it help—or not—to have classmates nod, vocalize, or make eye contact in class? What forms of responsiveness are helpful—or unhelpful—in virtual classrooms?

Discuss

- Invite students to share their thoughts from the "brainstorm" questions.
- Ask: How can we carry over the helpful aspects of embodied presence into a Zoom classroom? What would that look like, specifically? That is, how can we nod, respond, or otherwise show the body language of listening in an online class?
- What *other* ways are there of showing responsiveness to each other in an online class? That is, how can we compensate for the ways that Zoom limits our ability to show listening attention to each other? Consider other VCS features like chat, polls, whiteboards, emoji reactions, and cameras.
- Based on what has been shared and discussed, ask students to put together a set of class-discussion guidelines that would help to create a responsive environment in the virtual classroom. During the discussion, instructors may collect ideas on a whiteboard or in the chat, helping to consolidate similar ideas, summarize, identify patterns, or create categories.

Enact

- Working together in class discussion or in a collaborative document, generate a set of guidelines for strong community presence within the virtual class. The guidelines should include specific examples of what community presence looks like—for instance, will cameras be on or off? Under what conditions might students be expected to turn cameras on or leave them off? How will students show gestural listening during class? What other features of the software can students use to contribute to a sense of community presence?
- Establish a checkpoint sometime midsemester at which the class will revisit their guidelines for community presence. At the checkpoint, ask students to discuss or write a reflection on how the guidelines are working in the class so far. Invite students to suggest how they might change the guidelines for the second half of the term, including a rationale as to why.

5

Gestural Listening Currents beyond the Classroom

In 2018, Judge Rosemarie Aquilina of the Ingham County Circuit Court in East Lansing, Michigan, presided over an unusual, painful courtroom. The case was brought against Larry Nassar, a sports doctor infamous for assaulting hundreds of athletes during his tenure at the University of Michigan and USA Gymnastics. Notably, each athlete was allowed to speak freely, in the form of "impact statements" about the crimes they endured and those crimes' far-reaching half-lives. Around 150 people spoke over the course of the hearing, including parents and coaches of the affected athletes (Cacciola).

At the hearing, the layers of listening were thick: as the presiding judge, Aquilina listened. Others present at the hearing listened, too, some having just delivered their own impact statements or preparing to. Nassar himself sat in the witness box. Given that the proceedings were recorded and made available online, an untold number of other viewers have listened since. But in her court-room domain, Aquilina did not listen dispassionately, as one might expect of a judge. Rather, she was vocal in her support and encouragement of the athletes, and unstinting in her disparagement of Nassar.

This unusual juridical behavior garnered a range of reactions (Ford; Gowen; Simko-Bednarski; and Joseph). What I want to point out here, however, is that Aquilina's expressive listening powerfully shaped the discursive space in which

https://doi.org/10.7330/9781646428182.c005

the hearing took place—that is, her open support of the athletes influenced their willingness and ability to tell about their experiences. In her display of consequential listening to the impact statements, Aquilina found a way to center the victims' experiences and create an expanded, potentially worldwide audience for them (Ford; "Larry Nassar's"). She served as a listening force, bringing recognition to those affected by abuse and awareness to the exploitation of female athletes as a larger issue. Her gestural listening, radiating outward to touch speakers and other listeners, played an outsized role in this unique communicative situation.

In the last three chapters, I have endeavored to bring into focus the ways that gestural listening operates as a rhetorical force in classroom spaces: First, I discussed how it serves as a palpable conduit for respect, resistance, and self-regulation; next, I discussed how a preferred gestural idiom of the classroom refracts across aspects of difference. Then, my investigation of gestural listening with and through personal mobile technologies served to highlight the uncertainties of contextual multiplicity, digital underlives, and "absent presence," as well as how interface thinking and gestural listening together provide a framework to explain a phenomenon like Zoom fatigue. Altogether, a picture begins to emerge of listening as a quiet yet estimable rhetorical force. It is multidimensional in its impact, affecting the self and others. It retains special functions as a rhetorical strategy often, although not always, leveraged by subordinate players. It is effortful and complexly embodied, even when crossing into digitally mediated spaces. Woven in and through other facets of communication—speech, reading, writing—listening nevertheless is shaped by its own distinct cultural histories and operates in intricate, context-specific ways.

Focusing on gestural listening in educational settings thus far has allowed me to identify and articulate its attributes. After all, the classroom is a site that heightens the way power relations and citizenship are instilled in its participants. But just as the history I trace through chapter 1 of this book moves through sites and texts that encompass religion, performance, political demonstration, and therapeutic practice, so too does gestural listening exceed classroom spaces and act upon a wide range of other areas in which people listen together. In this chapter, I want to suggest, and begin to show, that gestural listening dynamics are not limited to classroom spaces, and I aim to illustrate some of what I perceive as the many possibilities for applying gestural listening to gatherings outside of formal education. At the start of this chapter, we see just one in the application of gestural listening to the Nassar hearing.

There are many possible sites we could focus on to illustrate gestural listening's group dynamics outside the classroom. In the rest of this chapter, I have chosen three main arenas that have in common their intentional gatherings of people, collectivities with their own specific purposes, traditions, and structures of authority: sites of protest, worship, and choral singing. Distantly echoing the gatherings of students in classrooms, in these other settings listeners leverage gestural listening in ways that expand upon dynamics I have previously explored, especially resistance, and that encompass other orientations, too: solidarity, recognition, and registering the presence of dissent within a group, among others. Gestural listening in these spaces is agential, both expressive and receptive. I hope to show how these types of gatherings while seemingly disparate share gestural and auditory overlaps that make them more similar than one might at first expect.

In examining gestural listening dynamics in settings outside the classroom, I am implying not only that protest, worship, and ensemble singing can be understood as linked to each other but also that all three may be influenced by, and in turn may influence, the gestural listening found in classroom spaces. While that may seem like an overly expansive claim, I operate on the assumption that listening is learned and practiced across many spheres in a life and that those spheres inevitably inform one another. In this sensibility, I draw upon the thinking of Paul Prior and his ideas about how learning occurs through and across what he describes as "laminated worlds," rather than in artificially distinct spaces. In "How Do Moments Add Up to Lives: Trajectories of Semiotic Becoming vs. Tales of School Learning in Four Modes," Prior demonstrates this orientation when he pushes back against what he identifies as "tales of learning," in which "learning happens inside specific territorial communities," where students "make their way to the centers (or fail to do so) by moving step-by-step along a sequentially graded curricular path." Prior locates an example of this distinctly territorial, graded curricular path in the Common Core State Standards Initiative, for instance, and their science-oriented counterpart, the Next Generation Science Standards. Prior argues, instead, that learning cannot realistically be extracted from its many organic, interconnected contexts in a person's life. "In contrast," he writes:

> The story I am calling "a trajectory of semiotic becoming" sees learning as embodied, dispersed, mediated, laminated, and deeply dialogic. Becoming happens not inside domains, but across the many moments of a life. Becoming happens in spaces that are never pure or settled, where discourses and knowledge are necessarily heterogeneous, and where multiple semiotic

resources are so deeply entangled that distinct modes simply don't make sense. (Prior)

When Prior writes that "becoming happens not inside domains," I believe he is not so much denying the power of the distinct, different spaces in which learning occurs but rather emphasizing that the domains people move through are not walled off. I would describe the domains in which listening is taught and learned—like school, family, theater, or church, for instance—as distinct from each other while still being porous, layered, variously overlapping. Even the relative centers of these spaces are never, as Prior puts it, "pure or settled"; rather, they are "heterogeneous" and require a willingness to think of learning as a kind of entanglement: of interconnected sites and of "semiotic resources." With the phrase "semiotic becoming," Prior describes a continuous, ongoing process rather than something learned immovably "once and for all." Becoming the "right kind" of gestural listener in any given environment, as I explore throughout this book, reflects the qualities of porousness, entanglement, and ongoingness that Prior brings to our attention here. With those qualities in mind, I refer to the dynamics of gestural listening that I explore in this chapter as "currents," through which I want to evoke the flowing and churning of moving water—its patterns broadly identifiable within a continual swirl.

The first sites that I focus on here are literally classroom adjacent: two college campus protests. In fact, the first, at Middlebury College in 2017, might be better described as a gestural demonstration of not-listening—of "audiencing" with extreme resistance. This protest illuminates how what we expect of students, especially listening characterized by obedience and respect, bleeds into how students' collective actions outside the classroom are perceived by the broader public. Specifically, it highlights accusations that the students "did not listen" to opposing views before engaging in resistant behavior. Journalist Laurie Penny helps explain how the accusation of "not having listened" often serves a particular rhetorical function, and the importance of decisions about who is given a platform—that is, who gets to be heard. The second protest I examine here, at Howard University and also in 2017, similarly shows resistant listening to the point of not-listening. But while the crowd at Middlebury was united in its determination to drown out the speaker, the Howard University protest also begins to show how gestural listening can convey the presence of multiple, often competing contingents within a group gathered to listen. In *Black or Right*, Louis Maraj's analysis of a racialized campus interaction between students and a staff member helps explain how the "semiotic resources" of gestural listening reveal affiliations and exclusions within groups.

Gestural listening that reveals the presence of dissent or multiplicity within a group is a theme that continues into the next site I examine here, also a scene of protest: the national anthem kneeling demonstrations made famous by Colin Kaepernick and the NFL in 2016. In these demonstrations, athletes turn the act of listening to the pregame national anthem into a gesturally and rhetorically rich moment, one that reflects the presence of multiple perspectives and priorities among teammates and that, upon closer examination, brings anthem listening not just into the gestural realm of protest but also into the embodied idiom of mourning, memorial, and prayer. Kevin Quashie provides context for the kneeling protests in his examination of another famous anthem-listening moment in sports history—the medal ceremony of runners Tommie Smith and John Carlos at the 1968 Olympic games—and unfolds, further, the role of Blackness in gestural listening that is both expressive and receptive, oriented to the external and the internal.

The gestural idiom of the kneeling protests overlaps significantly, if unexpectedly, with the embodiment of prayer. The embodied idiom of prayer, and sites of congregational worship more generally, combine layered valences of honor, surrender, and humility. In settings of congregational worship, the tools of gestural listening instantiate a different togetherness—the sense of a community's solidarity, and its role in recognizing moments in an individual's life, a collective witnessing. While I begin by detailing elements of Jewish religious practice to help me illustrate these aspects of solidarity, especially those related to mourning, I ultimately want to identify this phenomenon as "congregational listening" more generally, to suggest broadly how listeners in religious settings are shaped by its characteristic listening, types of listening that are reinforced by the spatial arrangements brought about by the built environment in many houses of worship. To that end, I draw upon scholarship in gesture studies and rhetoric, as I do in prior chapters but also findings in architecture and history, with the same "necessary eclecticism" that characterizes this book and its study of gestural listening as a whole. Adam Kendon's exploration of "proxemics" brings together built environments with the gestural idioms they produce and reinforce, while Richard Cullen Rath makes the connection between the architecture of houses of worship, and their attendant acoustics, with the values of those communities. Roxane Mountford's study of gender expectations in preaching, too, attends to the subtle movements of congregants in the context of their faith environment.

Deeply embedded into many religious practices, choral singing brings about intense forms of group listening. Here, too, we see gestural listening currents that are linked to those characterizing congregational gatherings but that also bring about their own rippling shapes. I suggest that choral singing, especially in its emphasis on coordinated breathing, creates a "somatic alignment" of its participants in a kind of gestural listening "net." Conductor and scholar James Jordan illustrates the role of breathing in his instructional book on choral conducting, *Evoking Sound*, while Deborah Kapchan describes the role of listening in the singing of the Sufi Qadirriya Boutshishiyya order.

Readers will see, too, in this chapter, expansions upon some of the aspects of my own life that I highlighted in chapter 1: underlying my attention to campus protest is my professionalization as a college professor; my illustration of listening practices in religious community settings is an extension of my time in synagogue Sunday school as a youngster; my preoccupation with acoustic architecture and choral performance is an outgrowth of my extensive participation in ensemble singing. That is, these are sites that are available to me as anchors for my observations about gestural listening—the "laminated worlds" within my life that have made gestural listening visible and palpable to me. Other sites will be available to other people. To aid others in their own investigations of gestural listening, I offer a set of questions at the end of the chapter designed to spur and guide further research.

The Currents of Protest, Part 1: Campus Demonstrations

In February 2017, students at Middlebury College in Middlebury, Vermont, staged a protest during a talk given by author Charles Murray. Although invited by a student group, Murray was an unpopular choice for a campus speaker overall. At the event, the students first interrupted the introductory speakers, then stood and chanted in chorus when Murray took the stage. In the minutes that followed, they continued to chant as they jumped up and down, held up signs, and crowded forward, arms raised in the air. Through their actions, the crowd of Middlebury students showed that a respectful gestural listening performance could not be taken for granted. Rather, they subverted the role of listening audience, and instead "audienced" with extreme resistance, actually disallowing the talk from happening.

In the days that followed, responses to the protest at Middlebury were strikingly negative: a writer for *The Washington Post* called it "brown-shirted thuggery," while Middlebury's own president, Laurie Patton, responded afterward that Middlebury students had "failed to live up to our core values" (Seelye; Volokh). Specifically, much of the backlash the Middlebury students received implied that they had foreclosed dialogue, that in refusing to hear Murray's ideas that day they reinstantiated the very exclusionary, silencing dynamics that they sought to protest. As is often the case, the whole story gets more complicated upon further investigation: the student protest was shadowed by the presence of antifascist groups not associated with the college. Dr. Alison Stenger, professor of political science at Middlebury, was injured when her neck was wrenched by a protest participant after Murray's talk, which was ultimately moved to a different room and made available to others via livestream. Murray's visit, according to more detailed accounts written later, served not only as a platform for protesting white supremacy against the backdrop of the ongoing Trump campaign but also as a lightning rod for an accumulation of slights sustained by Middlebury students in the weeks prior to the Murray event. Nevertheless, students' mobilization of protest techniques—expressive, defiant, and based on group participation—drew criticism in particular for the way it foreclosed listening.

Students, occupying a transitional role between adolescence and young adulthood, are particularly vulnerable to accusations of not having listened. Young, freshly introduced to new ideas, and preparing for—without having yet taken on—the economic imperatives of working life, students foment social change even as they are regularly lambasted for the idealism and disruptions to status quo that come alongside their stage of life. People in the role of students, as I have described in prior chapters, are also expected to manifest certain historically situated ideals about listening that reflect obedience and an awareness of hierarchy. So while they are especially likely to have these charges leveled against them, students are not alone in dealing with the charge of "not having listened," and the rhetorical purpose of that accusation warrants further reflection. In her 2018 article "No, I Will Not Debate You," journalist Laurie Penny investigates a pattern of public calls for the protection of free speech when rhetors are denied a platform—not being allowed to speak in a particular setting. Those rhetors often leverage the sense of rejection springing from "not being listened to" as a means of changing the larger conversation. Penny spotlights an experience in which she declined to participate as an invited speaker on a panel at *The Economist*'s Open Future Festival, during which Steve Bannon was also scheduled to be interviewed as part of a speaker series. Around the same time, a *New York Times* event that had programmed a live interview of Bannon changed course and disinvited Bannon from participating. Bannon, like Murray, was invited by one person or group within a larger organization (The New York Times organization and Middlebury, respectively), and then stopped from participating as planned by another. Already, changes in expected listening behaviors reflect the presence of multiplicity and competing values within one institution.

In the context of the Middlebury protest and others like it, students open themselves up to criticism that they didn't listen because they did not engage in the theater of debate, which heavily features the performance of listening. *The Economist*, keeping Bannon on the program, took a stance that put full faith in the power of open, fair debate, asserting that "the future of open societies will not be secured by like-minded people speaking to each other in an echo chamber, but by subjecting ideas and individuals from all sides to rigorous questioning and debate" (Penny). Penny's planned co-speaker, Laura Bates, in contrast, writes that Bannon's "deeply racist, misogynistic, white nationalist views pose real threat and harm to a large number of people, and that it is therefore irresponsible and damaging to provide him with the legitimacy of such a highly respected mainstream platform as *The Economist*" (quoted in Penny). In her stance, Bates points out that allowing Bannon to speak, to hear him out, to "just listen" to him, is already a choice in curating the roster of speakers that legitimizes a dangerous agent. As Penny writes later: "Curating debate participants is itself a political choice, because the terms of a debate inform public opinion as much as its content." According to Penny, responses to her withdrawal from the panel, and *The New York Times'* rescinded invitation, take on a familiar pattern: "If you won't debate, the argument goes, you're an enemy of free speech." As at Middlebury, a focus on how students disrupted the theater of listening replaced a potentially more constructive discussion about why they felt compelled to do so in the first place.

I have written that, on the one hand, students are expected to drive social change, and, on the other hand, they are expected to operate according to the societal expectation of students: obedient, receptive, respectful. Here, too, we see a conflict between the multiple, often competing roles that students occupy. Looking for instances of gestural listening reveals those conflicts. At Middlebury, the students' chosen form of protest fills the auditorium with their own sound and motion, preemptively crowding out others. The gestural vocabulary of their protest implies that a "passive silence" is the only alternative to speech, and they manifest an understanding of listening and vocalizing as opposing poles—with listening as a form of passive submission and speech its active, powerful opposite. As Penny teaches us, accusations of "not having listened" will often be made regardless, but an awareness of gestural listening opens up other alternatives that may head off such claims. Through the framework of gestural listening, performances of "passive listening" on the one hand, and vociferous protest on the other, do not emerge as the only available options—the kneeling protests I address in the next section, for instance, offer another. I focus on this example of the Middlebury protest not to critique the students' chosen form of protest: ultimately, demonstrations are a tool for when listening and dialogue have not led to acceptable solutions beforehand. Rather, I aim to highlight how gestural listening, with its blend of receptivity and expressivity, could play a useful role in a repertoire of bids for social change, potentially enriching both diplomacy and direct action.

Another university protest, one that requires an awareness of a full range of listening tools, took place in September of 2017, when a group of students at Howard University drowned out former–CIA Director James Comey as he rose to deliver Howard's annual convocation address (PBS Newshour). The students in the audience at Howard that day—a historically Black university—reportedly "sang and chanted continuously throughout the speech" (Nussbaum and Nelson). At Howard, however, the audience appeared much more ambivalent about the student protest than was visibly the case at Middlebury A Politico article on the event observes that "at one point much of the auditorium started their own chant: 'Let him speak.'" Politico also notes that the crowd of around 1,500, mostly students and faculty "seemed divided on the protest along generational lines" (Nussbaum and Nelson). Unlike at Middlebury, where the protesting crowd seemed fairly united in their antagonism toward Charles Murray, the responses of the audience at Howard University reflect competing currents of sentiment dueling within the audience itself. The protestors and counterprotestors in the audience made visible and audible the complexity of differing attitudes toward listening that can exist within one group of people. Some chanting, "Let him speak" may have wanted to hear the content of Comey's talk, for instance, while some may have wanted to preempt the inevitable accusations that dog the Middlebury students and the rhetors that Penny investigates: accusations of "not having listened."

In both cases, audience members could have chosen not to attend the events featuring speakers they found problematic. But an awareness of gestural listening reminds us that attending resistantly is different from being absent. While listening often starts as a receptive stance, as at Howard, it can quickly become a form of expression flowing in many directions—from the audience to a speaker, and between audience members and their fellow audience members. The expressive dynamics of resistant listening allow for a gathered group to express itself to itself, manifesting complex, mixed currents of feeling and response. In *Black or Right*, Louis Maraj examines spontaneous moments of resistance by students on college campuses as they assert their belonging within complex institutions that often contain competing parties and values. Looking at video footage of a tense encounter between police, university administrators, and students bringing food into a campus building for other students conducting a sit-in demonstration, Maraj describes a situation in which a gestural vocabulary—including elements of gestural listening—figures significantly. Maraj begins by identifying the racialized elements of the situation at hand: Black and Brown students trying to enter a campus building with food for demonstrators are described paternalistically by the police and administrators as "disruptive" and "scary," ostensibly alarming toward employees working in the building. In response to being called "disruptive," Maraj observes: "one Black woman quite audibly notes, 'Some of us are people of color, so . . .' slapping her knees, as the administrator looks away from the group in nonresponse to the point" (115). Here, when the Black student points out her own racialized treatment by the administrator and slaps her knees, she shows what Tamika Carey calls "rhetorical impatience," which Carey defines as "performances of frustration or dismissal and time-based arguments that reflect or pursue haste for the purpose of discipline" (270). Comprising an approach that Carey locates in Black women's advocacy and self-preservation practices, acts of rhetorical impatience are auditory and gestural in nature, "enacted through bodily, tonal, and verbal indicators and arguments of exasperation or displeasure," and encompass strategies like "talking back" and "calling a thing a thing" (270). In response to the student's deployment of rhetorical impatience, the administrator looks away from the students. The administrator's look away can be understood as a gestural listening behavior, one the administrator deploys to show refusal and defensiveness, unwilling to accept the student's callout. In all, the gestural and auditory dimensions of this scenario show a back-and-forth trade of rhetorical pressures that throw each party's alignment with parts of the institution into relief: students enter a building to participate in a sit-in; in doing so, they claim the right to demonstrate as "citizens" of the university. Stopped by staff members working in the building, the students respond with rhetorical impatience, and one administrator parries with a moment of gestural refusal that aligns them with the aspects of the institution they aim to defend, that is, the stability of their working environment. Their clash of gestural currents reveals what Maraj aptly calls the "fracture between them" (115).

Gestural listening as a rhetorical force is a framework that can help to explain incidents like the protests at Middlebury and Howard. Understanding the cultural history of where "good" listening comes from, especially for students, may further aid us in seeing how college campuses are places that possess fertile soil for demonstrations that call for large-scale change but that are also made vulnerable by those generative conditions. Moments of encounter and rupture on college campuses, like the ones I describe in this section, highlight the conflicting roles that students play. They also often give rise to gestural listening that reveals the presence of competing parties, values, and goals within a group. But campus protests are not the only places where gestural listening reveals the presence of multiple currents within a gathering.

The Currents of Protest, Part 2: The Meanings of Kneeling

In the last section, I write that gestural listening can potentially enrich bids for change that occur both through diplomacy and direct action. So if we invite the vocabulary of gestural listening into public acts of resistance, what might a "listening protest" look like? Since 2016, the "kneeling protests" of NFL football players have illustrated one example of a listening-focused demonstration, on one of the biggest American stages. Taking place during the playing of the national anthem before game-time, these moments of collective listening are used by kneeling protestors to call attention to unequal experiences of being American, without drowning out the anthem or covering their ears to it. It would be a very different gestural performance if protesting players covered their ears during the national anthem, or if they absented themselves by remaining inside the locker room for instance. But during an anthem kneeling protest, those kneeling are still, ostensibly, listening.

The multiple meanings layered into embodied postures like kneeling and standing make them deceptively simple positions. Accordingly, acts of standing and kneeling during the anthem have sparked a range of reactions in viewers. Standing tends to be more effortful than sitting and puts the stander at their full height. When viewed this way, standing emerges as a sign of respect. Those who perceive standing for the national anthem before sporting events as an act that honors the United States military and its veterans are likely to respond negatively to kneeling protests. Kneeling, however, which puts a person lower to the ground yet still upright, also contains age-old connotations of respect, deference, and even humility. Those who see the kneeling demonstrations as protesting racial injustice, especially in the form of police brutality toward black Americans—which was the goal of the protest as stated by Kaepernick himself—are more likely to feel that Kaepernick's actions drew necessary attention to an important issue with another respectful posture. While it may seem like a drawback that gestures like standing and kneeling lack exactness or specificity, in fact their respective composites of meanings imbue them with special depth that warrants our attention, as I hope to show.

In tracing the trajectory of Kaepernick's protests beginning in the preseason of 2016, there is a turning point when Kaepernick moved from sitting as a form of physical protest to kneeling. Initially, Kaepernick sat on the bench, during the anthem before a preseason game in 2016. His change to kneeling was evidently brought about by a conversation with a fellow NFL player, Nate Boyer. Boyer, who served as a United States Army Green Beret before entering the NFL in 2015, spoke with Kaepernick about the intentions of his demonstration and its gestural idiom. In a 2018 interview with NPR, Boyer states that he and Kaepernick met to discuss "our situation, our different opinions about all this" and that they landed upon a "compromise" between sitting and standing. Following this interaction, Kaepernick began to "take a knee," now the predominant gestural choice for this type of protest. In Boyer's words, kneeling contains special valences of respect and honor. In the same interview, he notes: "People kneel when they get knighted. You kneel to propose to your wife, and you take a knee to pray. Soldiers often take a knee in front of a fallen brother's grave to pay respect" (Boyer). Especially with the image of kneeling by a fallen soldier's graveside in mind, Kaepernick's kneeling posture during the playing of the national anthem comes to seem like a mournful gesture of respect, like flying a flag at half-mast in recognition of a recent loss. Boyer's explanation of the kneeling posture further acknowledges the multiple connotations that can be layered into the kneeling posture: knighthood, marriage proposal, prayer, grief. None of these intentions preclude listening.

And yet, the pregame kneeling protest does challenge existing norms when the kneelers are seen alongside standers. Throughout this book, we have seen how what constitutes "good" listening derives from traditions and expectations in each context where listening occurs. Kneeling during the "Star-Spangled Banner" represents a marked change from currently accepted conventions for pregame anthem listening, making that posture, in addition to its other connotations, a gestural-listening act of defiance and refusal. It's a gestural choice that disrupts the desired vision of unity during a moment of national pride and highlights multiple perspectives within a group, moving the gestural idiom from one, all standing, to two—those standing and those kneeling.

Especially notable in the Kaepernick-led kneeling protests is the kneel's resemblance, even overlap, with the gestural idiom of prayer. In fact, a Snopes article from September 2017 investigates a photograph of the Navy Midshipmen football team apparently kneeling together on the field (Evon). The original poster initially thought, as indicated in her caption, that the picture was of a Kaepernick-style kneeling protest during the national anthem. Snopes reports from an email exchange with Chris Maxon, director of the Golden Hurricane Club, on whose field the match took place, that the team was, in fact, kneeling in prayer, not in protest and not during the national anthem. Nevertheless, this post and subsequent investigation shows how easily the acts of taking a knee in protest can be mistaken for the readily recognizable kneeling posture of prayer. In fact, "mistaken" may be the wrong word. Rather, the knee-taking of protest overlaps with and even references the kneeling of prayer, as well as the kneeling of deference to an honored individual or group. This reminds us that gestures are complex, and historically and culturally situated.

The history of political protest in sporting events, to which the kneeling protests are connected, is a long one. In *The Sovereignty of Quiet*, Kevin Quashie turns his attention to one of its most famous instances: the raised fists of 1968 Olympic runners Tommie Smith and John Carlos as they listen to the national anthem during the medal ceremony in which they are awarded gold and bronze. Quashie interprets the athletes' gestural listening in this photograph through his theorization of the term "quiet." To Quashie, "quiet" is not simply "synonymous with silence" and "the absence of sound or movement" but rather is an almost contradictory display of the interior, in a public forum, without revealing what that interior might contain (21). Quietness, in Quashie's formulation, refers to a sort of dimensional outline of a vessel whose actual interior is still hidden from view. He writes: "This expressiveness of quiet is not concerned with publicness, but instead is the expressiveness of the interior. That is, the quiet of a person represents the broad scope of his or her inner life; the quiet symbolizes—and if interrogated, expresses—some of the capacity of the interior" (21). In Quashie's eyes, the podium photograph captures a moment of quietness, in which the athletes listen in their own ways, caught in an act of expressiveness that indexes their own interiorities, inner realms apparent yet simultaneously hidden. What interior experiences do their quiet outer displays suggest? Tommie Smith raises his right fist into the air with a visible, contained tension in his neck and shoulders. His raised arm makes a straight line like an arrow knocked on a bowstring. To his left, John Carlos raises his left fist with a slight bend to his elbow, the tilt of his head and right shoulder conveying a softer posture. Both angle their faces slightly downward, gaze lowered. Smith and Carlos unite in their salute, even as their respective bearings point to different interior experiences. Zooming out further on the scene, the duo forms a countercurrent to the listening of the other men in the frame, silver medalist Peter Norman and the two officials standing next to the podium; all of them gaze directly forward with arms by their sides. In microcosm, this photograph shows how Smith and Carlos bring multiplicity to the gestures of public anthem-listening, increasing the range of its quiet, embodied idiom. Kaepernick would build on this precedent when he increased its range yet again by kneeling in 2016.

In the examples that I've explored in this chapter so far, protest overlaps with other, seemingly separate modes of being and expression, like prayer and rest. Through their gestural overlap, we start to see how listening flows through and connects these states of being. In the next section, I move to examine collective gestural listening in congregational settings. I hope to show how elements of defiance and multiplicity remain, as do the particular communal relations that arise between members of an assembled group. Listening in religious contexts shapes and coheres co-present groups through ritual, even as it highlights differentiated social roles.

The Currents of Congregational Listening

In the last section, I focused on the multiple connotations that layer into the gestures of kneeling and standing, both of which carry meanings that encompass respect, deference, and honor. Kneeling, in particular, overlaps with the gestural idiom of prayer and the body language of mourning. With that in mind, it should come as no surprise that the choreography of standing, sitting, and kneeling figures prominently in sites of congregational worship, especially when it comes to its group practices related to mourning. From a gestural listening perspective, then, sites of congregational worship can, after all, be seen to laminate with scenes of protest.

Allow me to give one example of how gestural listening figures in the congregational listening of a Jewish prayer service, one of the "laminated worlds" that have brought gestural listening into focus for me. At the recitation of the Mourner's Kaddish in a Jewish service, those in mourning and those observing a jahrzeit, or the anniversary of the death of a family member, are invited to stand. The rabbi and the mourners recite the whole prayer together in unison, with those in mourning standing along with the rabbi, while the rest of the congregation remains seated. The entire congregation generally joins in on one line of text only, toward the middle of the prayer. At that point in the prayer, a group of voices rises like a wave around the standing mourners.

Gesturally and aurally, the choreography of the Mourner's Kaddish highlights the role of communal listening in Jewish tradition, as mourners and congregants listen to and for each other. Seated congregants provide the listening, "earwitnessing" force of the Kaddish, while mourners hear the presence of their community members. Standing serves as a sign of respect to those being mourned but also makes the mourners visible to the rest of the community. At the collectively spoken line, mourners hear the presence of the congregation around them. By being present and listening, congregants enable the mourner to fulfill their obligation to say the Kaddish, providing a witnessing quorum that acknowledges the grief of the mourners. In fact, certain prayers and practices in weekly Jewish services cannot take place unless a minyan is present, which refers to the assembly of ten adults (traditionally male but now including women in non-Orthodox denominations). In this sense, Judaism requires the presence of listeners—"earwitnesses"—to fully complete certain rituals. Jewish tradition further requires that mourners be surrounded with people every evening for a week during the shiva period immediately following a death, and then the mourner is required to attend weekly services for a month, during which they continue to say Kaddish. In these ways, Jewish tradition builds in recognition of grief through the presence of congregational listening during periods of bereavement.

The forms of gestural listening found in Jewish practice that I describe here carry palpable valences of respect and recognition, like the kneeling protests. At the same time, they do not carry meanings of defiance or refusal. Rather, they seem to emphasize the multidirectional, horizontal relationships that can arise in such gatherings: the formation of a congregation and its social cohesion, the solidarity that arises from gathering as congregants who are led by a rabbi but who ultimately serve each other through their participation in the (aptly named) service. And yet, the horizontal, networked relationships between congregants that I describe here are simultaneously entangled with more vertical, hierarchical relationships that take shape in those very same moments and spaces. In prior chapters, I describe how students in classroom spaces gear their gestural listening to the instructor in displays of respect and resistance but also to each other, often in ways that are intertwined. Similarly, congregants generally fall into hierarchical relationships with the congregation leader even as they show up for each other.

Some of these hierarchical relationships are instantiated and reinforced by the spaces themselves in which congregational worship takes place—the actual built environment of synagogues or churches, for instance. Especially when attempting to examine congregational listening dynamics that characterized centuries past, for which there may be little written documentation, attending to the built environments of houses of worship provides a different way to get at how people may have listened together. Some scholars—working at the intersections of rhetoric, cultural studies, and architecture—who have looked closely at the built environments of religious spaces, especially churches throughout Europe and America, help to reveal how particular group-listening dynamics may have been reinforced for centuries through acoustics and architectural design. Even as congregants' listening may reach laterally to serve their fellow community members, as I have illustrated through the Mourner's Kaddish, discussed earlier, we also see spatial arrangements in many houses of worship that manifest and reinforce rank relationships.

Take pews, for instance. Although rows of seats are something we may take for granted in the construction of most churches—so normal as to be almost invisible—pews instantiate a choreography of listening with attendant power dynamics. To explain this dynamic, the gesture theorist Adam Kendon draws upon the framework of "proxemics"—how people arrange themselves in spaces and how those arrangements reflect the values in play within those spaces. Proxemics, as an analytical lens, might explain how and when people stand closer together (to share a private conversation, e.g.) or when people might space themselves apart (when waiting in line at the bank or when staking out a place to sit on the beach, for instance). Proxemic factors include how many people are involved in an interaction, their social relation to each other, and what activity they are engaged in, among others. Proxemics also take into account aspects of the built environment like built-in seating or the shape of a room. In fact, in "Spacing and Orientation in Co-Present Interaction," Kendon further notes that "furniture arrangements, set up in various ways, provide a kind of permanent scaffolding for interactional occasions and, in some degree, take over the boundary-defining work that is done in unstructured environments by the bodies of the participants" (14). In other words, if features of a space cannot be easily changed, those features organize and delimit the types of interactions that take place inside them. The sanctuaries of many houses of worship such as churches and synagogues fit this description: the built-in seating of pews predetermines how congregants space themselves out, what direction they face, and how many may sit together in one row. It organizes congregants in a rowed group facing forward to where the service leader stands to conduct the ceremony. It puts congregants in a proxemic arrangement that reinforces their duty to listen to the service leader.

Interestingly, with a nod to how these two worlds are laminated, Kendon turns to the classroom as an example of a proxemically similar space. He describes classrooms as "spatial arrangements typical of occasions when there is an unequal distribution of rights to initiate talk or action" (11). Spatially echoing each other, similar hierarchies and "distribution of rights to initiate talk or action" tend to characterize the physical arrangements of students in school and worshippers in congregations. Kendon illustrates how the proxemics of school and congregational worship reflect similar social order and some similar values. Further exploring proxemics, acoustics, and societal values, Richard Cullen Rath attends to the sounds of churches to understand how people listened together in the past, arguing that "acoustical spaces reflected the beliefs underlying social order" (131). Writing about pre-Reformation European churches, he notes that "sounds bounced around echo upon echo upon echo rather than reaching the listeners' ears all at once" (132). "This created a powerfully moving effect," he explains, "one that amplified the voice and enriched the tone, but at the cost of clarity" (132). Later, the Reformation brought about changes in acoustic preferences that reflected changes in ideology. High ceilings were draped to dampen echoes, and pulpits were centered to be closer to the congregation, as Anglican ministers were instructed to preach from where congregants could hear most clearly (133). Speaking in the pews was discouraged, as, Rath writes, "whisperers stole the minister's rightful audience" (132). We get the sense of a move, acoustically and ideologically, from an emphasis on awesome emotional impact to the centering of more precise, clearly conveyed messages requiring silence in the pews and fewer majestic echoes. Rather than being immersed in a swirl of voices and music, congregants adapt to a more careful, exact hearkening.

This more direct, subdued setup may also enable congregants to show more overt resistance through their gestural listening, however. In one of her sites of study in *The Gendered Pulpit: Preaching in American Protestant Spaces*, Roxanne Mountford describes how a resistant form of gestural listening takes shape when a Protestant congregation has difficulty accepting their new pastor. The conflict between old-guard members of the congregation and their new leader, Pastor Janet, plays out along auditory and spatial lines, with congregants complaining of not being able to hear Pastor Janet as she spoke from the pulpit. Mountford, observing, writes: "While I had no trouble hearing her, some members of the congregation complained to me that they sometimes couldn't hear her sermons. Pastor Janet laughed when I told her about this complaint and said, 'I don't know how many times when I first got here, they're like 'We can't hear you!' It's just that they're not used to listening to a woman'" (144). It may indeed be that the architecture of the sanctuary put Pastor Janet's voice at an auditory disadvantage, as Rath and other researchers into the acoustics of sacred spaces teach us that acoustics correspond to accepted religious norms over time, including the gender of the preacher. Here, however, Pastor Janet's response shows that there may be more to the story. She is confident that the congregants' inability to hear her may not really be an issue of projecting her voice loudly enough to be audible; rather, the congregation's difficulty in hearing her has more to do with her gender and, by extension, their sense of a woman's acceptability in the role of preacher.

In Mountford's account, Pastor Janet chooses to preach from the pulpit, which, like the pews in many houses of worship, is built immovably into the sanctuary itself. Someone suggests leaving the pulpit to move closer to the seated congregation, but Pastor Janet, aware of how some congregants are signaling their resistance to her, feels that leaving the pulpit would reflect the wrong values. Mountford writes: "In fact, Pastor Janet did not indicate that she had changed her style to accommodate them but rather that they learned to 'crane forward,' as she put it, to listen to her . . . Pastor Janet was conflicted about moving closer to the people. *She wanted the people to move closer to her*" (144). Rather than allowing the congregation to retain their established gestural listening norms, Pastor Janet wants them to incline themselves forward in order to hear. Through "craning forward," Pastor Janet indicates her expectation that congregants be willing to destabilize themselves, to literally "stretch" themselves, to meet her partway as a female preacher. Mountford affirms Pastor Janet's expectation, locating the act of leaning forwards within the gestural idiom of Protestant church tradition. She writes: "This movement of the people toward the priest/divine is the normal, preordained motion in mainline Protestant church life: in liturgical services the people go forward to receive communion; in evangelical churches they walk to the altar to confess their sins" (144). Because moving forward represents the normal relationship between congregant and clergyperson within Protestant tradition, according to Mountford, the congregants' initial resistance to it further emphasizes the way they had been subtly leveraging their gestural listening to make a point. Here, we see a respect/resistance dynamic in gestural listening playing out, much as we did in classroom spaces in prior chapters.

Gestural listening in the sites of congregational worship that I examine here, emerges as having at least two major currents: it emphasizes "horizontal" relationships of solidarity and community witnessing among gathered congregants, yet it demonstrates, like the classroom spaces I examine in prior chapters, the push and pull of respect and resistance in its more "vertical" authority structures. It also serves as a kind of weathervane for the norms of acceptability within communities, as Roxane Mountford illustrates through Pastor Janet's experiences. Of course, many other remarkable examples of listening in religious settings exist that merit closer attention in further research but that are outside the scope of this book: the Catholic practice of confession comes to mind, for example, as does the peaceful, nonconfrontative listening of a Quaker Friends meeting. In the next section, however, I look more closely at a practice of intense listening often embedded into the congregational worship of many religious traditions: choral singing. While also emphasizing aspects of the communal in similar ways to congregational acts of listening, choral singing calls even greater attention to the multidirectional, somatic aspects of gestural listening.

Currents in Choral Listening

Choral music and performance, long integral to many religious traditions, is a "world" truly laminated to congregational settings. Tied to the church for centuries prior, secular choral music is thought to have developed in Western musical tradition only with the beginnings of opera in the seventeenth century ("Choir"). When it is taught in schools today, as it often is, choral singing laminates, too, with formal schooling environments. The first chorus I sang in was in school, where I took in a social and embodied curriculum alongside a musical one. I was taught, along with my classmates, how to stand and sit and hold sheet music while singing, how to breathe for optimal vocal production, and how to enunciate words. We learned how to walk onto risers set up in our school's gymnasium, to space ourselves evenly in rows, to wear only black and white during performances, and to refrain from touching our clothing or hair until we were offstage again. In order to coordinate all the actions of choral performance, we learned, perhaps above all, to watch the conductor. With the conductor, and with each other, we entered into a particular gestural and auditory relationship.

Conducting in choral performance depends upon gestural listening. Effective choral conductors use gesture to evoke sound from the singers, embodying the tone and style of the music even as they cue the first downbeat. But sensitive conductors also respond to the choir's sound with their gestures. Think of a conductor making a "shush" shape with their mouth if the choir attacks a musical phrase too loudly, or using a beckoning "come on!" gesture with one hand if the group is singing too softly. In this way, a conductor can manage several aspects of the choir's performance: the choir's balance (the relative volume of the different voice parts), and even intonation. If the choir is singing under pitch, for instance, conductors can often be seen to make their gestures more buoyant, sometimes raising their eyebrows and hovering on tiptoe, influencing the group sound to become lighter, more energized, and better in tune. Conductors of children's choirs can sometimes be seen to gently shake their heads or use a hands-up "slow down!" gesture when eager young choristers sing an up-tempo piece, holding the group's tempo in check and preventing the singers from pushing sharp.

We can see these types of motions, typical to the idiom of choral conducting, as a specific and refined example of gestural listening, one that is distinctly somatic, especially in its intentional focus on coordinated breathing. A champion of responsive choral conducting is conductor and scholar James Jordan, whose 1996 book *Evoking Sound* remains a classic of choral conducting pedagogy. In his guidelines for conductors, he writes:

> *When you conduct other persons, let the sound be your teacher.* As you conduct with your partner or a group of persons, remember that the sounds you hear are directly reflective of your body and gesture . . . If the sound is not what you want, you must be willing to accept that the sound is a mirror image of your conducting. When the sound is not "good," try to change it toward your ideal by understanding the interrelationship of gesture to sound. (77)

While it may seem natural to think of the conductor as establishing or producing the sound of the choir, Jordan conceptualizes conducting as an ongoing act of responsive listening. In particular, conductors in Jordan's school of thought must learn to respond to their choir's breathing: "When conductors listen to their choir's breath," Jordan writes, "they instinctively synchronize and coordinate their own breath with that of their ensemble" (72). Here, the conductor is at times actually cued by the choir, not the other way around: "When heard, the sound of the inhalation signals to the conductor when the choir should release sounds from their bodies" (72). The sonic clue of audible inhalation helps the conductor know when and how to subsequently signal the choir. Then, an "aural sensitivity to the breath provides conductors with the opportunity to 'set the sound' of the choir and insure a proper 'attack' " (72). So while the conductor communicates the time to inhale to the choir at first, they must also respond to the audible breath of the choir. Sometimes when watching a choral performance, viewers can see conductors visibly open their mouths to breathe along with the choir throughout the musical phrases, although they typically do not sing along—even seeing the conductor breathe, it seems, helps bring about a gestural and auditory give-and-take in a choral setting.

The gestural listening "currents" that can be found within a choir take on multidirectional shapes. Jordan emphasizes that listening takes place not just between ensemble and conductor but crucially between members of the ensemble, too: "Not only must the conductor listen to the breath in the choir," he writes, "but choir members must listen to each other breathe so as to establish an ensemble sense" (76). Again emphasizing the somatic tool of the breath, he continues: "That sense of ensemble begins in the communal breath" (76). To hear each other's breathing, members of a choir need to "listen out" or "listen around" themselves, attending to each other as well as to the conductor's gesture. So, for instance, members of the soprano section listen to each other in order to enter together and blend their voices, while, at the same time, all the sopranos together listen to the tenor section as a whole to match their sections' volume appropriately. The "currents" of gestural listening in a choral setting may at first seem to resemble spokes on a wheel, with each singer dyadically connected to the conductor. But when Jordan reminds us about the need for choristers to listen and respond to each other, too, the current begins to better resemble a net, with many interconnected nodes. Choral singing makes visible and palpable a multidimensional or "net-like" model of gestural listening that is distinctly somatic, especially in its emphasis on coordinated breathing.

The dynamics that Jordan highlights here in the context of choral singing are reminiscent of the intertwined flows of responsiveness in the audience at Howard University's commencement, and to the horizontal relationships of solidarity and witnessing that are reinforced by listening in congregational contexts. As choral singers tune in to each other and synchronize their breathing, so audience members, or congregants, hear each other and respond to each other, communicating in a moment-to-moment give-and-take. Choir, however, heightens even further the cooperative, somatic coordination of singing. Gestural listening in choir ushers participants toward a type of "somatic alignment."

As I mention earlier, choral singing has long been deeply embedded in many religious practices. The somatic alignment brought about by the "net-like" gestural listening of choral settings helps to explain the affective power of ensemble singing in devotional spaces. In "Listening Acts: Witnessing the Pain (and Praise) of Others," ethnographer Deborah Kapchan describes a striking example of how somatic alignment, through singing and listening, operates among members of the Sufi Qadirriya Boutshishiyya order. Kapchan notes that members of this particular order are generally not fluent speakers of Arabic. She observes that for these women, who have not grown up with the melodies or words of Sufi devotional music, but rather have come to them later, listening emerges as the primary means for learning sacred music. She writes: "Not being Arabic speakers, they would primarily listen deeply to their peers, rhythmically reiterating first the beginnings and the ends of phrases where the stress was most obvious, then incrementally weaving in more text" (280). "Listening deeply," order members gradually begin to produce phrases of language and music, as though taking on, catching and reproducing, the lines of the prayers. Importantly, order members are not just learning language and musical phrases in a rote or decontextualized way but are also learning the physical "stresses" of the prayers, "rhythmically reiterating." Through this approach, order members acquire a new, specific, embodied way of being. But not only is listening (rather than reading the music from a score, for instance) the primary means of learning the music; Kapchan argues further that the listening characterizing the order's ceremonies creates and transmits a particular "somatic attention" (277). She writes: "Just as one person looking at the sky will cause others to direct their gaze upward, one deep listener in a room will first change the vibrations of her own body and then affect the somatic attention of other bodies, sentient and non" (277). In the context of devotional singing in the Qadirriya Boutshishiyya order, gestural listening brings about a transformation into a devotional state, which is accompanied by a blurring of individual boundaries, a collapse of subject and object, and an entrance into "another way of being":

> *Sama'* is both the genre of Sufi music as well as the verb "to listen" in Moroccan Arabic. *Sama'* contains both subject (listener) and object (sound) in its very meaning. Indeed, the performers of this music are not called "singers" (*mughaniyyin*) as in other musical genres, but are called "listeners" (*musama'yyin*). It is not an ordinary listening, however, but a genre of listening informed by the intention (*niya*) to find another way of being. (279, emphasis added)

Here, the gestural listening of ensemble singing brings about a profound somatic alignment, one that figures prominently in the order's devotional practice. This "genre of listening" becomes a gestural and auditory tool for the order members—listening to each other even as they sing—to seek "another way of being" (279). A means of learning, aligning, and invoking the sublime, the listening on display in the Qadirriya Boutshishiyya order demonstrates gestural listening's rhetorical capacities in concentrated form. The somatic alignment brought about by gestural listening, as it takes on a multiply interconnected shape, or current, provides a tool for thinking about the power of choral singing and provides insight into the way it laminates with congregational and devotional settings.

Questions to Guide Gestural Listening Inquiries

The examples of gestural listening currents that I discuss in this chapter are far from exhaustive—much more can be said about their rhetorical impact in these arenas and many others. Rather, I aim to point briefly to the presence of gestural listening in an array of sites, and I hope that other authors in the days to come will build upon my start here by analyzing currents of gestural listening within their own "laminated worlds." Through my examination of protestors, congregants, and choral singers in this chapter, however, I hope to have shown further how listening can affect communicative situations in a variety of ways. Those ways can be dually receptive and expressive, defiant, multiple within a single group, and potentially transformative. In gatherings, listening can perform important social functions through its capacities for witnessing and somatic alignment.

Moreover, I hope readers take away the idea that analyzing certain events with gestural listening in mind can be fruitful, and may even be necessary to arrive at a fuller understanding of some rhetorical situations. For readers who want to begin developing projects that may incorporate an awareness of gestural listening, I offer the following list of key questions to consider when thinking about how gestural listening operates as a rhetorical force.

1. How will gestural listening in this situation be recognized? We have seen that gestural listening is challenging to capture and measure, so it is important to articulate what counts as listening behavior in the setting you are analyzing. Is it nodding, or making eye contact, or note-taking? Something else? Specify what gestural listening elements seem to be of special importance in the event you are looking at.

2. What gestural listening "currents" may be flowing in this situation? What group and/or subgroups can you identify? Do these currents

seem to compete and clash? Or on the other hand, do they seem to unify and align their participants? Do they take on a different shape, or dynamic, entirely?

3. In the situation being observed, is gestural listening being taught or learned in some way? If so, what type of gestural listening is being cultivated or promoted, and to what ends? What is "good" listening here?

4. What traditions or cultural histories may shape the gestural listening you observe in this situation?

5. What aspects of identity may come to bear on the gestural listening you observe?

6. In the gestural listening behaviors you observe, are there any ruptures, disruptions, or subversions of existing conventions taking place? Is there a departure from some preexisting expectations about gestural listening occurring here?

7. What does the gestural listening you identify in the situation bring about? What effects does it seem to produce?

8. What does an analysis of gestural listening enable you to do that other types of analysis don't? That is, why take special note of gestural listening in this setting? What in particular might it reveal?

Conclusion

Listening Configurations

Some years ago, I visited an exhibition in Pittsburgh's Mattress Factory Museum. After waiting in a long line, I walked through a short hallway and entered a booth much like a theater box, furnished only with two chairs facing into total darkness. I stepped in, sat down, and waited—waited for something to happen. You might say that it never came: there was no flash of light, no voices, no movement to catch my attention or tell a story. Instead, what happened had to do with my own sensory apparatus and with the way that I, like everyone who entered the box before and after me, have learned to behave in space. Even before my eyes fully adjusted to the dark, I realized that I was in a much bigger space than I thought. Eventually, I determined that it was a cavernous room as big as a stripped-out movie theater. And there I was, holding myself obediently still, facing forward with hands on my lap, making no sound except for my breathing, gazing out expectantly. There was no rope preventing me from climbing over the side of the box or from doing a few jumping jacks, but I didn't do either.

The exhibit called attention to the embodiment of my listening. I sat there, ready to receive even as my ears seemed to reach out into the darkness, trying to learn more about the space I had entered. From experience, I knew that galleries are for looking and listening, and occasionally touching. Nothing to touch

https://doi.org/10.7330/9781646428182.c006

was forthcoming here, and my sight was dimmed by the darkness, so it was the act of listening that crystallized and came forward. The exhibition included no intentional sound, however, so I was left only with listening's embodied idiom: I felt poised, as though straining forward and outward—ready, open, unsure.

To even consider the embodiment of listening as something taught and learned, something enculturated, is already to step outside of a habitus that naturalizes and renders it invisible, something too obvious to be noted. When we begin to notice that there are, in fact, many embodied, gestural ways of listening, we gain access to a rich site of analysis. The Czech philosopher Vilém Flusser looks for the gestures of listening carved into stone sculpture, and hints at what might be possible when gestural listening is taken seriously as a site of rhetorical encounter: "If we take a look at mediaeval iconography from the standpoint of gesture," he writes, "then we are confronted with the gesture of listening as one of the central themes. It is Mary's gesture at the conception, the gesture of being fertilised by the word (logos). Mary 'receives,' that means she hears a voice" (21). Flusser goes on to bring still more specificity to the depicted gesture of Mary's listening as it changes over time: "We can learn something from observing how the gesture changes with the onset of the Renaissance. In the Gothic period it is the gesture of someone who is surprised and called; in the Renaissance it is that of the resolved, hearing Mary" (21). Gothic depictions of Mary are "surprised and called," whereas the listening of Renaissance Mary emerges as "resolved"— states of intention and readiness that may reflect on aspects of gender, faith, and responsiveness that warrant scholarly attention. Implicit in these distinctions is the idea that listening is not a passive or homogenous act but rather that it has the potential to be creative, formative, and constitutive to communicative situations. Flusser understands listening—as I do—as a palpable force working in many different rhetorical encounters, as much as the more traditional sites of rhetorical analysis: speaking and writing.

When I write that listening can be "constitutive," I suggest that gestural listening is more than just a tool to be deployed in certain situations but rather a way of carving out a particular space, or set of conditions, for further encounter. In the exhibition that I have just described, the visitor is placed literally at the edge of an unknown, blinking expectantly into a dark room that gradually appears to take shape. The gestural idiom of listening, regardless of what is immediately heard, establishes a field of reception for whatever will come next. And because that field is not a neutral one, it also plays a role in shaping the rhetorical impact of whatever will be said, expressed, communicated. The exhibition enacts one vision of what Gemma Corradi Fiumara means when she writes that "the ability to listen, which allows us to hold firm and remain vigilant at the borders of obscurity, might be the condition that makes it possible for us to remain open to further linguistic and theoretical fields of concern" (91). The space is already there, and we enter into it. But for a moment, it is almost as though the gestures of listening actually create the space. In rhetorical encounter, I want to suggest that it does, in fact, establish the space, or conditions, for what will be spoken, argued, shared.

Perhaps it's here that my conception of listening intersects most with Krista Ratcliffe's, as she defines her notion of rhetorical listening as a "stance of openness that a person may choose to assume in relation to any person, text, or culture" (17). A "stance" is indeed what the exhibition I describe brings about most clearly—I write earlier that I held myself still, hands in my lap, eyes forward. While I have focused quite literally on physical stances of listening through this book, Ratcliffe refers more strongly to an internal stance. In that internal stance of listening, we temporarily quiet ourselves, making space within for the thoughts and ideas of another. Paul Kameen, looking for the contours of a "rhetoric of pedagogy" in *Writing/Teaching*, puts it this way: "If I can properly clear a space from which I can hear another voice, I become open not only to what is going to be said, but also to my own prospect for change in response to it" (252). Kameen gets at the dual nature of listening as a rhetorical force here—something that moves outward to affect others, as I have argued throughout this book, but also something that changes the listener.

So what type of rhetoric is gestural listening? I call it a sensory rhetoric, spanning the aural, visual, and haptic, and in this sense I echo Steph Ceraso, who coins the term "multimodal listening," referring to listening that engages the whole body kinesthetically, not just the ears. "Thoughtfully engaging and composing with sound," she writes, "requires listeners to attend to how sound works with and against other sensory modes to shape their embodied experiences" (103). I call it a rhetoric that can operate in both micro- and macro-ways, as a strategically deployed technique that may invite, or even pressure, another entity to express themselves; but also as a more fundamental, mutually constitutive capacity, creating a field of encounter. I call it a rhetoric that emphasizes a flow between speaker and receiver, in which the audience becomes an agent of expression even in its receptive stance—a rhetorical framework in which a listener can be as much a rhetor as the speaker or writer, albeit in ways that are densely layered with various, overlapping historical conceptions of listening.

Approaching listening in these ways lends itself to an awareness of what I will call new "listening configurations." When I speak of a "listening configuration," I refer to ways of marking out rhetorical situations that espe-cially attend to the flow of listening as a rhetorical force. I have outlined many listening configurations throughout this book, analyzing rhetorical situa-tions inside and outside the classroom by highlighting their listening dynam-ics. Thus far, I have focused mostly on acts of gestural listening in real-world sites—education (both in-person and online, virtual spaces), protest, worship, and performance.

But a framework of gestural listening as a rhetorical force also has impli-cations for textual study, too. With the idea of listening as a rhetorical force in mind, we can begin to locate listening configurations on the page, as well. Listening configurations on the page may well be located most readily in tradi-tions of poetry. Discussing his "Zen-inspired" translations of the Psalms, for instance, Norman Fischer writes: "Shakespeare's sonnets, whose power come from the fact that they are passionately addressed to a 'you' who is forever unknown, have always impressed me, and I believe the whole sense of the lyric in Western poetry (beginning with the Psalms) has its source in this notion of a passionate writing addressed to a nonexistent or supra-existent listener" (xxi). In Fischer's view, the writer of the Psalms conjures up the presence of a listener to beseech or praise, but at the same time, in a circular, supra-existent flow, the presence of that listener seems to actually call forth, to occasion, the Psalmist's expressions. The presence of listening catalyzes, draws out, gath-ers; and Fischer suggests this as one of the basic assumptions undergirding Western poetry. In a similar vein, in the preface to her collection of poems entitled *Stories I Ain't Told Nobody Yet*, Jo Carson writes that for her poems, she never "sat at her desk and made them up"; rather, she "heard the heart of each of them somewhere . . . I am an eavesdropper and I practiced being invisible to get them" (xi). The precondition of her poetry is listening. What she calls "practicing being invisible" may indeed involve hiding out of sight while people were speaking, but it may also include, more likely, Carson's ability to be pres-ent while clearing space for others' idiosyncratic expressions of self—spaces that others feel invited to step into, which draw forth their speech. She further notes that the poems' "layout on the page has to do with how the pieces should sound" (xii). With ample white space floating her quick-exchange paragraphs or the deliberate monologuing of her speakers, Carson seems to use the space of the page to evoke a co-present listener, with line and paragraph breaks pro-viding the gaps for a listener's nods and nonverbal backchanneling. The white space—which comes first and shoots through and co-creates the text of a writ-ten poem—implies the presence of a listener, and even transmutes the reader into that listener. In the final poem of the collection, which begins "I am asking you to come back home," the speaker addresses a long-absent and yearned-for listener and concludes with a jarring, equal parts silly and sad image of gestural listening, warning: "When I am dead, it will not matter how hard you press your ear to the ground" (93). Gestural listening as a rhetorical force provides a framework for articulating the communicative dynamics at work in these texts and others. It enables us to configure Fischer's "supra-existent" listener with the writer of the Psalms and with their readers, Carson's readers with her poem's speaker and aboveground listener.

In *The Heroine with 1,001 Faces*, a response to Joseph Campbell's classic about the "monomyth" and the hero's journey, Maria Tatar identifies a strain of folktales that include the presence of a "listening stone," sometimes called a Stone of Patience. These stories generate striking examples of listening configurations, with inanimate objects both "standing in" for human listeners and also creating particular opportunities for impactful listening. In this subset of folktales, a protagonist narrates her plight not to another person but to an object. In some of these tales, the stone is not a stone exactly; it is, rather, another object—a stove, a doll—to which the heroine tells all. In one, the protagonist is a princess who has been forced into a life of servitude by another woman, who has stolen the princess's identity and married her intended bridegroom. The princess tearfully spills her story to an iron stove, but her self-reflexive "idio-narrative" is overheard by the king, and thus the truth is out. In others, a character tells a doll, a pet dog, or a literal stone the story of their reversal of fortune. In each, the story is overheard by another, whose eavesdropping brings about the ability to restore social order. The eavesdropper is often a king, prince, or baron, though other times simply a person, like a king's maid, whose position makes it possible for them to bring about change upon learning the truth.

It would be easy to interpret these stories as evidence that the listening of an authoritative man is necessary for a person of lesser status to be liberated, or, in a particularly popular narrative, that the need for a protagonist to "find her voice," even if only confessing to a stone, is the only meaningful rhetorical move. But an awareness of listening configurations allows for different ways to understand these tales. The "listening" of the stone or other object creates an opportunity to tell that would not have existed otherwise. From this perspective, it is a listening presence, in the first place, that allows for speech, which draws out revelation. A more exact description would be that the characters in these tales construct opportunities for listening that allow for the truth to be known and for action to be taken to correct an injustice. The listening stone, or object, allows for a listening configuration to take shape that overrides the social conventions of the time, which likely do not allow a young "Goose Girl," for instance, to confront a king with the story of who she really is. Often, in the stories that Tatar collects, the person speaking to the stone does not know they are being overheard. This is an important detail, because when this is case, the eavesdropper can be assured that the teller of the tale is truthful—they could have nothing tangible to gain, after all, by recounting their story to a rock. A listening configuration that includes a stone, stove, or doll becomes significant when a certain hero or heroine might not otherwise be believed. Here, the crucial rhetorical act is in the listening, and especially in assembling effective listening configurations.

In one of the stories that Tatar features, an Armenian tale called "Nourie Hadig," the rhetorical force of listening is on display in particularly dramatic fashion. The listening configuration includes a Stone of Patience, to whom Nourie Hadig—also the victim of a malicious stolen-identity plot that prevents her marriage to a prince—narrates a woeful chain of events that has brought her to her current position. This Stone of Patience has a special capacity, though: if spoken to by someone whose troubles are truly great, the stone will swell in size. If used by a person who "makes much of only slight grievances," however, the complainer themselves will swell and burst. Overheard and witnessed by the prince, Nourie Hadig tells her story to the stone, which swells at each turn. Here, the Stone of Patience not only creates the listening configuration that allows for the truth to be known but also confirms by its physical response the veracity and emotional weight of Nourie Hadig's tale. It enacts a stony gestural listening—if I may—that serves a rhetorical function by conveying crucial information to the prince. This story throws into relief the significance of becoming the "right kind" of listener—even a rock takes on qualities of human response when engaged in listening.

In the absence of the right kind of human listener, or the right rhetorical situation, the characters in Stone of Patience tales turn to objects. We don't have to look far for a modern parallel to the listening stone—to do so, Tatar draws, as I do in chapter 4, upon Sherry Turkle's ideas about how contemporary technologies are changing listening configurations. In particular, Tatar mentions Turkle's observations about how people interact with the ELIZA computer program, an early chatbot developed in the 1960s, trained to respond to user input with open-ended, Rogerian therapy-style responses. Turkle observes how users quickly begin to disclose deeply personal, emotionally charged information to the ELIZA program, and Tatar goes on to interpret ELIZA as a

"modern day patience stone that promises therapeutic emotional release" (92).
It goes without saying that ELIZA and her ilk do not have bodies that can enact
nuanced gestural listening in the way I have described throughout most of this
book. But in fact, it may be a computer's lack of embodiment that users seek in
a listener. Indeed, a computer program will not blink with fatigue or sigh its
impatience. It won't take off its glasses and rub its eyes in exasperation. A user
does not need to apologize for being late, needy, distant, or disorganized. From
this perspective, the draw of a listening configuration involving a program like
ELIZA is not hard to understand. Today, of course, anecdotes abound about
people turning to ChatGPT and other large language model chatbots when they
need a responsive, yet disembodied listener. The attendant ethical quandaries
are beyond the scope of this postlude, but listening configurations involving
artificial intelligence should give us pause, especially as we hurtle forward,
seemingly unstoppably, into its widespread use.

Still more listening configurations can be observed, however, when we
know to look for them, and artificial intelligence is not the only form of technology in play. I have argued for an expansion of what are considered to be
recognizable gestural listening ways-of-being, especially in classroom spaces,
and I have proposed that practices of gestural listening can function as forms
of subversion and resistance to community norms. In his 2017 *Schooling New
Media: Music, Language, and Technology in Children's Culture*, Tyler Bickford eth-
nographically explores the quotidian, yet deceptively powerful, gestural listening practices of friendship between children. In particular, Bickford illustrates
how the students of Heartsboro Central School listen to music together on MP3
players by sharing earbuds between them, coordinating their movements as
the earbud cord marks out their social relationships. In doing so, they generate
new gestural listening practices that their peers and teachers learn to recognize
with increasing precision. In one instance, two girls, close friends, wander
onto a middle-school soccer field crowded with boys during recess. He writes:
"Amber and Kathy walked right into the middle of the game, listening together
to Amber's iPod. Intently oblivious to the action around them, they stopped,
talking, listening, and completely ignoring the boys who loudly complained at
the obstruction—the girls' private interaction dramatically intruding on the
public activities of the schoolyard" (Bickford 84). Through their tethered listening, the girls renegotiate the terms of the space they move through, and through
their "turned-in stances" they project outward toward others the nature of their
bond, and what Bickford recognizes as the "status and privilege claimed by
older girls" in this middle-school schoolyard (84). Their gestural listening duet,

driven and enabled by the shared, corded earbuds, co-constitutes the two girls at the same time as it moves outward to signal the strength of their dyad to others. Here, they playfully create a new gestural listening way of being, and a new listening configuration.

They also suggest alternatives, springing from children's playful embodiment and unique material culture, to the "absent presence" usually suggested by personal devices in school. In developing their own collaborative listening practices with their favored MP3 players, the students in Bickford's study quietly yet consistently defy prevalent understandings of headphones by media theorists as technologies that individualize and privatize public spaces. Pulling apart wired headsets and using earbuds as tiny room speakers, among other forms of "tinkering and tethering," as Bickford puts it, they bend what may otherwise seem like hermetically sealed technologies to the dynamics of their social lives—their friendships, their gendered practices, their negotiation of authority in school. Rather than allowing software and hardware interfaces to dictate practices in school, as we saw in chapter 4, the students reenvision and jerry-rig their devices in improvised, unassumingly subversive listening behaviors.

There will be many more changes to come as in-person listening and listening with-and-through-technology come to further inflect each other, and as what it means to be a student continues to take shape in the twenty-first century. I expect to witness the covert, "digital underlives" of students evolve ongoingly in ways that I imagine will take some time to recognize, even as my own listening practices grow and change. But I urge instructors to recognize new forms of gestural listening as they coalesce and to suspend judgment, at first, about what counts as "good" listening in acknowledgement of how ingrained assumptions about good listening have served some more than others, and not always in the ways we might expect. "Vigilant at the borders of obscurity," we can aim to be ready for listening's next chapters.

Acknowledgments

Believing in a project about the quiet, "other side" of speech, something subtle and challenging to measure, was not always a sure bet. I'm truly grateful to have had a chance to listen and be listened to by those who saw the potential in this work.

The road to this book has been a long one, and tracing its roots leads me to my undergraduate years at Bryn Mawr College, where Jen Callaghan's Writing Center and Gail Hemmeter's "Teaching of Writing" course set me on my current path.

This project first took discernable shape at the University of Pittsburgh, where I had the good fortune to learn from my professors and mentors in the English Department, all of whom guided me as I undertook research and situated my own voice within a field of study for the first time. At Pitt, the culture of respect for student writing informed my respect for student listening. It mattered to me to do my graduate "apprenticeship" among people who both conveyed, and simply enacted, the idea that the classroom is a special and important site of encounter. Cory Holding's "Rhetorical Gestures" class first suggested the rich intersection of rhetoric and gesture to me, and hers has been a "moving presence" that has inspired and sustained my scholarship since. Neepa Majumdar's careful questions about sound and listening, and

https://doi.org/10.7330/9781646428182.c007

her injunction to use the time available to me to read more deeply and widely, enabled me to assert and clarify my own intellectual contributions. Steve Carr also encouraged me to read, and then to stop reading—in order to write, and then to keep writing. His deep knowledge of our field and his skillful mentorship have shaped my teaching, my writing, my thinking, and my ability to convey all of those things to others. Paul Kameen, with his usual apparent effortlessness and good cheer, "cleared a space" for my ideas, reading and responding to early versions with his characteristic generosity, expansiveness, and erudition. I'm especially lucky to have shared space with my classmates in the graduate program at Pitt. I benefited greatly from walking with them as we conversed, argued, teamed up, and showed each other the way to becoming scholars and teachers.

The next step in my professional journey took place at Juniata College, where I'm especially grateful for the support, care, and collegiality of Jim Tuten, David Hsiung, and Donna Weimer. Elliot Hirshon and Münire Bozdemir played a key role in the development of the ideas in chapter 4. I was urged along by Kat Hart's encouragement and perspectives on higher education, while my thinking was strengthened ongoingly by Jared LaGroue's insights into the ethics of listening and the ownership of sound. The milieu at Juniata makes the concerns of this book feel truly alive.

I want to extend special recognition and gratitude to my friend, colleague, and collaborator Hannah Bellwoar. Her influence can be felt in every chapter of this book, from its orientation toward research to its pedagogical focus. A consummate teacher, researcher, and program-builder, Hannah continues to show me how many aspects of work and life are done with grace and integrity.

At Penn State Harrisburg, I've been extremely lucky serve in the School of Humanities alongside Russell Kirkscey, and all those whose commitment to our program have made it possible for me to put the necessary time and attention into this book.

At the University Press of Colorado, I have been fortunate to have Rachael Levay, Nate Bauer, Michael Spooner, Michelle Chen, and Skylar Cooper work with me on ushering this book to its audience in the world. I appreciate the careful readings and comments of my two anonymous reviewers, whose suggestions made this book a better one.

It's unlikely that I would have completed the journey of this book without the warmth, tenacity, good humor, and wisdom of the "Six Degrees" writing group, assembled and sustained by Moriah Kirdy, a tireless organizer of writerly community and practice. Among the wonderful practitioners I have met recently, I am especially grateful to Ericka Russell, whose expert feedback on later drafts of this book clarified its focus, style, and inner continuity.

I've named many teacher-scholars here whose input contributes to the best aspects of this book. I claim any of its errors or limitations solely as my own.

Perhaps most important, I would like to acknowledge all of my students, past and present. Although you are too many to name, sharing the endeavor of teaching and learning with you has been formative and profoundly meaningful. You are the main characters here, and I am proud to have known your "student selves."

Finally, I'm grateful, as always, to my family for their love, support, and good counsel.

Works Cited

Abeele, Mariek M. P. Vanden, Marjolijn L. Antheunis, and Alexander P. Schouten. "The Effect of Mobile Messaging during a Conversation on Impression Formation and Interaction Quality." *Computers in Human Behavior*, vol. 62, 2016, pp 562–69 https://doi.org/10.1016/j.chb.2016.04.005.

Ahern, Kati Fargo, and Ashley Rose Mehlenbacher. "Listening for Genre Multiplicity in Classroom Soundscapes." *Enculturation*, no. 26, 2018.

Aly, Götz. *Why the Germans, Why the Jews? Envy, Race Hatred, and the Prehistory of the Holocaust.* Metropolitan Books, 2014.

Astor, Maggie. "Kamala Harris Faced a Double Standard on the Debate Stage." *The New York Times*, 8 Oct. 2020, https://www.nytimes.com/2020/10/07/us/politics /kamala-harris-faced-a-double-standard-on-the-debate-stage.html.

Attali, Jaques. *Noise: The Political Economy of Music.* University of Minnesota Press, 1985.

Bailenson, Jeremy. N. "Nonverbal Overload: A Theoretical Argument for the Causes of Zoom Fatigue." *Technology, Mind, and Behavior*, vol. 2, no. 1, 2021, pp. 1–6. https://doi .org/10.1037/tmb0000030.

Barrick, Elyssa M., Alixandra Barasch, and Diana I. Tamir. "The Unexpected Social Consequences of Diverting Attention to Our Phones." *Journal of Experimental Social Psychology*, vol. 101, 2022. https://doi.org/10.1016/j.jesp.2022.104344.

Bercovici, Debra. "Autistics and Eye Contact (It's Asynchronous)." *Embrace Autism* 13 Apr. 2023. https://embrace-autism.com/autistics-and-eye-contact-its -asynchronous/.

Bickford, Tyler. *Schooling New Media: Music, Language, and Technology in Children's Culture*. Oxford UP, 2017.

Black, Michael L. *Transparent Designs: Personal Computing and the Politics of User-Friendliness*. Johns Hopkins UP, 2022.

Boyer, Nate. "The Veteran and NFL Player Who Advised Kaepernick to Take a Knee." *All Things Considered*, NPR, 9 Sept. 2018, https://www.npr.org/2018/09/09/646115651/the-veteran-and-nfl-player-who-advised-kaepernick-to-take-a-knee.

Brueggemann, Brenda Jo. *Lend Me Your Ear: Rhetorical Constructions of Deafness*. Gallaudet UP, 1999.

Bull, Michael. *Sound Moves: IPod Culture and Urban Experience*. Routledge, 2011.

Bulwer, John. *Chirologia, Or, The Naturall Language of the Hand C: Composed of the Speaking Motions, and Discoursing Gestures Thereof: Whereunto Is Added, Chironomia, Or, The Art of Manual Rhetoricke, Consisting of the Naturall Expressions, Digested by Art in the Hand . . . : With Types, or Chyrograms, a Long-wish'd for Illustration of This Argument*. London: Printed by Tho. Harper, and Are to Be Sold by Henry Twyford . . . , 1644.

Cacciola, Scott. "Victims in Larry Nassar Abuse Case Find a Fierce Advocate: The Judge," *The New York Times*, 23 Jan. 2018, www.nytimes.com/2018/01/23/sports/larry-nassar-rosemarie-aquilina-judge.html.

Campt, Tina M. *Listening to Images*. Duke University Press, 2017.

Carey, Tamika L. "Necessary Adjustments: Black Women's Rhetorical Impatience." *Rhetoric Review*, vol. 39, no. 3, 2 July 2020, pp. 269–86. https://doi.org/10.1080/07350198.2020.1764745.

Carson, Jo. "I Am Asking You to Come Back Home." *Stories I Ain't Told Nobody Yet*. Theater Communications Group, 1993.

Ceraso, Steph. *Sounding Composition: Multimodal Pedagogies for Embodied Listening*. U of Pittsburgh P, 2018.

"Choir." *Encyclopædia Britannica*, Encyclopædia Britannica, Inc., www.britannica.com/art/choral-music. Accessed 17 May 2025.

Cohn, Jenae. "'Devilish Smartphones' and the 'Stone-Cold' Internet: Implications of the Technology Addiction Trope in College Student Digital Literacy Narratives." *Computers and Composition*, vol. 42, Dec. 2016, pp. 80–94. https://doi.org/10.1016/j.compcom.2016.08.008.

Comstock, Michelle, and Mary E. Hocks. "Voices in the Cultural Soundscape: Sonic Literacy in Composition Studies." *Computers and Composition Online*, 2006. http://cconlinejournal.org/comstock_hocks/index.htm.

Corbett, Edward P. J. "The Rhetoric of the Open Hand and the Rhetoric of the Closed Fist." *College Composition and Communication*, vol. 20, no. 5, 1969, pp. 288–96. http://doi.org/10.2307/355032.

Corbin, Alain. *Village Bells: The Culture of the Senses in the Nineteenth-Century French Countryside*. Columbia UP, 1998.

Corfman, S. Brooke. "On Not Knowing Students' Genders, Nor Being Able to Predict When or How They Will Change." *College Composition and Communication*, vol. 73, no. 2, Dec. 2021, pp. 261–86.

Crary, Jonathan. *Suspensions of Perception: Attention, Spectacle, and Modern Culture.* MIT Press, 1999.

Daughtry, J. Martin. *Listening to War: Sound, Music, Trauma, and Survival in Wartime Iraq.* Oxford UP, 2020

Detweiler, Eric. "Sounding Out the Progymnasmata." *Rhetoric Review*, vol. 38, no. 2, 2019, pp. 205–18. https:/doi.org/10.1080/07350198.2019.1588567.

Diop, Arimeta. "It's the End of the iPhone-Notes-App-Apology Era." 12 June 2020, https://www.vanityfair.com/style/2020/06/notes-app-apology-instagram.

Drucker, Johanna. "Humanities Approaches to Interface Theory." *Culture Machine*, vol. 12, 2011, pp. 1–20.

Duffey, Suellyn. "Student Silences in the Deep South: Hearing Unfamiliar Dialects." *Silence and Listening as Rhetorical Arts*, edited by Cheryl Glenn and Krista Ratcliffe, Southern Illinois UP, 2011, pp. 239–306.

Emerson, Lori. *Writing Reading Interfaces: From the Digital to the Bookbound.* U of Minnesota P, 2014.

Eustachewich, Lia. "Kamala Harris' Facial Expressions during Vice Presidential Debate Go Viral." *New York Post*, 8 Oct. 2020, https://nypost.com/2020/10/08/kamala-harris-facial-expressions-during-vp-debate-go-viral/.

Evon, Dan. "Fact Check: Did Army Football Team Kneel in Protest during the National Anthem?" Snopes, 2 Oct. 2017, www.snopes.com/fact-check/army-football-team-kneel-protest-national-anthem/.

Fauville, Geraldine, Mufan Luo, Anna C. M. Queiroz, Jeremy N. Bailenson, and Jeff Hancock. "Nonverbal Mechanisms Predict Zoom Fatigue and Explain Way Women Experience Higher Levels than Men." *SSRN*, 2021, pp. 1–18. https://doi.org/10.2139/ssrn.3820035.

Faris, Michael J. "Queer Kinesthetic Interlistening." *Peitho*, vol. 23, no. 1, fall 2020, https://cfshrc.org/article/queer-kinesthetic-interlistening/.

Feibush, Laura. "Gestural Listening and the Writing Center's Virtual Boundaries." *Praxis: A Writing Center Journal*, vol. 15, no. 2, 2018.

Feldstein, Stanley, and Cynthia L. Crown. "Psychological Correlates of Silence and Sound in Conversational Interaction." *Perspectives on Silence*, edited by Deborah Tannen and Muriel Saville-Troike, Ablex Pub., 1985, pp. 31–54.

Felepchuk, Erin. "Stimming, Improvisation, and COVID-19: (Re)negotiating Autistic Sensory Regulation during a Pandemic." *Disability Studies Quarterly*, vol. 41, no. 3, 2021. https://doi.org/10.18061/dsq.v41i3.

Ferguson, Kennan. "Silence: A Politics." *Silence and Listening as Rhetorical Arts*, edited by Cheryl Glenn and Krista Ratcliffe, Southern Illinois UP, 2011, pp. 113–29.

Fischer, Norman. *Opening to You: Zen-Inspired Translations of the Psalms.* Penguin Compass, 2003.

Fisher, Judith L., and Mary B. Harris. "Note Taking and Recall." *The Journal of Educational Research*, vol. 67, no. 7, Mar. 1974, pp. 291–92.

Fiumara, Gemma Coradi *The Other Side of Language: A Philosophy of Listening.* Routledge, 1996.

Flusser, Vilém. *Gestures.* University of Minnesota Press, 2014.

For Harris and Trump, Facial Expressions Did Much of the Talking during Presidential Debate, AP News, 11 Sept. 2024, apnews.com/article/facial-expressions-trump -harris-debate-photos-70347bc693b14377de63e905e937f6e6.

Foss, Sonja K., and Cindy L. Griffin. "Beyond Persuasion: A Proposal for an Invitational Rhetoric." *Communication Monographs*, vol. 62, no. 1, Mar. 1995, pp. 2–18. https://doi.org/10.1080/03637759509376345.

Ford, Bonnie D. "After Larry Nassar: The Journey of Judge Rosemarie Aquilina," *ESPN Internet Ventures*, 12 July 2019, www.espn.com/espn/feature/story/_/id/27156746 /journey-judge-rosemarie-aquilina.

Gergen, Kenneth J. "The Challenge of Absent Presence." *Perpetual Contact: Mobile Communication, Private Talk, Public Performance*, edited by J. E. Katz and M. A. Aakhus, Cambridge UP, 2002, pp. 227–41. http://doi.org/10.1017/CBO9780511489471.018.

Gilmore, Perry. "Silence and Sulking: Emotional Displays in the Classroom." *Perspectives on Silence*, edited by Deborah Tannen and Muriel Saville-Troike, Ablex Pub., 1985, pp. 139–64.

Glenn, Cheryl. *Unspoken: A Rhetoric of Silence*. Southern Illinois UP, 2004.

Glenn, Cheryl, and Krista Ratcliffe, eds. *Silence and Listening as Rhetorical Arts*. Southern Illinois University Press, 2011.

Goldin-Meadow, Susan. *Hearing Gesture: How Our Hands Help Us Think*. Harvard UP, 2005.

Goodman, Steve. *Sonic Warfare: Sound, Affect, and the Ecology of Fear*. MIT Press, 2009.

Gowen, Anne E. "Larry Nassar Judge Aquilina's Remarks Undermined Justice," *Time*, 26 Jan. 2018, time.com/5119433/larry-nassar-judge-rosemarie-aquilina-justice/.

Green, McKinley. 2019. "Smartphones, Distraction Narratives, and Flexible Pedagogies: Students' Mobile Technology Practices in Networked Writing Classrooms." *Computers and Composition*, vol. 52, pp. 91–206. https://doi.org/10.1016/j.compcom .2019.01.009.

Gross, Daniel M. *Being-Moved: Rhetoric as the Art of Listening*. U of California P, 2020.

The HarperCollins Study Bible (New Revised Standard Version). Edited by Harold W. Attridge. HarperCollins, 1989.

Harrison, Carol. *The Art of Listening in the Early Church*. Oxford UP, 2013.

Hawhee, Debra. *Bodily Arts: Rhetoric and Athletics in Ancient Greece*. U of Texas P, 2004.

Hawhee, Debra. *Moving Bodies: Kenneth Burke at the Edges of Language*. U of South Carolina P, 2012.

Henriques, Julian. *Sonic Bodies: Reggae Sound Systems, Performance Techniques, and Ways of Knowing*. Continuum, 2011.

Hirschkind, Charles. *Ethical Soundscapes: Cassette Sermons and Counterpublics*. Columbia UP, 2009.

Holding, Cory. "The Rhetoric of the Open Fist." *Rhetoric Society Quarterly*, vol. 45, no. 5, 2015, pp. 399–419. https://doi.org/10.1080/02773945.2015.1058973.

Jairam, Dharma, and Kenneth A. Kiewra. "An Investigation of the SOAR Study Method." *Journal of Advanced Academics*, vol. 20, no. 4, 2009, pp. 602–29.

Jordan, James Mark. *Evoking Sound: Fundamentals of Choral Conducting and Rehearsing*. GIA Publications, 1996.

Kajimura, Shogo, and Michio Nomura. "When We Cannot Speak: Eye Contact Disrupts Resources Available to Cognitive Control Processes during Verb Generation." *Cognition*, vol. 157, Dec. 2016, pp. 352–57. http://www.sciencedirect.com/science/article/pii/S0010027716302360.

Kameen, Paul J. *Writing/Teaching: Essays Toward a Rhetoric of Pedagogy*. U of Pittsburgh P, 2000.

Kapchan, Deborah. "Listening Acts: Witnessing the Pain (and Praise) of Others." *Theorizing Sound Writing*, Wesleyan University Press, 2017, pp. 277–93.

Keith, Tamara, and Rachel Treisman. "Facial Expressions Spoke Volumes When Mics Were Muted in the Presidential Debate." *NPR* live blog, 11 Sept. 2024, www.npr.org/2024/09/11/nx-s1-5107965/kamala-harris-expressions-memes-donald-debate-2024.

Kendon, Adam. *Gesture: Visible Action as Utterance*. Cambridge UP, 2004.

Kendon, Adam. "Spacing and Orientation in Co-Present Interaction." *Development of Multimodal Interfaces: Active Listening and Synchrony. Lecture Notes in Computer Science*, edited by A. Esposito, N. Campbell, C. Vogel, A. Hussain, A. Nijholt, vol. 5967, Springer, pp. 1–15. https://doi.org/10.1007/978-3-642-12397-9_1.

Kress, Gunther. *Multimodality: A Social Semiotic Approach to Contemporary Communication*. Routledge, 2009.

LaBelle, Brandon. *Acoustic Territories: Sound Culture and Everyday Life*. Continuum International Publishing, 2010, ProQuest ebrary, 14 June 2015.

"Larry Nassar's Survivors Speak, and Finally the World Listens—and Believes." *Believed*, NPR, 10 Dec. 2018, https://www.npr.org/2018/12/07/674525176/larry-nassars-survivors-speak-and-finally-the-world-listens-and-believes.

LeMesurier, Jennifer Lin. "Winking at Excess: Racist Kinesiologies in Childish Gambino's 'This Is America.'" *Rhetoric Society Quarterly*, vol. 50, no. 2, 2020, pp. 139–51. https://doi.org/10.1080/02773945.2020.1725615.

Maraj, Louis Maurice. *Black or Right: Anti/Racist Campus Rhetorics*. Utah State UP, 2020.

Mason, Jeff. "Tone and Body Language at the Harris-Trump Debate Speak as Loudly as Words." *Reuters*, 11 Sept. 2024, www.reuters.com/world/us/tone-body-language-harris-trump-debate-speak-loudly-words-2024-09-11/.

McCarthy, Anjanie, Kang Lee, Shoji Itakura, and Darwin Muir. "Cultural Display Rules Drive Eye Gaze during Thinking." *Journal of Cross-Cultural Psychology*, vol. 37, no. 6, 2006, pp. 717–22. http://doi.org/10.1177/0022022106292079.

McCullers, Carson. *The Heart Is a Lonely Hunter*. Houghton Mifflin, 2000.

McNeill, David. *Hand and Mind: What Gestures Reveal about Thought*. University of Chicago Press, 1996.

Misra, Shalini, Lulu Cheng, Jamie Genevie, and Miao Yuan. "The iPhone Effect: The Quality of In-Person Social Interactions in the Presence of Mobile Devices." *Environment and Behavior*, vol. 48, no. 2, 2016. https://doi.org/10.1177/0013916514539755.

Mitchell, Alanna. "Bioacoustics: What Nature's Sounds Can Tell Us about the Health of Our World." *Canadian Geographic*, 12 Aug. 2022, https://canadiangeographic.ca/articles/bioacoustics-what-natures-sounds-can-tell-us-about-the-health-of-our-world/.

Mountford, Roxanne. *The Gendered Pulpit: Preaching in American Protestant Spaces.* Southern Illinois UP, 2005.

Mueller, Derek N. "Digital Underlife in the Networked Writing Classroom." *Computers and Composition,* vol. 26, no. 4, Dec. 2009, pp. 240–50. https://doi.org/10.1016/j.compcom.2009.08.001.

Myers, Nancy. "Purposeful Silence and Perceptive Listening: Rhetorical Agency for Women in Christine de Pizan's *The Treasure of the City of Ladies.*" *Silence and Listening as Rhetorical Arts,* edited by Cheryl Glenn and Krista Ratcliffe. Southern Illinois UP, 2011, pp. 56–74.

Nadler, Robby. "Understanding 'Zoom Fatigue': Theorizing Spatial Dynamics as Third Skins in Computer-Mediated Communication." *Computers and Composition,* vol. 58, Dec. 2020, pp. 1–17. https://doi.org/10.1016/j.compcom.2020.102613.

Nakamura, Takashi. "The Action of Looking at a Mobile Phone Display as Nonverbal Behavior/Communication: A Theoretical Perspective." *Computers in Human Behavior,* vol. 43, Feb. 2015, pp. 68–75. https://doi.org/10.1016/j.chb.2014.10.042.

Nolan, Jason, and Melanie McBride. "Embodied Semiosis: Autistic 'Stimming' as Sensory Practice." *International Handbook of Semiotics,* edited by Peter Trifonas, Springer Publishers, 2015, pp. 1069–1078. https://doi.org/10.1007/978-94-017-9404-6_48.

Nussbaum, Matthew, and Louis Nelson. "Protestors Disrupt James Comey's Howard University Convocation Speech." Politico, 22 Sept. 2017. https://www.politico.com/story/2017/09/22/protesters-james-comey-howard-university-speech-243023.

Palmatier, Robert A., and Michael J. Bennett. "Notetaking Habits of College Students." *Journal of Reading,* vol. 18, no. 3, Dec. 1974, pp. 215–18.

Pattermann, Juliana, Maria Pammer, Stephan Schlögl, and Laura Gstrein. "Perceptions of Digital Device Use and Accompanying Digital Interruptions in Blended Learning." *Education Sciences,* vol. 12, no. 3, 2022, p. 215. https://doi.org/10.3390/educsci12030215.

PBS NewsHour. "WATCH: Former FBI Director James Comey Delivers Convocation Address at Howard University," *YouTube,* uploaded by PBS News, 22 Sept. 2017, https://www.youtube.com/watch?v=Z8z35T7_b5g.

Penny, Laurie. "No, I Will Not Debate You," Longreads, 18 Sept. 2018, longreads.com/2018/09/18/no-i-will-not-debate-you/.

Prior, Paul. "How Do Moments Add Up to Lives: Trajectories of Semiotic Becoming vs. Tales of School Learning in Four Modes." *Making Future Matters,* edited by Mary P. Sheridan and Rick Wysocki, Computers and Composition Digital Press, Aug. 2018, ccdigitalpress.org/book/makingfuturematters/prior-part-1.html#content-top.

Przybylski, Andrew K. and Netta Weinstein. "Can You Connect with Me Now? How the Presence of Mobile Communication Technology Influences Face-to-Face Conversation Quality." *Journal of Social and Personal Relationships,* vol. 30, no. 3, 2012, pp. 237–46.

Quashie, Kevin Everod. *The Sovereignty of Quiet: Beyond Resistance in Black Culture.* Rutgers UP, 2012.

Ratcliffe, Krista. *Rhetorical Listening: Identification, Gender, Whiteness.* Southern Illinois UP, 2006.

Rath, Richard Cullen. "No Corner for the Devil to Hide." *The Sound Studies Reader,* edited by Jonathan Sterne, Routledge, 2012.

Reda, Mary M. *Between Speaking and Silence: A Study of Quiet Students.* State U of New York P, 2009.

Robinson, Melia. "A Deaf Artist Explains the Rules of 'Sound Etiquette'—and Why She's Kicking Them to the Curb." *Business Insider Australia,* 23 Oct. 2015, https:// www.businessinsider.com/deaf-artist-christine-sun-kim-2015-10.

Rogers, Carl. *Carl Rogers on Personal Power: Inner Strength and Its Revolutionary Impact.* Trans-Atlantic Publications, 1978.

Rogers, Carl R., and Richard E. Farson. "Active Listening." 1957. *Communication in Business Today,* edited by R. G. Newman, M. A. Danziger, and M. Cohen, Heath and Company, 1987.

Royster, Jacqueline Jones. "When the First Voice You Hear Is Not Your Own." *College Composition and Communication,* vol. 47, no. 1, 1996, pp. 29–40.

Seelye, Katharine Q. "Protesters Disrupt Speech by 'Bell Curve' Author at Vermont College," *The New York Times,* 3 Mar. 2017, www.nytimes.com/2017/03/03/us /middlebury-college-charles-murray-bell-curve-protest.html.

Senju, Atsushi, Angélina Vernetti, Natasa Ganea, Kristelle Hudry, Leslie Tucker, Tony Charman, and Mark H. Johnson. "Early Social Experience Affects the Development of Eye Gaze Processing." *Current Biology,* vol. 25, no. 23, 2015, pp. 3086–91, http:// www.sciencedirect.com/science/article/pii/S0960982215012476.

Shoshan, Hadar N., and Wilken Wehrt. "Understanding 'Zoom Fatigue:' A Mixed-Method approach." *Applied Psychology,* vol. 71, no. 3, 2021, pp. 827–52. https://doi.org /10.1111/apps.12360.

Simko-Bednarski, Evan, and Elizabeth Joseph. "Attorney General Backs Judge in Nassar Case against Accusations of Bias," *CNN,* 1 Aug. 2018, www.cnn.com/2018/08/01 /us/nassar-attorney-general-response/index.html.

Sinclair, Molly. "Students Close Gallaudet U." *The Washington Post,* March 7, 1983. https://www.washingtonpost.com/archive/politics/1988/03/08/students-close -gallaudet-u/439dff39-836b-4787-ad75-777f9f2c4cc8/.

Smilges, J. Logan. "Bad Listeners." *Peitho,* vol. 23, no. 1, fall 2020, cfshrc.org/article /bad-listeners/.

Sterne, Jonathan. *The Audible Past: Cultural Origins of Sound Reproduction.* Duke UP, 2006.

Stewart, Rozella. "Should We Insist on Eye Contact with People Who Have Autism Spectrum Disorders?" Indiana Resource Center for Autism, 2000, https://www .iidc.indiana.edu/irca/articles/should-we-insist-on-eye-contact-with-people-who -have-autism-spectrum-disorders. Accessed 23 Oct. 2016.

Stoever, Jennifer Lynn: *The Sonic Color Line: Race and the Cultural Politics of Listening.* NYU P, 2016.

Stone, Jonathan. "Listening to the Sonic Archive: Rhetoric, Representation, and Race in the Lomax Prison Recordings." *Enculturation,* no. 19, 2015.

Suter, Lisa. "Living Pictures, Living Memory: Women's Rhetorical Silence within the American Delsarte Movement." *Silence and Listening as Rhetorical Arts*, edited by Cheryl Glenn and Krista Ratcliffe, Southern Illinois UP, 2011, pp. 94–112.

Tannen, Deborah. "Silence: Anything But." *Perspectives on Silence*, edited by Deborah Tannen and Muriel Saville-Troike, Ablex Pub., 1985, pp. 93–112.

Tatar, Maria. *The Heroine with 1,001 Faces*. Liveright Publishing Corporation, 2022.

Thompson, Emily Ann. *The Soundscape of Modernity: Architectural Acoustics and the Culture of Listening in America, 1900–1933*. MIT Press, 2008.

Tóibín, Colm. *House of Names*. Scribner, 2017.

Trevisan, Dominic A., Nicole Roberts, Cathy Lin, and Elina Birmingham. "How Do Adults and Teens with Self-Declared Autism Spectrum Disorder Experience Eye Contact? A Qualitative Analysis of First-Hand Accounts." *PloS One*, vol. 12, no. 11, 2017. https://doi.org/10.1371/journal.pone.0188446.

Turkle, Sherry. *Alone Together: Why We Expect More from Technology and Less from Each Other*. Basic Books, 2017.

Volokh, Eugene. "Protesters at Middlebury College Shout down Speaker, Attack Him and a Professor." *The Washington Post*, 4 Mar. 2017, https://www.washingtonpost.com/news/volokh-conspiracy/wp/2017/03/04/protesters-at-middlebury-college-shout-down-speaker-attack-him-and-a-professor/.

Waite, Stacey. *Teaching Queer: Radical Possibilities for Writing and Knowing*. U of Pittsburgh P, 2017.

Walters, Shannon. *Rhetorical Touch: Disability, Identification, Haptics*. U of South Carolina P, 2014.

Yergeau, Melanie. *Authoring Autism: On Rhetoric and Neurological Queerness*. Duke UP, 2018.

Young, Vershawn Ashanti. *Your Average Nigga: Performing Race, Literacy, and Masculinity*. Wayne State UP, 2007.

Index

An f after a page number refers to a figure.

About the Author

Laura Feibush is Assistant Professor of Rhetoric and Composition at Penn State Harrisburg, where she teaches first-year writing, public and professional writing, writing across media, and writing in the disciplines. Feibush earned her BA from Bryn Mawr College and her MA and PhD from the University of Pittsburgh. Her research, which focuses on listening as rhetorical praxis, has been published in venues such as *Peitho*, *Composition Forum*, and *Praxis: A Writing Center Journal*.